THE DIVIDE

THE DIVIDE

HOW FANATICAL CERTITUDE IS DESTROYING DEMOCRACY

TAYLOR DOTSON

The MIT Press
Cambridge, Massachusetts
London, England

The MIT Press would like to thank the anonymous peer reviewers who provided comments on drafts of this book. The generous work of academic experts is essential for establishing the authority and quality of our publications. We acknowledge with gratitude the contributions of these otherwise uncredited readers.

This book was set in Bembo Book MT Pro by Westchester Publishing Services. Printed and bound in the United States of America.

Library of Congress Cataloging-in-Publication Data

Names: Dotson, Taylor, author.
Title: The divide : how fanatical certitude is destroying democracy / Taylor Dotson.
Description: Cambridge, Massachusetts : The MIT Press, [2021] | Includes
    bibliographical references and index.
Identifiers: LCCN 2020041674 | ISBN 9780262542715 (paperback)
Subjects: LCSH: Democracy--Moral and ethical aspects. | Truthfulness and
    falsehood--Political aspects. | Fanaticism--Political aspects. | Polarization
    (Social sciences) | Communication in politics.
Classification: LCC JC423 .D6795 2021 | DDC 321.8--dc23
LC record available at https://lccn.loc.gov/2020041674

10   9   8   7   6   5   4   3   2   1

CONTENTS

ACKNOWLEDGMENTS

This book would not have been possible without support from my wife, Rachel, and encouragement from my friend and colleague Michael Bouchey. I also owe a great deal of gratitude to friends, relatives, social media strangers, and everyone else whom I subjected to repeated attempts to provoke more democratic disagreements. I am grateful for the encouraging comments made by two anonymous reviewers, who saw value in my arguments, and for feedback I received from David Caudill and Andrzej W. Nowak at the Society for Social Studies of Science conference in New Orleans in 2019. Moreover, I am forever indebted to my mentor Ned Woodhouse, without whom I would have never had any of these ideas in the first place. Finally, I thank the editorial and production team at MIT Press, especially Katie Helke, Virginia Crossman, and Laura Keeler, for making this book happen.

1

IF THE TRUTH IS ON YOUR SIDE . . .

There are three sides to every story: yours . . . mine . . . and the truth. No one
is lying.
—Robert Evans, *The Kid Stays in the Picture*

"I cannot believe how misinformed you people are." The old woman sneered
into the microphone, "the sheer ignorance . . . I'm hearing." The atmosphere
at the public meeting was as tense as it was for many of the other congressional townhalls that followed Donald Trump's victory in the presidential
election of 2016. My district's seat was then held by Steve Pearce—a Republican who greeted Trump's electoral success with considerable enthusiasm.
Like countless other Americans, I got up early to drive to my district's townhall meeting because the election results had inspired me to be more active
in local politics, to match my social media rhetoric with action. The process
of reacquainting myself with public deliberation, however, was disquieting.
Many of my experiences made me worry about the prospects for American
democracy. This townhall meeting was no exception.

"My question to you, representative, is," continued the woman, "what
will you do to prevent the United Nations from using Agenda 21 to come
and take away our property?" The irony of someone calling other people
misinformed while rehearsing the tired conspiracy theory that a nonbinding UN agreement would lead to an authoritarian world government was
not lost on many of the attendees. The part that most stunned me was how
seriously Representative Pearce took her question, emphasizing the need
to read international agreements carefully. He treated the question more
earnestly than he did most of those asked by his more liberal constituents.
When citizens expressed reasonable worries about how Republican Party
health-care changes affected insurance premiums or expressed concern
about the consequences of budgetary or tax issues, Pearce would coldly ask

them if they had any "documentation" to back up their statements. Pearce's dismissiveness, seemingly justified by his portrayal of dissenting constituents as lacking the right information, was maddening.

Such interactions seem increasingly commonplace. Citizens respond to political disagreements with the assumption that they are caused by people being misinformed or, even worse, indoctrinated or corrupt. One thinks of actress Rose McGowan publicly deriding Trump voters as the victims of "cult brainwashing."[1] When people talk about everything from genetically engineered crops and climate change to gun control and minimum-wage laws, as I will show, they tend to fall back on the belief that only one side of the conflict (theirs) is capable of reasoning rationally. Why have we become a nation seemingly obsessed with the cognitive deficits of political opponents?

TRUTH AND DEMOCRACY

This book explores the role of truth in the practice of democracy. Specifically, how can democracy be possible when people believe outrageous things—or at least things that the other side thinks are outrageous? How can a populace fundamentally divided over the basic facts, assumptions, and ideas about the environment, human nature, and society hope to govern themselves collectively?

Many, if not most, people are fairly pessimistic. A good portion of the university students I teach believe that the United States would be a better place if it were ruled by a benevolent dictator or perhaps by a committee of scientific and engineering experts. *Politics* for them is a dirty word; democracy mere fancy.

Numerous scholars and commentators likewise bemoan the apparent slide into a "post-truth" era, fretting about the perception that "objective fact" no longer guides politics. The policy scholars Jennifer Kavanaugh and Michael D. Rich, for instance, diagnose American politics as suffering from "truth decay," a process by which opinions come to "crowd out and overwhelm" facts.[2] They see the roots of truth decay in the cognitive and educational shortcomings of citizens, disinformation and media echo chambers, and political polarization writ large. Tom Nichols has similarly proclaimed the "death of expertise," contending that the populace has become anti-intellectual, ignorant, and self-absorbed to the point that democracy itself is at stake. The result, according to Nichols, is a kind of vapid relativism in which emotions are seen as equal in weight to expert judgement.[3]

Others have claimed that the problem really lies with one particular subset of the population. Journalist Chris Mooney has written an entire book that suggests that differences in Republicans' brains leads them to "deny science." Alex Berezow and Hank Campbell have responded with the claim that it is really the progressives who are antiscience. They argue that progressive advocacy of organic foods over genetically engineered crops, green energy rather than fossil-fuel extraction, and a whole host of other policy positions are rooted more in emotionally laden "feel-good fallacies" rather than in reason. Then there are the more brazen and polemical commentators, who dismiss universities as factories for brainwashing youth with leftist nonsense or claim that "social justice warriors always lie" and disregard reality.[4] The problem, it seems for many political commentators, is that the "other side" poisons the public sphere with their ill-founded, ignorant, or supposedly intentionally deceptive ideas. If only all Americans could think like Republicans (or Democrats or . . .), the nation would finally progress—or so readers are told.

A common theme running through many laments about the state of politics is the idea that once the "truth" of a matter becomes discernible, the political process will be over—or at least the role of politicking and negotiation should be sharply reduced. As soon as scientists mostly agree about the existence of anthropogenic climate change, some claim, the only thing left to do is act to completely eliminate fossil fuels from people's lives. Similarly, President George W. Bush, upon winning reelection in 2004 by winning 51 percent of the vote—but only around 30 percent of eligible voters—declared that he had earned a "mandate" to make his policy preferences law.[5] Bush's dismissive view of the need to negotiate and compromise is shared by many other officials and voters, who have come to see election results as exposing the true "will of the people." Political actors on opposing sides of different debates appear highly motivated to shut down disagreement—a core feature of democracy writ large—as quickly as possible.

Patience with democracy seems to have been waning for some time. Studies have found that the majority of Americans see little point to political debate or discussion. They tend to agree with statements such as "Elected officials would help the country more if they would stop talking and just take action on important problems" and "What some people call compromise is really just selling out on one's principles."[6] This annoyance with disagreement and negotiation results in an indignant form of politics. Citizens become outraged when politicians fail to follow through with promises, as if elections were like a vending machine where political preferences are punched in at the voting booth and then immediately delivered through the right policies. The idea that people's views might change in light of opposition by others or in response to ongoing learning becomes unthinkable. Bargaining is no longer viewed as an essential part of doing democracy but as an impediment to progress.[7]

At least some of the intolerance for politics appears to come from the ever higher status of science within contemporary societies. The sociologist Nina Eliasoph found that political conversations among ordinary people get shut down by the belief that "political questions . . . can and should be decided by lining up the right technical facts."[8] Within this view, there is no point to discussing public issues because most citizens are not experts. As a result, people talk in ways that hide or ignore the deeper value disagreements at work, thus reducing multifaceted political beliefs into mere self-interest or clichéd concerns over tax dollars or their children's well-being. In turn, rich conversations about how different people's aspirations for a good society come into conflict and how those conflicts may be resolved, at least in part, do not happen.

Declining tolerance for political disagreement also comes from the idea that a very different kind of knowledge can end petty politicking: common sense. In response to survey data in 2019 showing that a majority of Americans favored stricter gun laws, Representative Tulsi Gabbard (D–HI) declared the debate to be over: gun control was no longer a "partisan issue," and the task now was simply to pass "common sense" laws.[9] It has become commonplace to hope that truth writ large—in the form of either scientific facts or common sense as revealed through elections or public polling— will end disagreements and produce harmony, a hope the historian Sophia Rosenfeld describes as "one of the oldest dreams around."[10]

Even otherwise intelligent scholars and writers appear to yearn for a truth so powerful and indisputable that it reduces contention, allowing for more civil and ostensibly rational political discourse. Graham Saul blames the paltry success of the environmental movement in part on environmentalists not having a coherent statement of purpose, not having a vision that provides a "truth that can't be denied."[11] The legal scholar Amy Chua searches for a similar kind of truth when lamenting that "no one [is] standing up for an America without identity politics, for an American identity that transcends and unites."[12] Her account of polarization and others like it hope for an America where citizens recognize the truth of their commonality. Yet it seems unfair to expect an inner-city African American man to feel commonality with a white suburbanite who wants to kick him out of Section 8 housing, increase police surveillance of his home, reduce funding for the public transportation that he relies on to get to work, and turn his son's ordinary schoolyard transgressions into police matters. Citizens suffer real harms when their opponents win an electoral or legislative victory. Nevertheless, calls for a language or an identity that transcends difference get increasingly loud as people become ever more divided. Why does the existence of seemingly ineliminable cleavages in citizens' identities and political interests provoke such anxiety?

Increasing political polarization no doubt has consequences. Political divisions become starker and more underlain by anger. On the one hand, anger per se is not a problem for politics. Numerous social changes, from improved working conditions to expanded voting rights, would not have occurred without people channeling their indignation to force others to negotiate and compromise. On the other hand, political anger becomes dangerous when it is tinged with resentment and colored by a desire for revenge, leading political actors not simply to seek to win but rather to destroy their opponents.[13] Many Trump voters in 2016 did not just want to see Hillary Clinton lose but also to go to jail; a significant number of their opponents are little different, though, calling for much the same fate for President Trump. A large segment of rural voters has come to believe that they receive too little governmental help and have too little influence or respect compared to city dwellers, thus fueling a political culture of resentment that has resulted in support for policies that explicitly punish liberal professionals, higher-salaried public-sector employees, and urban welfare recipients.[14]

Such divisiveness has trickled down to shape people's social relationships. I have witnessed many of my acquaintances on social media unfriend or block others—including family members—when the latter utter and stick intransigently to contrary opinions. Twitter is full of posts by people leaving dates or breaking off relationships the moment an onerous viewpoint is spoken. Tweeters justify doing so by claiming that the attitudes are "toxic" and that it is not their "responsibility" to educate people who are self-evidently racist, sexist, or ignorant. I am sure that many readers have seen or experienced something similar. Whatever the benefits of leaving the table are for reducing stress levels, it is difficult to imagine such behavior leading to greater understanding; ever starker and solidified ideological divisions instead seem more probable. Of course, nobody is legally or morally *responsible* for changing other people's minds, but doesn't *somebody* have to step up and do it if it is going to happen?

Diagnoses and proposed remedies to polarization vary. Senator Ben Sasse blames declines in community cohesion for the rise of "us versus them" political attitudes.[15] That argument seems to have a kernel of truth to it. In my previous book, *Technically Together*, I describe how the thinning out of community life and its replacement by more diffuse and weakly rooted networked relationships have left many citizens forlorn and yearning for a sense of togetherness. They seek out, as a result, surrogates for community in television, extreme fitness, social media, and consumerism.[16] It stands to reason that many Americans now search for community in their political identities; they are not unlike their counterparts of the 1920s and 1930s, who sought relief from that era's myriad cultural and economic disruptions within fascism and other fanatical ideologies.

Although Senator Sasse and I share similar feelings regarding the current state of American communality and the same desire to reweave more tightly knit communal webs—albeit coming from opposite sides of the political spectrum—I do not believe that the thinning out of collective social life fully explains America's political problems. The United States and other nations have been beset by major political cleavages and instability before now, even when people were more rooted in local community life than they are today. Consider the violent clashes of the 1960s, with students taking over university buildings, the outright abuse of civil rights demonstrators, and physical confrontations in the streets and at the Democratic National Convention over the Vietnam War. I think Sasse and others misdiagnose what ails American democracy by overstating the uniqueness of the present.

Just as polarization is nothing new, post-truthiness has arguably been a constant feature of public life. Sophia Rosenfeld outlines a number of examples of how outright falsities influenced politics, from salacious rumors about Marie Antoinette to conspiracy theories involving Jewish cabals. She quotes George Washington, who lamented at the end of his presidency that the gazettes of the era "teemed with all the Invective that disappointment, ignorance of facts, and malicious falsehoods could invent, to misrepresent my politics and affections, to wound my reputation and feelings, and to weaken, if not entirely destroy, the confidence that you [the public] have been pleased to repose in me."[17] Moreover, one should hardly need be reminded of the dubious claims that have underwritten many of America's wars, from claims of newborns being tossed out of incubators and Saddam's "weapons of mass destruction" to reports that the Spanish sabotaged a US warship and that a US gunboat was attacked in the Gulf of Tonkin.[18] It is unclear whether we have ever really been in a "truth era."

People in other times and places navigated political conflict just as pathologically as citizens do today—if not more so. Civil disagreement was so absent in the sixteenth-century Holy Roman Empire that a peace treaty between German Catholics and Lutherans made religious discussions punishable by death. In the lead-up to the US Civil War, gag rules were passed that prohibited even the discussion of antislavery petitions or resolutions in Congress. In other conflicts, participants were just as quick to point to their opponents' supposed cognitive deficits. One German writer in 1929 wrote that Munich's status as the dumbest city in the world was clearly proven by its support of Hitler, which in turn was explained by its citizens' excessive beer consumption. The Nazi propagandist Joseph Goebbels claimed to be protecting common sense when holding a bonfire of Jewish books, arguing that "extreme Jewish intellectualism" had a corrupting influence on "the German spirit."[19]

Although the political pathologies examined in this book are not unprecedented, they are probably exacerbated by recent sociocultural and technological changes, including social media. But blaming the internet or "kids these days" obscures how today's crises are merely the most recent manifestations of perennial political dysfunctions. Regulating Facebook does nothing to fix the root cause of polarization: the belief that only one's own side knows the truth of a matter and that politics and disagreement can only distract from what needs to be done.

IS (POST)TRUTH THE ENEMY OF DEMOCRACY?

Although the idea that Truth with a capital T should be more powerful than politics has likely always shaped public debate, its impact on the practice of democracy is too rarely considered. What happens to democracy when participants come to believe that their side is in unique possession of the truth?

In my own field—science and technology studies—the response to the perception that Americans now live in a "postfact" era has left something to be desired. There has been some self-flagellation, attempts at self-absolution, and finger-pointing, with a few commentators blaming the field itself for the weakening influence of facts.[20] Science studies scholars have written detailed studies of how science really gets done, exposing how subjective judgments and even cultural ideas influence the creation of scientific truths. However, to suggest that a few hundred esoteric research papers on the sociology of science have single-handedly reshaped the political cultures of democracies across the globe probably overstates the impact of academic scholarship. In any case, the philosopher Steve Fuller has recommended that people simply embrace living in a postfact world, treating knowledge as just another power game.[21] At the same time, the French theorist Bruno Latour has hesitantly suggested that we employ the idea of objectivity "strategically"—that is, when it aligns with solving global challenges such as climate change.[22] I am unsure if treating knowledge as just another power game is the right move, at least not without seriously considering the broader consequences if a Machiavellian view of truth became widespread. Likewise, I doubt my colleagues would appreciate others wielding "strategic objectivity" for issues that left-wing academics tend to be more skeptical about: genetically engineered crops, nuclear energy, natural gas fracturing, and so on. Neither reducing truth to just another political power game nor pursuing an uncritical albeit strategic use of "the facts" seems like a satisfying answer.

I find the prescriptions of scholars in other fields equally unconvincing. In the conclusion of her incredibly perceptive and insightful account of the historical tension between elite knowledge and ordinary common sense, Sophia Rosenfeld sees the answer in cultivating a culture of "truth-telling" and lie-detecting within journalism and public life, regulating media to prevent the spread of disinformation, securing voting rights, and ensuring an independent judiciary.[23] Both the insistence that democracy must rely upon and aspire to the truth and the belief that judges and journalists can be independent or nonpartisan strike me as overly simplistic. Only the most opportunistic politicians and media commentators are completely indifferent to the truth. Most partisans sincerely believe that they are grasping a reality that eludes their opponents, despite the existence of what others would see as obvious biases. Judges and journalists are merely human, and, as far as I know, scientists have yet to discover a truly objective person. Even worse, years of fact-checking President Trump's claims—or those of other politicians—do not seem to have brought Americans any closer to a more productive democracy. The tensions between truth and democracy are here to stay.

Could it be that the ideal of Truth is the problem rather than the fact that people rarely live up to it? Does it ask too much of democracy to expect it not just to settle disputes imperfectly and tentatively but also to validate an objective reality? What happens to democratic politics when Truth becomes gospel, but no one can agree on the catechisms?

AN OUTLINE

This book seeks an alternative answer to the apparent dilemma between truth and democracy, an answer that avoids the contradictions and pitfalls that infect other perspectives. Can we avoid overly idealizing expert knowledge while also refraining from romanticizing the beliefs and preferences of the "average" citizen? Can politics be grounded in and supportive of democracy both without sanctifying truth and without falling prey to a stultifying form of post-truthism?

I start my exploration in chapter 2 by critically examining the intersection of science with politics. In asking "Can science settle political questions?" and "What does the belief that science can settle political questions do to politics?," I find that the border between science and politics is far fuzzier and grayer than is commonly acknowledged and argue that this fuzziness undermines epistocratic or technocratic proposals that put experts in the driver's seat of the policy process. I find that the belief that the facts should determine policy amounts to fanatical scientism, which undermines the practice of democracy. Most importantly, I contend that productive and intelligent politics is not a product of embracing truth but of a pluralistic democratic process.

In chapter 3, I examine the reactionary countermovement to fanatical scientism: the belief in the superior weight of common sense. Commonsensical truths have always worked in tension with expert facts and should be taken equally seriously. How does the idea that policies should simply instantiate the down-to-earth judgments of "the people" affect democratic politics? I find that common sense functions like "the facts," spurring an equally fanatical view of and approach to governance.

Chapter 4 surveys other fanatical narratives: nature, progress, and the market. I illustrate how sanctifying these ideas depresses democratic politics and obscures what really matters to people. I end by exploring the roots of the preoccupation with truth in politics, tracing them to a philosopher whose sympathies lie with anything but democracy.

Not content to merely diagnose what ails politics in the United States and increasingly elsewhere, in chapter 5 I focus on the question "What would more democratic disagreements look like?" I outline three different strategies that would help citizens' political disputes be more productive. Such strategies are not totally new or surprising, yet they are obscured by the belief that certitude and rationality can steer politics. Put together, they amount to a form of democratic civility. Because calls to be civil can become just as stifling as a preoccupation with truth, however, I also explore how fanaticism can play a positive role within a democracy.

Chapter 6 begins with the recognition that citizens' political interactions are not going to become more democratic simply by force of argument. The myth of Truth has come to dominate people's political imaginaries largely because so much of everyday life implicitly teaches or reinforces it. Realizing a more democratically pluralistic society would take reforms to political structures, adjustments to media systems, and dramatic changes to schooling, childhood, the workplace, and other institutions. The dominance of fanatical truthism is largely a result of myriad thoughtless and unintentional acts of social engineering. The remedy lies in being more circumspect and intelligent with our attempts to shape society.

Again, I do not argue that there is something unique to our time or that some golden age existed when citizens were more civil and better at conflict. Democracy has faced similar challenges throughout its history, and pathological variants have waxed and waned over time—although conflict and incivility are arguably on the upswing in our current moment. Yet most proposed solutions to an ever more gridlocked and polarized democracy fail to address underlying causes and even risk exacerbating the situation. To the extent that experts dominate policy decisions, government seems increasingly distant and unresponsive, sowing discord among ordinary citizens. At the same time, idealizing the beliefs of laypeople or mythologizing "the majority" creates anxieties among experts and other important decision makers, worries that can motivate attempts to centralize power. Any hope for a democratic future lies in finding a way out of the regress produced by a preoccupation with a monolithic Truth.

WHITHER DEMOCRACY?

I have written the word *democracy* quite a few times in this book already. For many readers, the concept might seem fuzzy and abstract, little different from other "feel-good" terms such as *freedom* and *community*. Uses of the word vary considerably for the largely unsurprising reason that describing things as democratic makes them seem more important, if not essential, for a good life or society. The internet, so we were told, would democratize the planet—a claim repeated earlier for electricity, radio, and television.[24] Claiming that a technology, a practice, or an ideal such as Truth is necessary for democracy often ends up being a way to protect it from scrutiny.

In any case, the main risk in defining a foundational word such as *democracy* is that definitions can hinder critical thinking rather than provoke it. Consider Yascha Mounk's characterization: "A *democracy* is a set of binding electoral institutions that effectively translates popular views into public policy."[25] This seems uncontroversial. Democracy in such terms means using voting or polling technologies to ensure that policies are rooted in the preferences and beliefs of a sizable plurality, if not a majority, of citizens. However, this definition does not seem to go deep enough. It is mainly a description of how many nations currently practice democratic politics, and it is a rendition that largely fails to convey democracy's more fundamental purpose. Mounk goes on to define *liberalism*: "*Liberal* institutions effectively protect the rule of law and guarantee individual rights such as freedom of speech, worship, press, and associations to all citizens (including ethnic and religious minorities)."[26] In this view, liberalism is a check on democracy, ensuring that translating popular views into policy do not come at the cost of individual rights.

The problem with Mounk's definition is that by essentially equating democracy with elections and majoritarian decision making, it gives too little recognition to matters of process. Are the "popular views" instantiated into policy the knee-jerk preferences of citizens or perspectives developed after deliberating alongside other people, including opponents? Because Mounk's definition of democracy leans toward the former, it implicitly

makes liberal institutions necessary by default. Unreflective, nondelib-
erative majoritarian electoral systems seem destined to violate individual
rights. Thus, the only means of protecting minorities—ostensibly from
democracy itself—is via written, formal rights and "guardian" institutions
(e.g., the Supreme Court), which should, at least according to advocates, be
politically neutral. Political guardians, as a consequence, become the arbiters of truth regarding the rights and liberties afforded by national constitutions. Mounk's definition almost begs the question by making liberal
guardian institutions the inevitable answer to the limitations he builds into
the concept of democracy from the outset.

I use a different conception of democracy, not because I think it is more
objective or true but because I think it challenges our thinking about what
it means to have a democratic society and demands that advocates of liberal institutions develop better arguments. Democracy should be viewed
as something more complex and fundamental than the mere translation
of popular opinion into policy. It should be defined as a system wherein
people have a significant influence on the decisions that affect their lives.
Although the distinction might seem esoteric and nitpicky, it helps ensure
more precise thinking. Consider how the philosopher Jason Brennan claims
to demonstrate the undesirability of democratic decision-making by using
a definition very similar to Mounk's and pointing out that it would not
stop a political majority from making the self-evidently unjust decision to
permit the molestation of children.[27] Brennan states that this hypothetical vote comes out of an "ideal deliberation," but he says little about the
character of the conversations between opponents or whether the process includes the potential victims of the policy. It is incredibly difficult
to imagine such a law being passed if children themselves were afforded
substantial influence.[28] Without their inclusion, the deliberation and vote
would not be democratic but rather epistocratic: "experts" in the form of
supposedly more enlightened adult citizens would be deciding for kids. A
democratic process would in contrast have empowered children to be able
to voice their opposition either directly or indirectly via representatives
and enabled them to develop a political coalition capable of challenging or
curbing the power of a pro-molestation alliance.

In my view, a society that runs roughshod over the rights of minority
groups can do so only because it is insufficiently democratic per se; otherwise, that minority would have been able to influence the process enough
to limit or prevent their own victimization. As I argue later in this book,

oppressive, insensitive, or unintelligent policies are more often the result of processes that are insufficiently inclusive rather than too democratic.

An additional advantage of defining democracy in terms of influence is that it expands one's horizon with respect to politics, leading to the recognition that *governance* is not something done solely by *governments*. The organizational structure at most workplaces is a kind of government as well, one in which bosses and managers often unilaterally make decisions with significant consequences on the lives of workers. Similarly relevant to the life prospects of the average person are the behind-closed-doors decisions made at large corporations and by those who develop new and highly consequential technologies such as nuclear power, artificial intelligence, and three-dimensional printers.[29] Defining democracy solely in terms of electoral politics hides the fact that a sizable portion of the choices affecting citizens' ability to pursue fulfilling lives remains in private hands. Once influence is seen as core to democracy, countries such as the United States can be recognized as democratic in only a relatively weak sense of the word.

In any case, my goal in defining democracy as a system wherein citizens have the ability to shape the decisions that affect their lives is to leave open the challenge of discerning the maximum feasible extent of democratic politics. If Americans and citizens around the world are to ensure a future for democracy, they will need to be far more innovative with respect to their major institutions. As my PhD mentor Ned Woodhouse would often say, if few people would want to be treated with eighteenth-century medicine, why is it reasonable to keep a stubborn commitment to eighteenth-century political designs?

I have written this book primarily with the hope of inspiring ordinary citizens, activists, and policy makers to think more deeply about the potential for democratic politics. As a result, I do not provide a detailed exposition of all the different philosophical theories on democracy or politics. It is very difficult to write a book that both is useful to people outside of academia and includes copious references to the literature and clever theoretical jargon in order to please academic audiences. I have deliberately chosen to lean toward the former. I delve deeply enough into political thought to provide context for my arguments and raise complex questions but at the same time keep my reasoning accessible. If I am at least partly successful, readers should finish this book with a greater understanding of how truth narratives affect democratic politics and with a clearer sense of what they might do to bring about a far more productive democracy.

THE FACTS

Science can be a powerful political tool. Consider a hearing on climate change, "Data or Dogma," held in 2015 by the then chairman of the US Senate's Space, Science, and Competitiveness Subcommittee and soon-to-be presidential candidate Ted Cruz. Senator Cruz characterized himself in his introduction as a defender of the truth writ large. As the son of two mathematicians and scientists—both of his parents earned bachelor's degrees in mathematics[1]—he claimed that he was interested only in ensuring that public policy followed from "the actual science and the actual data." In Cruz's view, however, the actual data demonstrated that there was little to no threat from global climate change, contrary to the "alarmism" of mainstream climate scientists.[2]

The rightness or wrongness of Cruz's understanding of climate science in his hearing is not the focus of this chapter, although it is an important consideration. Rather, I am interested in what fact-oriented speech does to the character of contemporary politics. Science no doubt plays a necessary role in policy. Officials would not be able to set standards for highway construction or water treatment absent the guidance of research data. The notable feature of Cruz's rhetoric during his hearing was not simply his appeal to scientific evidence but the underlying narrative of science being threatened by politics. Cruz ironically framed his argument in much the same way that his political opponents do: extoling the benefits of open scientific debate and expressing the desire to move past the kinds of partisanship that can cloud a supposedly clear-eyed view of the facts. Yet in Cruz's view mainstream climate scientists, not skeptics, were the ones guilty of stifling criticism and being overly wedded to a convenient political narrative. Cruz depicted the political problem of anthropogenic climate change as one that can be overcome—fortuitously in the policy direction he prefers—if people were finally to know about the real data: the "inconvenient" facts he presented in his hearing.

It would be much too easy to dismiss speeches like Cruz's as nonsense, as examples of petty political theater that would not persuade a reasonable person. Yet such talk clearly resonates with some members of the public. In the digital spaces where many conservatives go to learn about and discuss politics, mainstream climate scientists are frequently portrayed as both politically biased and scientifically incompetent. Writers for online magazines, blogs, and websites such as *Reason*, *Watts Up with That*, and Breitbart contend that mainstream climate scientists are "scamsters" using "pseudoscience" and science that "is not yet settled" to force unsound policy on the rest of the country.[3] Such language is nearly the same as that used to describe climate "denialists." It often seems as if each side of any contentious issue is absolutely convinced of being on the "right side" of science.

The focus of this chapter is the most frequently claimed conflict between democracy and truth: people's lack of respect for scientific data. What happens to politics when citizens begin to believe that science should settle public disagreements and when rhetorical appeals to "the facts" start to dominate people's justifications of their political worldviews and actions? Can science actually play the role in solving contentious disputes that people expect it to? In this chapter, I not only illustrate the consequences of what I term *political scientism* but also question the assumptions about science and politics that underlie it.

THE POLITICIZING OF SCIENCE

Some areas of science provoke considerable controversy simply because of their subject matter: genetically engineered (GE) crops, climate change, vaccines, and so on. When a scientific practice or the results of a study have political consequences, the science and the scientists themselves are viewed much more skeptically or are subjected to more pressure by industry and governments than they would otherwise be. These avenues of science are seen as having been *politicized*.

Consider a study by a trio of Cornell scientists in 1999 suggesting that the *Bacillus thuringiensis* (*Bt*) bacteria produced by one species of GE corn threatened monarch butterfly populations.[4] Despite the study passing peer review at one of the most prestigious scientific journals, *Nature*, the reaction among some scientists, especially those with industry funding, went beyond a healthy degree of skepticism. Subsequent commentary dismissed the study as a "false report,"[5] and follow-up studies have downplayed the risks posed to monarch butterflies by GE crops—though more recent research suggests that even those conclusions were premature.[6] The existence of routine limitations and uncertainties within the study took on special significance, especially in light of a sudden 10 percent drop in Monsanto's stock price. Industry officials heavily criticized the study on television and created a working group that funded numerous field studies to challenge the results. For advocates of GE crops, these new studies did not simply amend or improve the original study but "discredited" it, while GE skeptics in turn argued that the dominance of industry in the process prevented a fair risk assessment of *Bt* corn by the US Environmental Protection Agency.[7]

When scientific studies appear to threaten a profitable product, businesses frequently respond in ways that seem to undermine the traditional autonomy of academic researchers. The lead author of the monarch butterfly study received "visits" by scientists from major biotechnology firms, who would drop hints that publishing the article would endanger his career.[8] Syngenta went so far as to subpoena the emails of a researcher who found a correlation between birth defects and the concentration of one of the company's pesticide products in citizens' water and to undermine the reputation of another scientist.[9] GE opponents claimed that a $25 million relationship between Novartis and the University of California at Berkeley was behind the denial of tenure to Ignacio Chapela, a researcher who argued that transgenes had infiltrated traditional varieties of Mexican maize.[10]

Science is also politicized by governments. For instance, the North Carolina legislature, prodded by an alliance of coastal developers, homeowners, and businesses, forbade communities from setting regulations that used the state's own Coastal Resources Commission report on expected climate-change-induced sea-level rises; it even limited future reports to a 30-year timeline.[11] More recent events include the Trump administration telling US Department of Agriculture staff to avoid the phrase *climate change* and to use the term *weather extremes* instead, a kind of political language policing all too common within the history of "natural" disasters.[12] As in the case of North Carolina's legislature, many commentators view the administration's attempt to reframe the narrative on climate research as signaling the government's increasing willingness to micromanage scientific reports when their results are politically inconvenient.

In the eyes of climate-change skeptics, the behavior of scientists out of East Anglia in the 2000s showed that processes within the Intergovernmental Panel on Climate Change were no different. Stolen emails showed scientists, such as Phil Jones, openly discussing how to purposefully exclude skeptical papers from their literature reviews and data presentations to underplay the disagreement between historical temperatures measured via tree rings and those obtained in other ways. The scientists justified such moves in terms of conveying sufficient consensus so that policy makers would feel confident to act and in terms of making reasonable decisions meant to ensure that more minor problems in the data would not hold back legislation. Their defenders said that a few quotes were being taken out of context and misrepresented. Although official investigations cleared the scientists of any wrongdoing, skeptics saw the emails as evidence of politicization.[13] For all such cases, it matters little whether any impropriety on the part of business, governments, or scientific organizations actually occurred; the damage is done by the perception of undue political meddling.

There are numerous takes on the politicization of science, and almost none of them are positive. Any kind of explicit political influence is often treated as an indecent infringement on scientists' autonomy or as an inevitably corrupting force against objectivity. Are these assessments fair?

It is tempting to see the institution of science as pure and value free. One viral online cartoon presents the scientific method and the "political method" as stark contrasts: For the former, the question is "Here are the facts. What conclusions can we draw from them?," whereas the latter puts it as "Here's the conclusion. What facts can we find to support it?"[14] And the word *politics* itself seems to be most often uttered as a lament, with some distaste, especially when compared with the term *science*. Should we be surprised that levels of public trust and distrust for scientists are nearly the inverse of those for elected officials?[15]

In line with popular opinion, a number of recent books portray the problem of politics and science as relatively straightforward: too much politics. Science historians Naomi Oreskes and Erik Conway, for instance, have documented the efforts of tobacco companies and fossil-fuel corporations to artificially increase doubt over the existence of climate change, acid rain, ozone depletion, and the harmful effects of smoking.[16] Business lobbies and allied scientists have established institutes dedicated to questioning inconvenient scientific results, seemingly not with the intention of improving knowledge but rather of uncovering enough uncertainty in order to delay regulatory changes. Thomas McGarity and Wendy Wagner similarly depict the pipeline of scientific knowledge into the policy sphere as being "contaminated" by outsiders.[17] For instance, industry-funded research is sometimes explicitly designed to produce favorable results. Gastrointestinal issues caused by the fat substitute olestra were hidden by intentionally doing experiments that were too short to uncover problems. Likewise, the fact that Merck only compared patients taking Vioxx against others using naproxen (rather than against a control group) allowed it to deny that Vioxx increased the risk of heart attack.

No doubt these scholars' observations regarding how powerful groups sometimes intentionally muddy public debate and produce biased data are important. But they tend to portray science as something that is pure only until tainted by corporate profit incentives, an image that is—ironically—at odds with much of the sociological and anthropological data on fact production itself. Science has always been political.

The science policy scholar Daniel Sarewitz subsumes the idea that scientific research is politically neutral—that is, guided purely by curiosity rather than by political need or cultural values—under the "myth of unfettered research."[18] Contrary to the popular image of scientists as monastic explorers of truth, science has been socially shaped and steered since its beginnings. The ancient Greek scientist Archimedes's role as a maker of war machines is paralleled today by the disproportionately high levels of funding awarded to fields such as physics, whose results are more readily relevant to the creation of new weapon systems. The rise in biomedical science funding was likewise not because such research areas suddenly became more evocative of curiosity but rather because of both the desire to improve public health and high expectations for patentable and hence profitable new treatments. Recognizing these influences does not mean that all science funding is so narrowly motivated but that funding generally accrues to fields with powerful constituencies, economic or political, or with appeal to broader values such as improved national economic competitiveness, military prowess, and the curing of disease.[19]

Furthermore, scientific results have been shaped by the traditional maleness of research. Male scientists generally excluded women from clinical trials, seeing their hormonal cycles as unnecessary "complications." Understanding of how drugs affect women's bodies has suffered as a result. Patriarchal ideals about feminine passivity led generations of biologists to ignore the active role that mammalian eggs play in the process of conception, capturing and tethering sperm rather than acting as, one set of writers put it, a passive "bride awaiting her mate's magic kiss."[20] Moreover, because medical research is so often privately supported or profit driven means that diseases afflicting affluent and/or white people get more attention. More is spent on cystic fibrosis and erectile dysfunction than on sickle cell anemia and tropical diseases.[21]

Values shape science at nearly every stage, from deciding what phenomena to study to choosing how to study and talk about them.[22] For instance, blindness related to vitamin A deficiency in developing nations could be solved by a variety of means. Ostensibly more "technological" approaches, such as genetically engineering "golden rice," tend to overshadow agroecological techniques, which emphasize increasing the diversity of crops grown, improving soil health, and reducing reliance on expensive biotech products. Golden rice would be unnecessary, say advocates of agroecology, if policies were instituted to reduce the poverty of subsistence farmers, to diversify their crops, and to help them become more self-sufficient. In any case, either approach not only entails doing very different science but also making different assumptions about how the world ought to work. Is it better to solve public problems via technologies that better adapt crops and farmers to the current agronomic system or via alterations to the system itself? Science cannot definitively tell us which approach is better; rather, the choice is invariably guided by political commitments (or perhaps resignation) to the makeup of a particular society.

Other scientific questions are equally and unavoidably value laden. Should safety studies on the chemicals inside consumer products (e.g., bisphenol A, or BPA, used in the production of food containers and hygiene products) be designed to avoid false positives or false negatives? How much data are sufficient to justify regulation? Which is worse: a potentially unsafe product ending up on the market or a safe product being mistakenly banned? Societies may want to avoid the latter not only because it could impose unnecessary costs on industry but also because banned substances may be replaced with alternatives that end up being worse in some respects. Likewise, should toxicological tests be designed to produce answers quickly or to be as accurate as possible?

Finally, values shape scientists' language. When environmental research-ers started to refer to boggy areas as "wetlands" rather than as "swamps," it helped persuade citizens that such places were not merely wasted space but rather served a purpose: supporting animal species, purifying groundwater, and improving flood control. Calling a chemical an "endocrine disruptor" rather than an "hormonally active agent" highlights its potential for harm. Scientists make value-laden choices every day regarding their terminology, research questions, assumptions, and experimental methods, which can often have political consequences.

Last, scientists themselves act politically with respect to their areas of study. They have strong commitments to the theories they develop and the experi-ments they conduct. Many scientists and philosophers see bias as a vital part of research rather than as always contaminating it. Lunar geologists interviewed by Ian Mitroff argued that "unbiased" scientists would fail to see their theories through tough times and likely abandon them much too early.[23] Similarly, without skeptics hoping to advance their careers by "jumping ship" when tra-ditional paradigms run into problems, new competing theories would often not get developed. Furthermore, contrary to the common view of science, many debates end up "settled" prior to the emergence of unquestionably solid evidence.[24] Einstein's theory of relativity gained adherents even though previ-ous theories had not yet been empirically disproven and a portion of the evi-dence supporting his ideas came from poorly conducted research. Although Einstein's vision was eventually vindicated by later experimental studies, many scientists supported it because they were attracted to the range of interesting predictions it made, not because of the accuracy of confirmatory data. In other controversies, such as the one over whether apparent lesbian behavior among whiptail lizards serves a reproductive function, scientists relied on political rhetoric as much as on their data to try to sway fence-sitters, denigrating oppo-nents' supposed lack of experimental competence. Wherever social scientists have looked closely, they have found elements of politics in the conduct of science.

Discerning exactly where science ends and politics begins is no simple matter. Although it is clear to most people that certain kinds of politics are problematic (e.g., sowing doubt in bad faith), other political influences go unquestioned (e.g., funding biases toward weapons and new consumer gadgets). The framing of science as pure until it is externally politicized

therefore prevents a broader debate of the question "What kinds of political influences on science are appropriate and when?" Improving women's
and minorities' ability to become scientists or directing science toward
more peaceful or life-fulfilling purposes is political in a different sense than
intentionally obscuring the harmful effects of smoking. But the myth that
science is inherently apolitical prevents a full consideration of such distinctions. Despite its problems, however, the belief that the normal conduct of
science is purified of politics nevertheless dominates people's political imaginations and drives attempts to scientifically "rationalize" policy. What are
the effects of such attempts?

SCIENTIZING POLITICS

> It is our responsibility to hold all policy makers . . . accountable for developing
> and enacting evidence-based policy.
> —March for Science website

Even though much of the public decries the explicit politicizing of science, few question the simultaneous effort to ensure that policy making is
"scientifically guided." In a recent viral YouTube video, for instance, astrophysicist Neil deGrasse Tyson claims that America's problems stem from
the increasing inability of those in power to recognize scientific fact. Only
if people begin to see that policy choices must be based on established scientific truths, according to Tyson, can we move forward with necessary
political decisions.[25]

In contrast to the cases described earlier, the movement to scientize
politics explicitly seeks to *depoliticize* contentious public issues—or at least
appear to do so. As one set of science policy scholars puts it, it is hoped that
putting scientific experts at the helm in policy decisions will "[clear] away
the tangle of politics and opinion to reveal the unbiased truth."[26] The scientizing of politics thus relies on the same assumption as attacks on the explicit
politicizing of science: that science and politics are totally distinct and that
the former is nearly everywhere preferable to the latter. Yet is there any reason to believe that scientized policy would be value free? Upon reflection,
it seems unreasonable to believe that any human endeavor—being carried
out by imperfectly rational persons—can be so. Even worse, evidence that a
large number of published scientific studies have been so poorly conducted

or designed that their results are not reliably reproducible suggests that even evidence-based policy is not guaranteed to be guided by reality.[27] There are plenty of reasons to doubt the visions expressed by Tyson and others who hope that science can provide a firm, indisputable basis for policy making.

It can be countered nevertheless that even though values and politics play a role in research, science should still be a dominant means of settling public issues. No doubt having some scientific research when deciding a complex issue is preferable to having none at all. Moreover, even if scientific results are sometimes biased or even completely wrong, scientific institutions at least value *trying* to improve the quality of knowledge.[28] It is difficult to quarrel with such a view in the abstract; however, one still wonders exactly how dominant a role scientific expertise should play in politics. In what ways might scientized policy fail to deliver the goods?

One question on this point is "Whose expertise?" New York Department of Health scientists thought they were being more objective when they made conservative estimates about the potential risks from the toxic-waste dump lying underneath Love Canal, New York—designing their analyses to avoid falsely labeling the neighborhood as unsafe.[29] But equally talented scientists allied with homeowners made the exact opposite assumption regarding the burden of proof. Who was being less objective?

People with advanced degrees, moreover, have no monopoly on insight. British physicists, for instance, did not bother to include local sheep farmers' knowledge when investigating the consequences of fallout from the Chernobyl nuclear disaster on the local agricultural ecosystem. As a result, the scientists recommended actions that the latter considered absurd and out of touch with the realities of sheep farming, such as having the sheep eat straw in pens rather than forage. They also failed to take advantage of farmers' understanding of how water moves through their fields, which resulted in the scientists' failure to measure where rainwater pooled and underestimation of the degree of nuclear contamination. Similarly, officials in Flint, Michigan, initially met residents' complaints of developing health problems and skin issues after being exposed to the municipal water supply with eye rolls and snide remarks, dismissing them as rushing to judgment on mere anecdotal evidence. But later investigation corroborated the residents' worries, finding that changes in the water system caused lead to leach out of local pipes and to introduce elevated levels of trihalomethanes. Corrosion even created geographical inconsistencies in chlorination, raising the risk of fostering Legionella bacteria. Scientizing public controversies often prevents the recognition that people without science degrees often have important contributions to make.[30]

Even experts from different scientific disciplines often see controversial phenomena in wildly different ways. Ecologists are more often critical of GE crops, given that their field emphasizes the complexity, potential fragility, and interconnectedness of ecosystems; in contrast, genetic engineering's role in transforming organisms for human purposes lends itself to a more optimistic view of humanity's ability to control transgenic species.[31] It is simple enough to argue that science should guide policy, but things quickly become more complex after recognizing that no single group of experts can give a complete and fair analysis of a problem.

Another question is "Can science even settle controversial disputes?" For instance, Silvia Tesh has described how scientifically proving that a substance has ill effects on human bodies is often very difficult, if not impossible.[32] For obvious ethical reasons, experimental tests are done only with nonhuman animals, whose reaction to different doses can vary wildly from humans' reactions. Thalidomide, which even in minute amounts produces birth defects in humans, affects dogs only in large doses. Epidemiological studies on populations exposed to toxic substances are even messier: it is hard to get an accurate measure of how much of a toxin people have been exposed to; information on harm (e.g., birth defects and cancer) is not always reliably or consistently reported; there are too many confounding factors (e.g., smoking, toxic exposure at other times and places); and exposed populations and increased rates of illness are often just small enough that under standard measures of statistical significance it is impossible to prove a relationship.

Digging deeply into any contentious case furthermore exposes a wealth of conflicting scientific perspectives. Consider the recent controversy over "shaken-baby syndrome"—more recently dubbed "abusive head trauma." Since the 1970s, it has been accepted within the medical community that a typical pattern of symptoms—including brain swelling and bleeding within brain membranes and retinas—can be produced *only* by abuse from a caregiver and not from other kinds of accidents or unrelated diseases. The trial of British au pair Louise Woodward in 1997 was the most visible case. The trouble with shaken-baby cases is that the alleged abuse is almost never witnessed. It is inferred that abusive trauma occurred when medical examiners judge that nothing else could have likely caused the damage.[33]

To scientists critical of this assessment, however, shaken-baby syndrome diagnoses are questionably scientific and are at high risk of falsely putting grieving parents in prison for the accidental deaths of their children. Critics contend that the decades of clinical studies that undergird the diagnosis of shaken-baby syndrome were prone to subjective biases and circular reasoning. Many cases were confirmed only by confession, which could have been extracted from caregivers through investigators' threats: "The facts show abuse. We know you did it. Why don't you confess and save yourself from a life sentence or the death penalty?" Other cases are considered "confirmed" simply based on a medical examiner's judgment of whether parents' alternative explanations were "reasonable" or not. To critics, the diagnostic model has in a sense been used to prove itself. Other skeptics point to biomechanical studies that purport to show that shaking is unlikely to produce the necessary g-force to significantly harm children. They reason that neck damage would be more often present if babies were actually violently shaken and that accidentally falling headfirst from a couch does more damage than shaking. But proponents of the dominant diagnostic model for shaken-baby syndrome contend that biomechanical studies are poor models of infant bodies because they use the pediatric equivalent of a crash-test dummy. Some go so far as to depict the skeptics' disagreement with the model as a "manufactured controversy" based on "shoddy science" and the public's lack of "data literacy." Whether the science is settled or not depends entirely on which set of imperfect methods and theories one decides to trust.[34]

The science policy scholar Daniel Sarewitz goes so far as to argue that science usually makes public controversies worse. His argument rests on the logical incompatibility of policy expectations and what science actually does—namely, that decision makers expect *certainty*, whereas science is best at producing new questions. That is, the more scientists study something, the more they uncover additional *uncertainties* and *complexities*. For instance, part of the controversy over siting nuclear waste at Yucca Mountain in Nevada involved discerning the rate at which water flows through nearby rock—a viable long-term storage site needs to be sufficiently "dry." Evidence accumulated by the US Department of Energy in the 1990s appeared to confirm that the Yucca Mountain site was suitably free of moisture, but that assessment was overturned later when other groups began to review and participate in the research—though their results, too, were far from consistent. Similarly, Swedish plans for long-term nuclear-waste disposal were upended when copper storage canisters were found to be far more prone to corrosion than originally believed. The persistence of serious uncertainties regarding the hydrogeology of Yucca Mountain, copper nuclear-waste storage canisters, climate change, and GE crops is characteristic of science more broadly: there are enough limitations and variabilities among studies to permit a variety of (partly politically motivated) interpretations of the data, especially when the political stakes are high.[35] Otherwise run-of-the-mill studies are subjected to higher levels of scrutiny, and inconsistencies that would normally be acceptable get transformed into irredeemable methodological flaws. Simply put, the more we try to make science settle a political dispute, the less it is able to do so.

Moreover, can we be sure that scientizing does not introduce its own biases? The sociologist of science Abby Kinchy found that privileging fact-based assessments tends to push out nonscientific concerns.[36] Controversy over GE crops is often narrowed to focus on only the likelihood of clear harm to the environment or human bodies. For many opponents, however, GE crops' more worrisome consequences are economic, cultural, and ethical, which stem from the difficulty of keeping GE crops in place. Growers of traditional maize varieties have witnessed GE corn genes infiltrating their breeds; farmers growing non-GE crops have been barred from saving seeds or have lost their certified-organic status when GE pollen and/or seeds contaminate their fields. Ignoring questions regarding the right of traditional societies or organic farmers to uncontaminated crops, simply for the sake of keeping the debate "rooted in science," advantages biotechnology companies at the expense of other groups. Furthermore, strictly scientizing debates over genetic engineering forecloses a broader conversation about whether GE crops can fit into an alternative vision of our agricultural system that is more oriented to small business than to corporate business. Because socioeconomic concerns are not scientific matters, they are not discussed.[37]

The scientized debate regarding driverless cars is similarly biased. Proponents' discourse is exclusively focused on predicting an automobile-based world without traffic accidents, and as a result it is rarely considered that a more desirable world might be based on mass transit, walking, and biking instead of on more highly computerized cars. Scientizing policy privileges the dimensions of life that are easily quantifiable and renders less visible the ones that are not.

Scientized debates also tend to be biased in terms of who bears the burden of proof. Many large businesses' lobbies have demanded that any regulation affecting their products should be rooted in "sound science."[38] On its surface, that demand seems reasonable. Why would anyone not want regulations to be based on the best available scientific knowledge? However, the implication of "sound-science" policy is that no restrictive regulation of an industry can be developed until proof of harm is conclusively demonstrated. As noted earlier, scientists are often not able to provide firm answers, especially for complex physiological and environmental phenomena—and typically not in the time scales appropriate to policy making. As a result, calls for "sound science" end up being a delaying tactic that provides an advantage to the industrial firms producing risky products at the potential expense of humans and nonhuman species—who may be needlessly exposed to potentially toxic substances during the decades spent "proving" harm. Scientists first learned in the 1930s that bisphenol A, a component in many plastics, mimicked estrogen in mammalian cells, but it was not until 1988 that the US Environmental Protection Agency began to regulate the use of bisphenol A and not until 2016 that manufacturers were finally pressured to remove it from their products.[39] In such cases, scientizing policy allows one group of political partisans to frame their more precautionary opponents as antiscience and to portray the debate as already settled by "the facts"—namely, the lack of "conclusive" proof of harm. Absence of evidence is taken to be evidence of absence.

GOVERNANCE AND EXPERTISE

The cases described in the previous section show that science and politics are invariably intertwined. Both the politicization of science and the scientizing of politics can advantage some groups over others. However, recognizing this does not tell us what a tighter relationship between science and politics means for governance writ large. No doubt it is important to recognize that appeals to the soundness of research results or demands for science-based policy are political strategies, but are they antidemocratic? Politicians and other political actors routinely employ a range of rhetorical tools in their attempts to beat their opposition. Are left-leaning citizens' claims that science demonstrates that abortion is not murder any less appropriate than pro-choice appeals to women's rights or than pragmatic arguments about dangerous illicit abortions as far as democratic politics or competent governance is concerned? What is wrong with letting scientific expertise lead and politics follow?

The perception that democracy and expertise are at odds is at least as old as American democracy itself. Federalists such as James Madison were suspicious of popular democracy. Indeed, he recommended that the Constitution of the United States be designed so as to prevent the ostensibly unenlightened masses from passing legislation to forgive debts or to ensure an equal distribution of property; representatives "whose wisdom may best discern the true interests of their country" would be used instead.[40] Alexander Hamilton was even more extreme, advocating a strong executive branch to ensure that wise decisions could be made—with wisdom being understood mainly as protecting the interests of the growing financial class.[41] Thomas Jefferson saw matters very differently. He decried Federalist policies, believing that they would lead the country toward plutocracy. Jefferson championed an egalitarian political system, where a relatively equal distribution of property ownership would create a citizenry with the capacities to govern well through popular democracy.[42] Contemporary desires to scientize politics pivot on a similar debate: Given the increasing technoscientific complexity of the world, can average citizens govern intelligently through democratic processes?[43] Or is it reasonable to believe that experts would invariably do any better?

EPISTOCRACY

Any answer to the question of expertise is no doubt shaped by what one understands to be the purpose of democracy and political governance more broadly. At one extreme, one might conclude that—even given the limits of science—rule by the scientifically literate is preferable to democracy. The philosopher Jason Brennan argues that because most American citizens are relatively uninformed, beset by cognitive biases, and excessively loyal to their own political party, the United States would be better off as an epistocracy—or a polity ruled by the more knowledgeable. According to Brennan, political involvement appears to have a corrupting influence on some people's thoughts and actions—resulting in gridlock-inducing tribalism and in policies that infringe on people's liberties. Because he believes that citizens have the right to "competent" government—one that is composed of people who are aware of, understand, appreciate the relevance of, and can correctly reason about the facts—Brennan contends that only those proving themselves sufficiently well informed and rational should be permitted to be involved in governance.[44]

Brennan is far from the first or only person to advocate epistocracy. More than two millennia ago, Plato, for instance, believed that a philosopher king would be the best form of government. The idea that expertise can free us from the undesirable features of politics also suffuses popular imaginations. One circulating meme calls for a combined presidential run from astrophysicist Neil deGrasse Tyson and science popularizer Bill Nye; one can even order a T-shirt emblazoned with "Tyson–Nye 2020" on Amazon. Tyson's call for a world government called "Rationalia," whose one-line constitution requires that policy decisions simply be settled by "the weight of the evidence," went viral on Twitter. An international Pew survey found that some 49 percent of respondents consider "rule by experts" to be a good form of governance.[45]

Apart from the obvious race- and class-based inequalities likely to result from epistocratic government, epistocracy's most significant problem is that experts are not immune from having their own narrow interests and cognitive limitations. Expertise by itself does not assure wise or unbiased decision making—to which anyone who has witnessed a university departmental or faculty senate meeting can likely attest. For instance, mid-twentieth-century physical and chemical scientists and allied bureaucrats, some motivated by technological enthusiasm and others hoping to right the wrongs caused by nuclear weapons, pressed a number of nuclear innovations—including uranium-powered jets and atomically fracked gas wells—into research and development despite clear risks and impracticalities.[46] The Nobel Prize–winning scientist and Atomic Energy Commission member Willard Libby infamously dismissed citizens' concerns with the statement that "people have got to learn to live with the facts of life, and part of the facts of life are [sic] [nuclear] fallout."[47] One also thinks of the irony of Secretary of Energy James Schlesinger testifying to Congress about the "inherent safety" of nuclear plants even as a partial meltdown was occurring at the Three Mile Island plant in 1979 or of the infamous Rasmussen Report in 1974, in which MIT scientists seriously underestimated the chances of a serious nuclear accident because they—according to critics—intentionally employed inappropriate methods.[48] Such cases undermine the presumption that experts are inherently wiser or less value biased than other citizens; epistocratic governments may simply amplify experts' own interests and values under the guise of improved "rationality."

Moreover, it is in no way assured that recognizing competence, deciding the relevant facts, and discerning "proper" reasoning in light of those facts would be relatively straightforward and apolitical. The fact that surveys find people become even more polarized in their disagreement over human-caused climate change and stem-cell research even as they become more scientifically literate or educated suggests that deciding who embraces the correct facts in the right way would be a much more complicated—and politically wrought—process than epistocrats such as Brennan recognize; indeed, some surveys of scientists find that they disagree among themselves as much as nonscientists do about the risks and benefits of contentious biotechnologies (such as GE crops).[49] Rather than solving the problems that befall democratic politics, an epistocratic system would likely just shift political contention, obscure the issues at hand, and polarize the debate over who gets to be declared competent enough to decide.

One possible solution would be to go with what a majority of scientists believe, despite what relatively "informed" or educated citizens think. Indeed, this answer is reflected in a common meme reporting that 97 percent of climate scientists believe that climate change is man-made. Yet such statements typically overlook the fact that considerable disagreement exists even among people who accept the existence of anthropomorphic climate change. The economist Bjorn Lomberg, for instance, has infamously declared that society's optimal response is to do nothing.[50]

Regarding other issues, too, the scientists are deeply divided, often along disciplinary lines. In the twentieth century, chemists and ecologists viciously disagreed with one another about the risks posed by the pesticide DDT, each motivated by incommensurable readings of Darwin and divergent understandings of humanity's role on Earth.[51] To many chemists at the time, humans were an embattled species, constantly threatened by insect hordes that could overwhelm and destroy "modern" civilization, as a result dismissing worries about environmental disruptions as antiscience. Ecologists, however, were guided by the contrasting understanding of nature as a web of balanced relationships. This view led them to put more emphasis on the negative effects of DDT on nonhuman species because they saw human- ity's lot as inexorably tied to that of other living things. It is far from obvi- ous how any kind of metric for competence or for being "well informed" would have avoided privileging the values of chemists over ecologists or vice versa.

The additional trouble with epistocratic proposals is that they presume a "truth tenet" regarding good governance.[52] That is, it is believed that some objectively "correct" outcome for political questions exists and is the main goal of politics. This assumption invariably scientizes policy, rendering it improper for a citizenry to reject the recommendations of a scientific sub- discipline. The right to self-governance is given second billing, and the nar- row concerns that scientific studies are reasonably well equipped to address are privileged over questions of values. In a sense, in an epistocracy citizens would be considerably less free insofar as their visions of a life well lived conflict with the visions of more scientifically literate epistocrats. If it were decided that agricultural scientists who prioritized narrow measures of yield per acre were more competent and objective than scientists more concerned with biodiversity, yield per unit of fossil fuel, or some other measure of sus- tainability, then an epistocratic society would be justified in banning or heav- ily discouraging organic or agroecological farming techniques. Departing from industrial-scale monoculture would be framed as irrational or sentimen- tal, needlessly raising costs because of nonscientific valuations of a more inti- mate relationship with nature or a less economically centralized agronomic system. The political values and technocratic visions of progress underlying support for industrial agriculture would remain privileged and outside the realm of debate.

In any case, the function of democratic political systems is not just to produce "competent" decisions but also to ensure the representation of citi- zens' interests. Many, if not most, people value feeling as if they have some influence over their lives and consequently over the political decisions that affect them. Even though nonscientists may not be able to evaluate scien- tifically the environmental risks of GE salmon, for instance, they are not being unreasonable when they resent never being consulted, informed, or included in the process of assessing those risks. Any complex technosci- entific undertaking can produce unintended consequences to the environ- ment, job markets, and human health, in which citizens themselves have a stake. Laypersons are no more experts in constitutional law than they are in genetic engineering, but few would contend that their opinions on hate-crime laws or gun control should not matter.

Epistocrats forget this facet of democratic systems when they decry "pseudoscientific" public outcomes, including everything from opposition to nuclear energy and GE crops to a legal settlement against Dow Corning regarding its silicone breast implants. They fail to recognize that political systems are primarily about creating *legitimate* social orders. People care about fairness, trust, and responsibility, not merely about quantitative estimates of benefits, costs, and risks. As such, it is not citizens' job to become quasi-experts capable of evaluating the technical merits of different pathways but rather to assess the *trustworthiness* of experts and whether technologies are compatible with their values; their task and goal are to enhance the "social rationality" of contentious policy changes and technologies.[53] Citizens oppose nuclear energy because the safety predictions of nuclear bureaucrats, scientists, engineers, and firms such as General Electric were seemingly contradicted by accidents at Three Mile Island, Chernobyl, and Fukushima. In many citizens' view, new nuclear-safety estimates are moot because they come from people who are no longer trustworthy.[54] Hesitancy about vaccines is similarly rooted in a loss of legitimacy rather than in simple public ignorance. Given signs that the US Food and Drug Administration has been "captured" by the pharmaceutical industry, can its experts be trusted to properly evaluate the safety of vaccines?[55]

The role of legitimacy is also frequently forgotten when it comes to court cases. Although some lamented the billion-dollar court decision against Dow Corning and the Food and Drug Administration moratorium on silicone breast implants in 1992, dismissing it as the product of a "misinformed campaign" and "pseudoscientific approach," the charges against the firm centered around claims of *irresponsibility*. Dow Corning overzealously marketed its implants at the same time that it failed to adequately follow up on early evidence of potential risks with more thorough animal studies, choosing instead to learn about such risks in the field. The firm even actively attempted to obscure the dangers, going so far as to intentionally deceive women who called into its information hotline about the rate at which the implants leaked.[56] The goal of such cases is to find evidence of negligence, not to settle the science. Imagine if lawsuits involving senior citizens breaking their hips on icy sidewalks focused on the physics of bone fractures and biomechanical gait analyses—attempting to discern whether victims were likely to have fallen regardless of the conditions—rather than on if property owners were sufficiently diligent in de-icing.

Similarly misdirected was the considerable uproar within the scientific community when six scientists were convicted of manslaughter—a conviction overturned on appeal—in the aftermath of the L'Aquila earthquake in central Italy in 2009. Critics of the case misidentified the motivation for the charges. The scientists were not blamed for failing to predict the earthquake but for neglecting to correct or contradict overly optimistic public reassurances regarding safety made after an official meeting, which led locals not to take their usual precautions. People were crushed to death by their collapsing homes because the scientists *failed* to intervene.[57]

The scientific question of how exactly to quantify risk or harm is often not the central concern for a public worried about uncertain science and technology; rather, the public is more concerned that experts, firms, and public officials are acting fairly and responsibly in light of their considerable privileges and power. An "evidence-based"—as opposed to legitimacy-based—political system would make it difficult to sanction irresponsible behavior until harms became clear and present; in some case, firms might be given carte blanche until scientific research can catch up with them—if it ever can. Concerns about fairness and trust would be given little representation.

In light of the risks posed by privileging expertise in policy making, some science studies scholars have proposed mechanisms for ensuring the compatibility of expert guidance and democracy. Harry Collins and Robert Evans contend that there is a moral responsibility for science to be a crucial input into policy making because the institution of science at least aspires toward providing reliable knowledge, even if individual scientists often fall short of the ideal.[58] Of course, they argue, science should not completely dominate. Citizens may decide against scientific recommendations for a variety of reasons. For instance, leaders of an African nation might choose not to subsidize a new AIDS drug from the United States if they feel that it would be more broadly beneficial to focus on reducing poverty, which is a strong contributor to HIV-positive people acquiring fullblown AIDS. Governments, moreover, could ensure that decisions do not become dominated by scientists' values by enabling social scientific experts to evaluate recommendations. Science studies scholars could help uncover latent values, conflicts of interest, and other kinds of biases, adjudicating the legitimacy of any apparent scientific consensus.

Collins and Evans's suggestion sounds promising, but there are significant barriers to its realization. As one can gather from the paltry support
given by the federal government to social research—less than 5 percent of
the National Science Foundation's research-and-development budget[59]—
the social sciences have nowhere near the same status as the natural sciences
and engineering. It seems unlikely in the short term that social scientists
would not only be permitted a stronger role in policy making but also be
allotted the ability to veto in part the recommendations made by experts
in a natural science subdiscipline. I would wager that such a change will
remain politically infeasible until the popular belief that policy can or
should be scientized is effectively lessened.

There is good reason to be skeptical of proposals favoring an epistocratic
form of government. By enshrining a mere portion of the population with
the power to govern, everyone else is rendered less free. Although policies
might become more sensitive to scientific consensus—wherever it might
actually exist—epistocratic processes risk forcing nonepistocrats to live
according to other people's values and worldviews without adequate representation. Moreover, given that scientific and technical experts—along
with their political colleagues and public fans—have been known to fall
prey to technological enthusiasm in the past, it is unclear whether decisions
would necessarily be any wiser. Attempting to make political decisions
solely on the weight of the evidence, moreover, would produce inaction
when the facts are far from certain and exclude full consideration of issues
such as fairness and responsibility. Finally, far from decreasing the messiness and unsavory political jockeying that often infects policy decisions, an
epistocracy would only shift politicking to the problem of what constitutes
genuine expertise or rationality. Apart from such problems, it is unclear
whether epistocrats' foundational assumption is justified. Is competent
decision making really incompatible with democracy?

DEMOCRATIC PLURALISM

The reality that people are often, if not usually, ill informed or suffer from
various cognitive impairments or biases does not mean that democracy itself
is unworkable. *Democratic pluralism*, in contrast to epistocracy, is rooted in the
recognition that even expert analysts generally lack the cognitive capacity
to fully understand complex problems; even if they do have such a capacity,
they typically do not possess adequate information, do not have enough time

or money to conduct sufficient study, and cannot provide a value-free perspective of the issue. As a result, pluralists argue that just as good, if not better, outcomes result from *mutual adjustments* among diverse groups of political partisans: activists, citizens groups, industry lobbyists, experts, and decision makers. In a pluralist democracy, various political coalitions debate, negotiate, compensate, defer, reciprocate, and otherwise strategize in order to achieve at least some facet of their desired outcome. It is through this ongoing fracturing and reforming of alliances around different conflicts and via the resulting compromises, concessions, and adjustments that a large segment of citizens' interests can be satisfied. The tendency for different groups to get at least some of their demands met produces more gradual policy changes. This gradualness helps ensure that unintended consequences remain relatively small, permits policy makers more flexibility later on, and ensures that changes can be more easily studied and understood.[60] Contrary to the idyllic images of harmonious democratic deliberation proffered by some political theorists, pluralists do not idealize consensus; too much agreement would be a sign that something has gone wrong, that citizens' thinking has been impaired so as to prevent critical thinking.[61] In short, pluralism articulates how collections of imperfectly rational, biased people nevertheless manage to produce intelligent decisions.

Although a theoretical statement of democratic pluralism can sound esoteric, most citizens have as much personal experience with mutual adjustment as they do with centralized planning. The political scientist Charles Lindblom asked readers to consider how masses of people negotiate a crowded intersection without someone barking out orders and assigning trajectories.[62] The answer is that pedestrians pick up on subtle cues regarding each other's decisions, adjusting their path accordingly in order to avoid collisions. One sees the same kind of mutual adjustment on the notoriously undersigned and seemingly chaotic streets in Mumbai and other Indian cities—where one finds pedestrians, farm animals, motorbikes, cars, and large buses and trucks all vying for space. A growing class of traffic engineers even argue that designing streets to require eye contact and subtle negotiation between drivers, cyclists, and pedestrians is more efficient and safer than enforcing a rigid adherence to explicit rules through signage and policing. Professional soccer and rugby teams likewise accomplish brilliant plays on the fly, without a coach giving orders via a headset—as is the case in American football. Even air-traffic control involves myriad negotiations and adjustments between pilots and controllers rather than decisions by an ostensibly all-knowing central authority.[63]

Although expert voices are no doubt vital to competent policy making, pluralists argue that it is diversity of thought and critical disagreement that produces intelligent choices. Simply put, more heads are better than one. This claim runs counter to the popular perception that bad decisions are the consequence of a purportedly ignorant public getting overly involved or of bureaucratic committees stifling the creativity of lone technoscientific geniuses. Indeed, the political scientists Joseph Morone and Edward Wood-house argue that the late twentieth-century demise of nuclear energy can be attributed to *too little democracy, not too much of it*.[64] If early champions of atomic technology had encouraged and included critical perspectives, then it might have been possible to better anticipate and prepare for later design problems. Overly enthusiastic engineers, scientists, and politicians might have more carefully reconsidered how persuasive the safety of light-water reactors that power today's nuclear plants would have been to citizens after an accident. They might have more strongly considered a greater diversity of reactor options, proceeded more gradually, and been more prepared to learn from experience rather than to plow ahead and be caught unawares by accidents such as Three Mile Island.

Indeed, it is often the mistaken belief that experts have complete, neutral knowledge and thus the subsequent exclusion of everyone else's input that leads to mistakes. One classic example is how a decentralized network of artisan craftsmen in Denmark produced far more reliable wind turbines in the 1980s than did the much better-funded, highly centralized, and NASA-supported effort in the United States. Despite having hundreds of millions in funding and some of the best minds and resources, the NASA effort was outdone by far less sophisticated designs created by people with back-grounds in building agricultural machinery. Part of what made the differ-ence is that the process used by the Danish wind-turbine builders enabled widespread but small-scale experimentation with traditional models. Builders also shared their frustrations and results through a widely circu-lated journal, which allowed them to learn more quickly from each other's experience and then to adjust their designs. The NASA engineers, in con-trast, had little respect for traditional turbines developed by artisans in the early twentieth century, believing instead that they could mathematically model their way to a more optimal design. This case shows how diversity of participation often trumps high-level technical expertise.[65]

Support for the idea that decentralization, diversity, and disagreement produce better decisions also comes from research on "high-reliability organizations," which successfully manage extremely risky technologies. For instance, even though the US Navy is a hierarchical and centrally run organization, an aircraft carrier's hierarchy flattens while crews launch and land jets.[66] Even the lowest-level serviceperson can halt an operation to avert disaster and can propose new ways of doing things. Rather than be dictated by a central officer's commands, safely launching or landing a fighter jet once per minute on a constantly rocking runway emerges out of the constant communication and mutual adjustments between groups of servicepeople—many of them just 18 years old. They even manage to do so among the ever-present dangers of hot jet exhaust, bombs and missiles, and steel wires moving at 170 miles per hour. Similar procedures have been present at the nuclear plant at Diablo Canyon. Employees are encouraged to maintain a constant critical attitude about the safety of the plant, and frequent meetings are called to carefully scrutinize what might at first appear to be routine maintenance or a minor error. Indeed, in high-reliability organizations, people who think they have it all figured out are the least-desirable members.[67] Bad decisions often result when certain people's judgments are treated as sacrosanct. Numerous airplane disasters, for example, have been the product of a copilot failing to question a poor decision made by the more experienced and senior captain.[68]

One only has to look to science itself, moreover, to see the potential of pluralist disagreement and mutual adjustment. Again, the lone-genius story is a deceptive myth. Philosophers of science instead contend that theories become more "objective" only by being subjected to scrutiny by scientists holding a variety of different competing viewpoints—perspectives influenced by their personal commitments to different theoretical paradigms, experimental methods, research goals, and base assumptions about reality.[69] Recall how feminist biologists and anthropologists have improved understandings of conception by pointing out hidden masculine biases.

Consensus in science, if it occurs, is almost always tentative or incomplete and rarely goes unchallenged; no researcher is considered too intelligent to have his or her claims accepted without skepticism, and new theories would be too slow to develop without newcomers positing what might initially seem to be outrageous reinterpretations of earlier results. Scientific adversaries even go so far as to publicly lambaste one another in order to ensure the survival of their own view of natural phenomenon.[70]

This state of endless conflict is held together by a tacit agreement to a shared set of value aspirations: replication, falsifiability, openness to criticism, and so on.[71] At the same time, peer reviewers exert real power in routinely forcing scientists to compromise—that is, to temper or note the limitations of their claims. Although untrue results frequently get published, scientific institutions generally produce *good enough* technical knowledge despite the fact that scientists suffer the same cognitive limitations and biases as the rest of us. In other words, scientific knowledge is usually reliable not because scientists themselves are especially rational but rather because of the process of productive disagreement between diverse groups of researchers.

One might argue that all of the groups mentioned here—scientists, turbine builders, nuclear operators—hold only a narrow range of values in common—truth, safety, reliability and so on—and therefore cannot teach us anything about democracy. But pluralism is visible in the partial resolution of many public conflicts. For instance, John Fleck has described how water policy for the Colorado River advances through the decentralized "network governance" of managers, engineers, lawyers, environmentalists, and representatives for agricultural interests, a process that is often far more productive and cooperative than the media depict it to be.[72] Although achieving cooperation between these disparate groups has not been easy, pluralistic water governance has produced ongoing partial successes, from the release of "environmental" flows from the Colorado River to ensure the continued existence of the Santa Clara Cienega wetland to the ever-improving water-consumption rates in some southwestern cities. Similar to how scientists with different understandings of "good science" can produce reliable knowledge through productive disagreement, political partisans with divergent views on the "public good" can achieve quality policy outcomes through mutual compromises and concessions.

One reason why pluralism can outperform expert analysis is that it ensures the representation of a wide range of values and viewpoints, thus helping to expose blind spots and faulty assumptions. Most of all, pluralism recognizes that people have as much, if not more, expertise regarding their own interests and lives as distant experts do. Recall the earlier example of English sheep farmers after the Chernobyl disaster. Recommendations were made that locals saw as detrimental to their way of life because British government scientists, despite having little to no knowledge of sheep farming, did not think to talk to the farmers. The government scientists assumed they knew what was best for local farmers, so they excluded the latter's expertise. Pluralism acknowledges that no amount of education can guarantee that an expert knows what it is like to live in another person's shoes. Moreover, just as a scientific fact might be accepted today only because it has not yet been subjected to sufficient scrutiny, political consensus may exist simply because those who disagree have been left out of the decision-making conversation.[73] By valuing disagreement per se, pluralism ensures broad enough participation to counter the cognitive limitations and biases of any individual group.

It is important to keep in mind that pluralism is both a description of what sometimes occurs within democratic societies and an ideal. The intelligence of pluralist democracy is no different than that of science: it is a *potential*. It is realized under the right circumstances. One of the most significant barriers to intelligent pluralism in contemporary democracies is the fact that some partisan groups are much more powerful than others. For instance, business occupies a politically privileged position in terms of having considerable financial resources, lobbying organizations at the ready, and more direct access to political officials.[74] The CEO of Exxon more easily arranges meetings with senators and the president than can leaders of large environmentalist groups. And even when the ears of decision makers are equally open to a variety of interest groups, industry groups often leverage their far deeper pockets to ensure that their opponents' victories remain small, are delayed as long as possible, or are eventually rolled back.[75]

In this view, the problem in cases where corporate lobby groups manufactured doubt (e.g., acid rain and cigarette smoking) was not so much that science was being contaminated by politics but that corporate interpretations of the evidence were given disproportionate weight in the political debate. Just as markets are competitive only if no producer, consumer, or other economic actor is so large that it can dictate prices, pluralist democracy exists only insofar as no political group is powerful enough to be able to unilaterally skew the agenda. It is a sign of the deficit in pluralism in the United States that Exxon's and its allies' political opposition to and claimed skepticism regarding climate change carry far more weight than the views of a broader coalition of concerned citizens and other partisan groups.

Business's privileged position means that firms need not even voice concern to influence policy; just the perceived possibility of a negative "market reaction" leads decision makers not to pursue or even to think of certain options.[76] How often do citizens hear that measures such as a living-wage requirement or efforts to mitigate the worst possible climatic changes cannot be implemented because financial markets would mutiny and corporations would take their business elsewhere, reduce investments, or cease to create jobs? Whether the implicit threat is realistic is rarely seriously considered; just raising it as a possibility is often enough to stifle debate. The Australian government, for instance, abandoned plans for a mining tax once it appeared to them that the industry had persuaded much of the population that the tax would jeopardize jobs and economic growth.[77] One political science study claimed to find that median citizens' opinion has mattered far less than that of business lobby groups and economic elites regarding whether a bill becomes a law—although the study's conclusions are disputed.[78] Hence, there is good reason to believe that better educating average people on the "right" facts is less important for moving policy forward for climate change or for other public scientific controversies than ensuring that some groups' political interests do not crowd out everyone else's.

Just because business occupies a privileged position, however, does not mean that corporate CEOs pull the strings on politicians as if they were marionettes. Rather, officeholders rely upon economic well-being and job growth—or the perception of it—for reelection. As a result, there is a strong incentive for the cries of the business sector to be more readily heard. But it is not guaranteed that business always gets its way. Public-administration scholars in Denmark have found that nonbusiness groups actually tend to be more influential than industry for laws and regulations dealing with public-sector services.[79]

Besides relative equality between partisan groups, pluralism also requires certain kinds of interactions between citizens. Indeed, if more intelligent public decisions are supposed to emerge out of mutual adjustments between diverse partisan groups, those groups must be willing to tolerate occasional compromise and concession. The political theorist Chantal Mouffe argues that pluralist partisans must see each other as "adversaries" rather than as "enemies" to be vanquished;[80] they must be willing to make and accept tentative compromises and must keep in mind that they might be able to force additional concessions in their own interests at a later time. Moreover, groups that might otherwise be enemies must be willing to ally themselves when their interests partly align, such as when hunters and environmentalists join together to advocate for the preservation of wilderness. These kinds of agonistic—rather than antagonistic—interactions are likely only if citizens are willing to give ground to or work with former opponents.

But agonistic politics cannot happen when citizens fall prey to dogmatism, whether that dogmatism is the result of advertising, propaganda, threats of social ostracism, or the gentle cognitive tyranny exerted by family socialization and education.[81] These processes give rise to convergences of opinion—absences of disagreement—that exist not because they are objectively or unquestionably superior but because they remain unchallengeable in people's minds. Recall the convergence among twentieth-century nuclear scientists and most of the public that unbridled nuclear innovation would provide for a better American future or the oft repeated claim that one cannot have a "modern" society without toxic chemicals.[82] Cognitively imprisoned within narrow thought paradigms, citizens become more intransigent in their opinions and political interests. Thus, when disagreement does emerge, it is transformed from a means for mutually adjusting toward more intelligent outcomes into a source of ongoing polarization and instability.

Such seems to be increasingly the case in the United States and across the world today. What role does political scientism—the belief that science determines one's own political view but not those of others—play in the declining productivity of public disputes?

POLITICAL SCIENTISM AND THE POTENTIAL
INTELLIGENCE OF DEMOCRACY

As I have depicted throughout this chapter, people frequently talk as if expertise were everywhere preferable to democracy in terms of delivering intelligent decisions, especially when it comes to technoscientific issues. Many groups act as if they believe "the facts" can do their politics for them. Some of these beliefs may be rooted in unrealistic expectations of scientific experts, whereas other partisans may be simply leveraging science's high status for political gain. Whether the debate is over climate change, GE crops, mandatory vaccinations, or gun-control legislation, political opponents routinely behave as if science has already vindicated their own position. They are not unlike opposing high school football teams who take a pregame knee to ask for divine intervention: both are utterly convinced that the universe is uniquely on their side.

The incompleteness of scientific knowledge and the complexity of reality, however, means that every partisan group's factual understanding of reality is invariably incomplete, an incompleteness filled in by the group's values. Moreover, even if total scientific certainty were possible, facts would still not be able to settle disputes. Suppose that scientists could prove that a fetus at a certain gestational age unequivocally possesses some level of consciousness. Advocates of legalized abortion would not disappear; they would continue to emphasize the need to prioritize the mother's health and her right to choose or concerns about the fetus's likelihood of having a good life. Although science cannot solve citizens' political disputes, the idea that it can do so still influences political interactions. How does the belief that our contentious conflicts can be settled by the facts alter the character of political debate?

The first consequence of political scientism is easily seen. Consider how one *Discover* magazine writer charged in 2013 that worries about GE crops are the result of people's brains being infected by "ignorance and ideology." An author on *Natural News* similarly argued that science-popularizer Bill Nye's more optimistic take on the environmental risks of GE crops was a product of Nye's alignment with the "greatest science fraud of the century."[83] My point here is not to defend a position for or against GE crops. Rather, my contention is that once people believe that their own political positions are just the result of "listening to the science," they tend to deride political opponents as uninformed, if not corrupt.

Although citizens of all stripes dismiss those who disagree with them as simply being ignorant of the facts, such dismissal is particularly prevalent in liberal rhetoric about conservatives. Comedian Rob Corddry quipped in 2004 that "the facts have a liberal bias," a line now repeated by columnists such as economist Paul Krugman. And there is no shortage of newspaper editorials and books that argue that poor and middle-class whites who vote Republican have been duped or brainwashed into voting against their own interests. The claimed liberal bias of facts, however, does not stop right-wing media outlets from professing a similar monopoly on truth. For instance, one Louder with Crowder network blogger asserts that facts never sway liberals because they feel rather than think through the issues.[84]

Although it is probably unavoidable that people develop negative views of their political opponents, the way that mental and cognitive deficits are placed center stage within political scientism is particularly harmful.

Consider one blogger's suggestion that being skeptical about vaccines "might be some sort of mental disorder" or a *Scientific American* writer's argument that left-wing opposition to nuclear energy is the result of ignorance, "bad psychological connections," and an irrational fear of the unknown. One author in the *New Republic* dismissed worries about nuclear energy as a product of "coordinated misinformation" and blamed safety concerns on citizens having watched *The Simpsons* and mistakenly believing that Homer Simpson represents the average nuclear-reactor employee. On his Netflix program, Bill Nye tackles controversial issues such as alternative medicine, antivaccination, and climate change primarily by presenting one side as in line with science and the other as beset by cognitive biases and ignorance.[85] Yes, people are often misinformed about the issues they care about, but narratives like Nye's and the others mentioned here portray disagreement as if it were always the result of cognitive deficiencies and conspiratorial thinking on one side or the other. The historian Ted Steinberg describes this tendency to blame political opponents' opinions on an underlying psychological ailment as "the diagnostic style of politics."[86]

The problem with the diagnostic style of politics is not simply that it is rude and condescending but that it encourages a fanatical approach to political disagreements. Opponents are no longer people who see the world differently but instead heretics who refuse to think "rationally" or accept objective science. Consider how one *Natural News* writer recently decried the environmental movement to limit carbon dioxide emissions as "not just a war on facts, but even a war on logic and reason" advanced via brainwashing.[87] These kinds of framings undermine the adversarial interactions at the root of pluralist politics. Those who disagree become enemies to be vanquished, not people to be negotiated with. The idea of sharing power or compromising with opponents becomes anathema.

Another cost of the fanaticism bred via political scientism is a loss in citizens' capacity to critically probe social problems.[88] The belief that one's own partisan group has a monopoly on truth prevents citizens' from inquiring too deeply into their own beliefs or political opponents' motivations. One writer for *The Federalist* did just this when she chided pro-choice advocates for "their lack of understanding or willingness to admit science proves life begins at conception"; according to the author, the resulting and logically fallacious pro-choice arguments have had a "disgusting" effect on the debate. Yet others such as Bill Nye have claimed to survey the same facts and come up with the exact opposite conclusion.[89] Such rhetoric leaves little room to consider the divergent understandings of rights, visions of a good society, and personal experiences that might shape someone's understanding of the topic. Contra political scientism, most people's views on issues such as abortion developed long before they took high school biology, and next to no one with a position on climate change, GE crops, vaccines, or nuclear energy risks has spent the months, years, or even decades necessary to review all the relevant literature on it—even if people were capable of doing so with a cool and rational detachment.

When debates are thought of as being settled by science, consideration of people's differing values, needs, and interests is crowded out. Why even try to understand the position of someone you consider deluded, ignorant, or indoctrinated? This lack of understanding was visible in the seemingly technical debate over whether private firms such as SpaceX can provide safer spaceflight than NASA. Advocates of government-driven spaceflight and champions of privatization measured safety differently: the former saw it in terms of dollar amounts dedicated to safety and operational experience, whereas the latter defined it in terms of meeting certain technical requirements and more quantitative measures of a successful track record.[90] As a result, opponents ended up talking past each other and so distracted politicians and the public from the main point of contention: Is a privatized space system something we should want?

Likewise, the Genetic Literacy Project purports to advance "science not ideology" and derides any negative viewpoint on GE crops as steeped in "pseudoscientific nonsense." Yet given that much of the project's funding comes from free-market-promoting philanthropic groups such as the Searle Freedom Trust, one suspects that genetic science literacy is really a screen for the project's underlying political aspiration: the "right" free-market thinking with regard to biotechnology. As a result, the project's participants mislead readers as they misunderstand opponents, failing to recognize that public opposition has as much to do with citizens' lack of trust in markets to ensure safe biotechnological products as with their purported deficits in scientific literacy.

Focusing on "the facts" obscures the broader value disagreements and political interests lying at the root of most controversies. Just look at the paltry progress made through decades of "just the science" climate-change communication. Climate activists have spent far too much time trying to make climate-change skeptics see the light rather than attempting to understand the deeper reasons for the skeptics' hesitancy.

The belief that one's own ideas are uniquely guided by science may even hinder critical reflection. The media theorist Neil Postman found that he could dupe many of his academic colleagues surprisingly easily. He could convince them that a relationship existed between jogging and reduced intelligence or that chocolate eclairs contained a special nutrient that helps people lose weight simply by claiming that it was the result of a recent scientific study reported in the *New York Times*.[91] Even highly educated people will accept the outrageous result of a purported scientific study as received wisdom rather than critically inquire into the study—that is, unless the result conflicts with their worldview. Survey results appear to show that opinions on anthropogenic climate change and other issues become only more increasingly polarized as people become more educated or scientifically literate. Such results are not all that surprising, given that people adept at scientific reasoning can just as well use it to confirm their own biases as not.[92] The French sociologist Jacques Ellul once quipped that "anyone holding [the] conviction [that he can distinguish truth from falsehood] is extremely susceptible to propaganda, because when propaganda does tell the 'truth,' he is then convinced that it is no longer propaganda . . . his self-confidence makes him all the more vulnerable to attacks of which he is unaware."[93]

Another cost of the fanaticism bred by political scientism is equally fanatical policy. For instance, the Australian Parliament passed regulations that not only eliminated thousands of dollars of welfare benefits for parents with unvaccinated children but also sought (via fines) to prevent them from enrolling their children in preschool or other child care centers; South Australia's minister for education and child development argued that although "there will be people who have . . . ideological concerns about immunization[,] I'm not particularly interested in hearing an argument that isn't based in science." One Maryland judge mailed letters to parents of unvaccinated children that threatened them with fines and jail time.[94]

Although vaccine advocates might applaud such moves, it is important to acknowledge the consequences of more fanatically punitive policy. Because fanaticism ignores or dismisses as illegitimate the value disagreements underlying a conflict, it can breed retrenchment. Many vaccine-wary parents, for instance, are not so much antiscience as dissatisfied with the lack of power they feel when interacting with the medical system.[95] As a result, achieving desired vaccinations rates through harsh punishments may end up being a Pyrrhic victory; even though it might be a net good for public health, vaccine-skeptical parents would likely become more distrustful of governmental oversight of medicine. Indeed, interview data from Australia and psychological experiments find that mandates and financial penalties tend to make vaccine-hesitant parents angrier and more committed to their "antivaxx" position.[96]

Fanatical policy, furthermore, hinders the process of mutual adjustment toward a more intelligent outcome. Imagine if pedestrians or car drivers stuck fanatically to their prechosen paths and took no consideration of others' decisions. Consider how good soccer or basketball teams often lose matches when "prima donna" players make little effort to coordinate their tactics with their teammates. Policy can be similarly hindered by fanatical participants.

From a politically scientistic viewpoint, alternative medicine and the antivaccination movement are nothing more than irrational quackery. How can policy be anything but harmed by engaging with skeptics of mainstream medicine or with antivaxxers who still cling to a long-retracted study on vaccines and autism? As a result of this scientism, vaccine advocates blind themselves to the underlying driver of opposition: the perception that pharmaceutical companies have an undue and dangerous level of influence in the medical system.[97] Likewise, when parents ask that decisions previously made unilaterally by doctors, such as vaccination schedules, now be more open, flexible, and transparent, their request reflects the growing illegitimacy of the "doctor decides, patient listens" mode of interaction. Women are disproportionately attracted to alternative medicine for similarly understandable reasons. Many of them have had underlying conditions that remain undiagnosed for years because mainstream doctors are likely either to dismiss their pain as psychosomatic or to be ignorant of gender variations in symptoms.[98] Political scientism would ensure that such problems within contemporary health care go unaddressed; if any failure to act according to "the facts" is simply heretical deviance, then there is little hope to develop alternative medical systems that can achieve public-health targets by better fostering trust.[99]

Health care is far from the only area of public life where political scientism prevents a fuller exploration of policy alternatives. Consider how little progress is made in gun control in the United States. No doubt part of that slowness is due to the privileged political position of the firearm business lobby acting via the National Rifle Association.[100] Another significant reason, however, is that each side seems totally convinced that the data vindicate its position. Whether a ban on assault weapons would actually decrease mass-shooting events in the United States is not assured by Australians' experiences when they enacted a similar ban after the Port Arthur massacre. Likewise misleading are conservatives' claims that ongoing violence in cities such as Washington, DC, and Chicago despite harsher restrictions proves gun control cannot work in the United States. Absent actual incremental changes whose results can be monitored and evaluated, it is anyone's—albeit educated—guess what effect a national ban on and buyback of assault weapons might accomplish. However, within the politically scientistic discourse, any proposed change running contrary to "the facts" is portrayed as pointless and irrational; the outcome is ostensibly already knowable. Policy predictions become dogma, preventing societies from experimenting.

Political scientism is thus profoundly unscientific. Again, science is about uncovering the complex layers of reality and continuing to question the tentative truths established by the previous generation; it is not about arriving at simple, indisputable facts. Politically scientistic discourse, in contrast, is characterized by a dismissive incuriosity regarding controversial claims, treating them as if the current state of knowledge were so good that further inquiry would be unmerited. For instance, despite ongoing concerns by some scientists that nonionizing electromagnetic radiation might pose adverse health effects, including cancer, the wireless communication industry and many self-described "defenders of science" nonetheless act as if the question is completely settled, as if continued skepticism can never be anything more than pseudoscientific piffle. Of course, assurances that Wi-Fi and 5G cell phone signals are entirely harmless seem reasonably well founded. Yet that does not mean that it is pointless to continue to look for potential harms or to proceed more cautiously when saturating public spaces with electromagnetic radiation.[101] I do not know what to call the treatment of certain beliefs about highly complex phenomena as if they were totally unassailable—"fundamentalist theology" maybe—but science it is not. No doubt, at some point it makes sense to deprioritize some areas of research, but that choice is as much political as it is scientific.

As Daniel Sarewitz has argued, "Politics isn't about maximizing rationality, it's about finding compromises that enough people can live with to allow society to take steps in the right direction."[102] Holding fanatically to one's own supposedly "fact-based" political opinion prevents the discovery of opportunities to negotiate new alliances and agreements. If one's political opponents are simply irrational or ignorant, what would be the point of arguing? It would be unreasonable to debate and compromise with a hopelessly deluded person. However, most people are not incapable of reason; rather they are imperfectly rational beings who see things differently than their opponents for a variety of legitimate reasons that are obscured by the narrative of "just the facts." By mistaking the source of disagreement as a lack of understanding *of truth*, opponents are decreasingly capable of recognizing and addressing the underlying deficits *in trust*. The dispute mediation scholars Lawrence Susskind and Patrick Field argued more than two decades ago that the collective hope that science can be an "objective arbiter" of our conflicts was a misguided one; scientific discourse was not up for the job, and the hope that it could be conceals the real challenge: earning public confidence.[103] Despite Susskind and Field's prescient observations, societies today seem no closer to managing public disagreements productively.

Given the limitations of scientized policy and epistocratic approaches to politics, it seems unlikely that sound political decisions can be made while simultaneously idolizing expertise. In light of how well pluralism functions in everyday life—in managing dangerous technologies and in the process of science itself—citizens should look for better governance via more democracy, not less. However, the hope that expert knowledge will be capable of solving the problem of political contention remains pervasive. This hope is self-defeating, though, ultimately undermining the preconditions for intelligent pluralistic democracy to exist. That is, epistocratic beliefs are a self-fulfilling prophesy: the more it is believed that only expertise and "the facts" can resolve political problems, the less democracies are capable of doing so. The barrier to intelligently addressing public issues, therefore, is not that citizens cannot be purely rational or objective; rather, it is the tendency to pathologize disagreement. Without diversity of thought and equally empowered oppositional partisan groups, there is little to stop ruling alliances from committing major mistakes in their enthusiasm for their own preferred visions of the good society.

In this chapter, I have charted one contemporary—and increasingly dominant—ideal regarding the relationship between truth and politics.

Motivated by the belief that science and the political world are entirely distinct, many citizens have begun to see science as something to be isolated and insulated from explicit political influence and politics as something to be almost entirely guided by scientific evidence. People act and talk as if a kind of apolitical scientific politics can steer controversial policy decisions, thus sidestepping or obviating differences in values or worldview. The resulting actions and talk are, however, far from apolitical but instead amount to a form of fanaticism. That is, political scientism starkly divides societies into friends and enemies, the enlightened and the ignorant. The solution to political disagreement under such a view is not to listen, debate, or—at least—explore possibilities for compromise or concession. Instead, political opponents are to be informed of the "correct" facts or truths, harshly sanctioned, or simply ignored. No doubt there are cases where fanaticism may be justified—an issue I take up in chapter 5—but political scientism risks turning *every* debate with a factual element into a fanatical one.

In any case, "the facts" are far from the only political discourse that makes disagreement intolerable. In the next chapter, I examine the parallel rise of "common sense," a discourse that directly challenges political scientism by attempting to disempower experts.

Political scientism has sown the seeds of its own undoing and given rise to its own nemesis. Competing narratives have developed in response to the growing political power of "the facts." Consider an exchange between President Trump's senior adviser, Stephen Miller, and the *New York Times* reporter Glenn Thrush:

> MILLER: Let's also use common sense here, folks. At the end of the day, why do special interests want to bring in more low-skilled workers? And why historically . . .
>
> THRUSH: Stephen, I'm not asking for common sense. I'm asking for specific statistical data.
>
> MILLER: Well, I think it's very clear, Glenn, that you're not asking for common sense, but if I could just answer your question.
>
> THRUSH: No, no, not common sense. Common sense is fungible. Statistics are not.[1]

In light of what I discussed in the previous chapter, it is clear that Thrush erred when he claimed that statistics are not fungible—statistical studies are routinely designed and interpreted in value-laden ways. They cannot provide a perfectly complete or objective answer to the question regarding the effects of low-skill immigration or any other complex social issue. In any case, despite Thrush's protests, "common sense" has become a popular rhetorical tool, one almost as powerful as "the facts" in shaping people's understanding of politics. But what is common sense really? And how does the veneration of common sense alter thought, debate, and action in a democratic society?

COMMON SENSE IN POLITICAL TALK

As Sophia Rosenfeld describes in her history of common sense, it has long influenced European and American politics.[2] Although the term *common sense* was originally used to describe nothing more than the ordinary capacity to learn about the world via the five human senses, a new meaning took shape throughout and after the eighteenth century. Radicals and conservatives alike appealed to the ostensibly irrefutable capacity of so-called true or common men for clear and objective reasoning and their ensuing acceptance of certain truths.

Such appeals were, however, born in contradiction. Common sense was implied to be something that unifies all people; yet only a distinct group was viewed as being in possession of it. The lower classes were often depicted as lacking the requisite good breeding or upbringing, and overly educated elites were seen as having lost touch with common sense. In his pamphlet *Common Sense* (1776), Thomas Paine claimed to be speaking only simple, irrefutable, and self-evident truths—in contrast to the bombastic and overly complex claims of philosophers and aristocrats of the time—when he argued that common sense dictated that the American colonies should separate from England. Of course, his opponents viewed themselves as being the ones truly in possession of common sense when they argued to the opposite conclusion.

The political promise of "common sense" is similar to that of the facts. The term is invoked to suggest that some objective answer to political questions exists and could be implemented if only all the noncommonsensical contaminants of people's thinking could be eliminated. It is believed, as Rosenfeld puts it, that under the guidance of common sense "politics itself will become simpler, clearer, and ultimately less contentious once all the complex speculation and obfuscating jargon associated with an exclusive political class are finally pushed aside and the *real* people are finally able to see it and tell it like it is."[3] That is, like political scientism, the narrative of common sense promises that some special kind of reasoning can replace the messiness of political conflict and offers the potential to escape contention through a depoliticized form of "rational" politics.

The trouble with common sense as a guide for public problems is that there is even less agreement on what it is than on what is scientific fact. Ronald Reagan simplistically portrayed conflict with the Soviet Union via "commonsensical" metaphors describing the Soviets as barbarous and immune to reason; such language was used to justify a national stance that risked provoking nuclear war in order to prevent the spread of communism.[4] It almost goes without saying that nuclear brinkmanship, for many people, never seemed commonsensical. Donald Trump similarly couched his policy proposals, from a multi-billion-dollar border wall to protectionist trade policies, in appeals to common sense, even as free trade and liberal immigration policy have become almost unquestionable in many university economics departments.[5] Gun-control advocates likewise defend assault-weapon bans and other measures as straightforward, commonsensical policy, only for conservatives in turn to mobilize their own appeals to common sense, such as the truism that gun laws punish the "law-abiding" gun owner and do little to prevent crimes from being committed with illegally obtained weapons.[6]

How can we hope to come to know reliably and fairly who exactly reasons commonsensically and who does not? The idea that rule by the commonsensical classes would obviate traditional political contention seems to move conflict from the public issue at hand to the question of who has common sense. Unlike the case for scientific expertise, however, there are no existing institutions that credential people in commonsensical reasoning. In any case, when most people invoke the term *common sense* in political conversations, the implication is that they, but not their opponents, are in possession of it.

Even though it is not clear who exactly exercises common sense, there is a recognizable pattern to who is portrayed as lacking it. Consider how one political cartoon depicts the climate-change debate: a scientist is shown standing by a chalkboard covered in calculations and conflicting messages about the global climate and looking on as a child writes, "It's called weather."[7] The implication of the cartoon is that apparent extreme climatic events are easily recognized as no different from normal weather variability; the problem is that scientists and climate-change proponents are overthinking the issue. Academics and other highly educated people are routinely depicted within the "common sense" narrative as adrift in a sea of theoretical abstractions, having long ago lost touch with concrete, everyday rationality.

The distrust of "overthinkers" explains why children are often portrayed as paragons of sound reasoning. Indeed, the underlying political message of episodes in the long-running show *South Park* is usually uttered by the character Stan, a fourth grader. The show's writers regularly depict adults, Hollywood elites, and political authority figures as "blinded by ideological filters," while the child protagonists see reality for what it is.[8] For instance, one early episode derides environmental activists working to protect rain-forest land as intolerantly imposing on others a naive and mythological view of nature as benevolent. According to the child protagonists, environmentalists do so only to feel good about themselves. In contrast, the construction firms bulldozing the rain forest exemplify the conservative commonsensical ideals of self-sufficiency and domination over nature.

In any case, the tendency for common sense to be defined in opposition to expert knowledge is unsurprising, given how politically advantageous scientistic political rhetoric has become. Portraying experts as being misguided by their education and too clever to think soundly helps wrestle back some of the rhetorical high ground from fact-wielding opponents. Common sense can be seen as a reactionary counterrhetoric to the perceived overreach of experts in politics. Conservatives try to reframe extreme climatic events as mere weather because of worries that the apparent scientific consensus on climate change provides left-leaning policy makers with a convenient crisis that gives them carte blanche to alter societies in far-reaching ways. Indeed, one commentator derides climate science as a "fad" that liberals have latched onto in order to implement "rule by experts." Another political cartoon depicts the acceptance of man-made global warming as a product of "drinking the Kool-Aid" sold by Al Gore, implying that a majority of Americans have rediscovered common sense by rejecting Gore's views; the cartoonist tellingly depicts the cost of the Kool-Aid as the "U.S. Free-Market Economy."[9]

In other instances, the appeal to common sense is used not just to denigrate experts but to deny the relevance of facts at all. In the lead-up to the presidential election in 2016, former Speaker of the House Newt Gingrich dismissed as immaterial the FBI statistics showing the US violent crime rate to be at a multidecade low; what truly mattered, Gingrich argued, was that "the American people" believed neither that crime was down nor that they were any safer.[10] As the political scientist Jan-Werner Müller has argued, claiming to represent common sense is a means to render one's position "immune to empirical refutation."[11] Given the political power imparted by appearing to be on the side of science and the fanatical rejection of disagreement evoked by politically scientistic narratives, it is no wonder that those placed on the wrong side of "truth" search for a rhetorical weapon of their own.

The rejection of expertise within the narrative of common sense rests on the assumption that there is an almost "natural" or objective kind of reasoning that exists independently of culture but nevertheless remains always at risk of being corrupted by it. In an apparent attempt to give scientific backing to a conservative notion of common sense, the evolutionary psychiatrist Bruce G. Charlton has argued that the high-IQ individuals who tend to hold left-wing political views have an overdeveloped drive toward novelty seeking and hence a tendency to try to misapply abstract logic to otherwise straightforward, everyday problems. That is, they see more complex novelties than really exist in the world. These left-leaning "clever sillies," as Charlton puts it, have overriden the ostensibly proper human reasoning system that has evolved through millennia of hunter-gatherer existence. Charlton argues that clever sillies continue to exist only because their intelligence signaling provides a sexual-selection advantage in societies that are "IQ-meritocracies."[12]

Charlton's argument, however, is a "just-so story." It is a seemingly scientific explanation of an evolved trait that sounds plausible but is unproven—perhaps even untestable—and is likely to be infected by the storyteller's cultural biases. One thinks of the many purportedly biological explanations used over the centuries to justify slavery and the subordinate position of women in society.[13]

Leftists can just as easily point to other evolutionary perspectives to uphold their own worldview as more natural. Indeed, in response to a study suggesting that both men and women having equal decision-making power—traditionally not part of conservative common sense—was the norm until the advent of agriculture, one commentator explains: "Sexual equality is common sense."[14] There is no shortage of "scientific" disagreement regarding whether humans' common sense should point them toward egalitarian societies rooted in cooperation and mutual sharing or toward hierarchy and competition-driven inequalities in status and wealth.[15]

The attempt to naturalize common sense runs into additional problems once one tries to compare across groups. The eminent anthropologist Clifford Geertz argues that common sense is the organized system of knowledge that founds a culture, not a way of knowing shared by all of humanity. Commonsense views regarding how to think about and treat intersex people—the very small percentage of the population born with both male and female sex characteristics—have varied considerably. Such people were viewed with horror in ancient Rome and twentieth-century America, while the ancient Greeks saw them as a mere peculiarity. Certain East African tribes have considered the existence of intersex individuals to be a simple mistake, and traditional Navajo culture interprets it as a wonder and a blessing.[16] Even ostensibly self-evident, almost "natural," intuitions such as whether time moves forward by moving from left to right or some other way—right to left, back to forward, or east to west—varies by culture, often matching the dominant conventions for writing and other practices.[17]

In any case, even though the narrative of common sense contains an implicit derision of intellectuals and valorization of lay reasoning, experts are usually still sought to give voice to proper reasoning on political matters. Indeed, Sophia Rosenfeld's history shows that even though advocates of "commonsense" arguments saw it as a more natural or uncorrupted form of reasoning, they still believed that commonsensical thinking had to be instilled or properly cultivated.[18] Partisan political pundits fill this role in contemporary politics, reiterating or confirming the right political reasoning for viewers and readers. Ben Shapiro and Jordan Peterson, for instance, have earned a substantial online following for their "commonsensical" conservative judgments on political issues, despite having educational pedigrees no less elite than the average college professor's.

POPULISM: "THE PEOPLE" AND DEMOCRACY

If there is some kind of reasoning that is universal to all humans, beyond mere trivialities such as knowing that water is wet and drawing basic inferences about cause and effect, social scientists have yet to find it. However, common sense does not have to exist for the belief that it does to affect political talk. Whereas political scientism undergirds an attraction to epistocratic forms of governance, the idolization of common sense drives populism. Whereas epistocrats make little to no (positive) reference to democracy in justifying their preferred form of governance, populism is frequently portrayed as a democratizing political movement. But is it really any more democratic than epistocracy?

At the heart of populism is what my PhD mentor Ned Woodhouse calls the *illusion of harmony*. Populist rhetoric is suffused with references to "the people." Populist movements champion their right to control the levers of power by counterposing "the elite," who are seen as corrupt, and the "average" citizen. The democratic process is viewed as having been distorted by the excessive power of elites, which prevents the commonsensical "general will" of the people from dictating policy. For conservative populists, the average citizen is the antithesis of the ethnic, racial, and sexual minorities who receive "excessive" welfare benefits or rights protections from the liberal state, whereas leftist populists commonly depict the conflict as between economic elites—bankers and businessmen—and the poor and working classes.[19] President Nixon appealed to the supposed general will of the American people with his rhetoric of the "silent majority," who were taken to be those citizens who were middle class, suburban or rural dwelling, primarily Christian and white, supportive of the Vietnam War, and not at all like the cosmopolitan intellectuals who seemed to dominate the Democratic Party.[20]

Populist sentiments on the left are apparent in phrases such as "the 99 percent," which portray "the people" as everyone below the top one percentile in income and wealth. And there is a broader tendency among the Left to see all corporations and business interests as inherently corrupted by greed and profit seeking and to depict most nations as being hoodwinked by an illegitimate class of business elites. In any case, the rhetoric of populism on both sides of the spectrum presumes that political conflict will end once "the people" retake power from a corrupt establishment.

As is also the case for epistocracy, populism promises a depoliticized mode of politics that ultimately suffers several democratic and practical deficiencies. To begin, to what extent does the "general will" exist? And, assuming it does, how would people know when they found it? The "general will" looks to be the populist analogue of the "truth tenet" upheld by epistocrats. It sets up the task of politics as simply to unearth and implement the "true" popular will.

The idea of the general will figured prominently in the work of the eighteenth-century political theorist Jean-Jacques Rousseau. However, whereas Rousseau claimed that the general will was the common interest of all citizens[21]—recognizable to them once they learned to set aside their personal interests or "particular wills"—populism frames the general will as unique to a subset of citizens. This makes populism inevitably exclusionary: it enhances the level of participation of whichever groups get subsumed under the idea of "the people" but leaves out all others.

Moreover, applying a populist lens to political contention does not really eliminate conflict but instead shifts conflict to the question of who really represents "the people." Political rhetoric between Democratic and Republican politicians frequently centers on this distinction. In the run-up of the presidential election in 2008, candidate for vice president Sarah Palin referred to the residents of small, rural, and primarily white and Christian towns in the middle of the United States as "the real America," despite the fact that people with those demographics constituted a mere 20 percent of the population.[22] Although Hillary Clinton has never been a populist in the way of Trump or Palin—she has made no reference to the putative existence of a corrupt, elite political class—her campaign's language was still defined by this element of populism. A representative of Hillary Clinton's campaign in 2016 dismissed primary wins by Bernie Sanders in places such as Minnesota as not representative of the "New America," ostensibly because they were insufficiently diverse. Likewise, in her infamous reference to certain Trump supporters as belonging to "a basket of deplorables," Clinton claimed that citizens who used language that she considered racist, sexist, or xenophobic were "thankfully . . . not America."[23]

Whether in the ultraconservative claim that white, rural, and Christian citizens are under threat by "socialistic" policy or in leftist populists' railings against corporate interests, the underlying thrust of populist movements is a loss of trust in the ruling regime. In this way, populism is the opposite of epistocracy, which in contrast denies wholesale the role and importance of legitimacy within politics. However, populism in practice rarely leads to the strengthening of democracy. The typical result, visible everywhere from Hugo Chávez in Venezuela to Recep Erdoğan in Turkey, is the centralization of power in a charismatic figurehead through the removal of constitutional checks on executive power.[24] Because at the heart of populism lies the belief that unerring political truth lies within the symbolic notion of "the people," as represented by the populist leader, democratic practices themselves become superfluous. As a consequence, the populist leader's own interpretation of the citizenry's needs dominates all other interpretations. So, in another sense, populism is almost a subform of epistocracy, one in which the expertise of the ruling class lies in deciphering the general will rather than in understanding scientific truths.

Populism in practice is as antidemocratic as epistocracy. It disenfranchises large swathes of the population for lacking the "right" reasoning skills, shifts contention away from the issues at hand toward the problem of certifying who is in possession of common sense, and leads to the centralization of political power. Still, it has its defenders. The political theorist Chantal Mouffe believes that the right form of left populism could strengthen democracy if "the people" could be constructed out of the currently disparate democratic demands of the working class, LBGTQ communities, and other groups.[25] Yet such a designation invariably relies on an "oligarchy" in opposition, a group that Mouffe never clearly defines. Exactly how such a populist coalition would act any differently from other populist movements, which typically respond to the interests of those who are defined as "the people" and attempt to silence everyone else, is not clear either. Although Mouffe's proposal is potentially promising, there is good reason to be wary of it because it still offers no answer to the historical antidemocratic risks of populism.

COMMON SENSE, POPULISM, AND DEMOCRATIC PLURALISM

Although populism—and the idolization of commonsensical knowledge that underlies it—is in some ways a corrective to epistocracy, its democratic credentials are equally questionable. But my argument is not simply that truth narratives are exclusionary but that they promote a fanatical approach to politics that undercuts democratic pluralism. How does populism compare?

When examining political scientism, I argued that truth-focused political language undermines democratic pluralism in three interrelated ways. First, it encourages the diagnosis of political opponents, not dialogue. Because opponents are viewed as cognitively deficient rather than simply as having different values or experiences, political groups tend to call for and instantiate more fanatical policies. As a consequence of partisan groups overestimating their own abilities to comprehend the world and disavowing compromise and concession with opponents, their policy demands not only deny that other groups have something to contribute but also leave little to no role for active learning—thus reducing the representativeness, legitimacy, and intelligence of political outcomes. Can the same be said for populism?

No doubt most readers have already witnessed or experienced the "diagnostic style of politics" when it comes to "common sense." It is a typical feature of online political memes. Facebook pages such as Liberal Loon and Liberal Logic 101 as well as Twitter feeds such as Millennial_Conservative and Liberal "Logic" feature memes deriding the "stupidity" of American liberals and claiming to uncover glaring logical inconsistencies in leftist positions. Web pages and Twitter feeds by media figures such as Tomi Lahren and Ben Shapiro, whose careers have been built on claiming to expose the supposed irrationality of leftists, are followed by millions of people. Tomi Lahren, for instance, has dismissed Representative Keith Ellison (D–MN) as a "wacko" who did not believe in "common sense." Ben Shapiro's tweets include references to the "stupidity" of leftists and the claim that their political beliefs are justified only through "pseudo-science."[26]

Moreover, within the conservative populist narrative, the argument is not simply that leftists are irrational but also that they actively seek to destroy young people's ability to exercise common sense. Consider the University of Toronto psychologist Jordan Peterson, who gained a large online following after publicly exclaiming his refusal to be required to refer to transgender students by their preferred pronouns. No doubt there is a legitimate debate to be had about whether Ontario's human rights code actually requires him to do so and if it should. But Peterson's main contribution to that discussion has been to warn his Twitter followers that "radical leftists are replacing education with indoctrination." Peterson has fueled the populist narrative that debate around such issues exists only because students' cognitive ability to exercise common sense has been compromised.[27]

Most online political media seem to be steeped in the diagnostic style. Contemporary conservatives can tune into the Common Sense Conservative YouTube channel, which has garnered more than 23 million views, for videos lambasting leftists. The channel's description laments the loss of "the ability of reasonable thought and common sense" and takes the mere existence of "liberals" as evidence of this loss. Videos here and elsewhere in the political web reinforce the diagnostic approach and claim in their titles that this or that conservative pundit "owns" or "destroys the logic" of an opponent. Former children's television voice-over actor Steven Crowder has built a small media network called Louder with Crowder featuring videos, podcasts, and columns with titles such as "Top 5 Liberal FAILS throughout History" and "Top 5 Idiotic Leftist Moments during Anti-gun Student Walkouts." As a video and radio host, Crowder adapts the smug rhetorical style pioneered by left-leaning comedic television news anchors such as John Stewart and John Oliver but uses it to skewer "liberals" and "social justice warriors" for their supposed inability to think rationally.[28]

Less comedic but no less dismissive of their leftist opponents are websites such as Breitbart, WND, TheBlaze, The Rebel, and Infowars, which in their different ways portray themselves as populist outlets combating the elite "liberal media."[29] A quick search of their homepages uncovers a heavy application of the diagnostic style. Stories, editorials, podcasts, and video clips on the more extreme websites do not simply cover events but also often frame liberal politicians as "unhinged" or full of "rage." Protesters are "far-left agitators" who "trash the streets," and political offices are full of "social justice warriors" taking advantage of crises to expand corrupt governmental overreach. Even when outlets such as TheBlaze employ more measured language, they are nevertheless selective in the curation of stories, never missing the opportunity to cover an event where a citizen with a concealed carry license seemed to be mistreated, a leftist politician called for a gun ban, a public-school student was required to do a project on Islam, or an organization required more LBGTQ sensitivity from their employees. The focus of such media is to diagnose leftists, or at least the world they aspire to build, as irrational.

Last, a plethora of diagnostic books have been published accusing the Left or Right of lacking common sense. The radio host Michael Savage went so far as to entitle one book *Liberalism Is a Mental Disorder*; Ben Shapiro refers to leftist university students as "brainwashed"; and Ann Coulter insists in a book title that "if Democrats had any brains, they'd be Republicans." Diagnostic books on the left include Leland Gregory's collection of anecdotes and quotes entitled *Stupid Conservatives* and Clyde Coughenour's *Anyone That Works for a Living and Votes Republican Is an Idiot*."

As I argued in the previous chapter, it is not the rudeness of such rhetoric that makes it problematic—democratic politics does not have to be nice. Rather, by recasting political conflict as a battle between those who can reason and those who cannot, it encourages fanatical policy and undermines the possibility for compromise and coalition building. That is, when one's political world is divided into enlightened friends and brainwashed or stupid enemies, there is little sense in permitting opponents an influence on policy and every reason to enact extreme legislative action against them. Research from Turkey suggests that a predominance of populist political rhetoric is directly tied to opponents being seen as unworthy. In fact, surveys find that a large portion of Turkish citizens do not want to live next door to, do business with, or even have their children play with the offspring of people who support a different party; many Turks feel morally superior to their political opponents and approve of fanatical policies that constrain their opponents' freedom of speech and privacy rights.[30]

In the United States, Republicans' and Democrats' views of each other have never been more negative. A large portion of them see people belonging to the opposite party as close-minded and dishonest and view the opponents' policy preferences to be not merely wrong but also a threat to the nation's well-being. Americans saying that they would be displeased if their child married someone belonging to the opposite party has increased from 5 percent of Republicans and 4 percent of Democrats in 1960 to half of Republicans and one-third of Democrats. For many Americans, those who disagree politically are not merely opponents but outright enemies. In light of such changes, it seems unsurprising that 25 percent of Americans support the idea of the president being "a strong leader who does not have to bother with Congress and elections."[31] Such correlations suggest a relationship between an affinity for antidemocratic populism and the tendency to dismiss opponents as unworthy of reasoned consideration.

If a populist embrace of "common sense" leads citizens to see opponents as dangerous and cognitively damaged enemies, one should find a tendency to propose and support more fanatical policy proposals. Consider the right-wing polemicist Dinesh D'Souza, whose recent *New York Times* best seller applies some questionable logic to validate the claim that the American Left has "Nazi DNA." D'Souza advocates that the United States be "denazified" by investigating and prosecuting—and one supposes imprisoning—Barack Obama, Hillary Clinton, and other Democrat politicians for unnamed abuses of power.[32] In Canada, Jordan Peterson has described much of the social sciences and humanities as infected with something he calls "cultural Marxism" and as "hellbent on demolishing the fundamental substructure of Western civilization." His writings convey a belief in a kind of commonsensical natural order with regard to social hierarchies and gender relationships as well as considerable anxiety that professors who are overly enthralled with French social theory will disabuse unsuspecting college students of that natural order. In a move that harkens back to Red Scare political tests, he has called for tracking any university courses with "corrupt" "neo-Marxist" ideas in order to steer students away from them.[33]

Even more extreme examples exist. One blogger for *The Federalist* scolded centrist Republicans for continuing to compromise with the Left, warning readers to be ready to "Fight to the Death" in order to avoid the "eventual socialist abyss" awaiting the United States. The editor of one Alabama newspaper argued that the Ku Klux Klan needed to "ride again" and lynch the "socialist-communists" trying to raise taxes, arguing that these "fake" Americans' false understanding of the Constitution resonated only with "the ignorant, the uneducated, and the simple-minded people."[34]

In nations where populist politicians have attained the highest office, fanatically antipluralist policies have ironically tended to follow. Venezuelan leftist populist Hugo Chávez dismissed most of his political opponents as "enemies of the people" and followed such pronouncements with policies ensuring that the opponents could not force him to make political concessions. Outgoing parliaments delegated legislative powers to him in order to prevent an incoming opposition party from being able to shape policy. And when Caracas elected a mayor from the "wrong" party, Chavez tied his hands by putting city policy under the supervision of a federal commissioner.[35]

Populism in the United States has not yet gone that far. Of course, President Donald Trump did portray his opponent Hillary Clinton as not merely wrong but morally corrupt, calling for—though not following through with—her incarceration. However, the unchecked centralization of power in the executive—typical in populist governments—has not yet occurred in the United States, though not for any lack of expressed desire by the president. He has threatened to sue journalistic outlets that criticize his policies, has fired insufficiently loyal bureaucrats, and frequently railed against checks on his authority.[36]

Whereas some see Trump's and other politicians' inability to instantiate fanatical policies as a sign that the US political system is working properly, others worry that the increasingly widespread disavowal of democracy and the broader demonization of opponents will eventually undermine the American government and other democratic governments across the world. As the political scientists Steven Levitsky and Daniel Ziblatt have pointed out, the reframing of political opponents as enemies of the people tends to coincide with an unwillingness to compromise and the tendency to utilize any and all available legal methods—including packing courts and bureaucratic offices with loyalists—in order to get one's preferred policies established.[37] The repression of political opposition in turn paves the path to autocracy. Some of these techniques were visible in Salvador Allende's leftist government in Chile in the early 1970s, in particular the utilization of legal loopholes to push reforms through a reluctant parliament. Allende's supporters labeled any naysayers as "enemies of the people." His American-backed opponents retaliated with an even greater degree of fanaticism, leading the nation into a downward spiral of polarization, declining legitimacy of the political process, and eventually a military coup.

The United States increasingly appears to share many of the same features of declining democracies, albeit in more inchoate forms.[38] To take one example, populist rhetoric increasingly undergirds a tendency to see the electoral process as illegitimate. When populist candidates lose, the only possible reason for that loss must be corruption, given that their representation of the "will of the people" is seen as established fact. Recall Donald Trump's claim that his setbacks in the Republican primary in 2016 were the result of fraud and his insistence that his failure to win the presidential vote in 2020 was due to a cadre of enemies collaborating to "steal" the election.[39] Although the United States has not yet suffered an authoritarian populist regime, such rhetoric is a worrying sign that it may be sliding in that direction.

The final feature of fanatical truth-focused politics is that policy is no longer designed to be intelligent. That is, by denying the complexities of political issues and deifying one vision of the will of the people, populist politics leaves little to no room for explicit learning. The right-wing populist prime minister of Hungary, Viktor Orbán, notably refused to participate in his country's election debates in 2010 and 2014. He argued that "no policy specific debates are needed now," claiming that what needed to be done was obviously discernible through (his) common sense.[40] In the 1980s, the British prime minister Margaret Thatcher justified her insistence that "there is no alternative" to conservative free-market politics through an equivalent appeal to "common sense."[41] The Stephen Miller anecdote with which I began this chapter and Newt Gingrich's dismissal of FBI crime statistics exemplify similar mindsets. The supposed consequences of immigration by low-skilled workers on jobs or the perceived changes to the violent crime rate are portrayed as so clear and commonsensical that introducing scientific facts can serve only to confuse the matter. Right-wing author Dinesh D'Souza encourages people to assume that "everything we get from progressive academia, the media, and Hollywood [is] false" and that "nothing could be more useless" than trying to persuade leftists that they are wrong, contending that a fanatically unyielding implementation of Republican policies is the only way to ensure a free country.[42]

It is difficult to proceed intelligently in developing and deploying new policy when anyone with a different vantage point is dismissed. Left populist policies in Latin America have had a tendency to lead to runaway inflation and capital flight because populist leaders—in their zeal to raise wages, nationalize industries, and redistribute property—neither heed conservatives' warnings about inflation nor learn from other countries' failures.[43] By declaring economic elites to be not of "the people," leftist populist leaders let themselves forget that they must still contend with the global capitalist system. The thing with political opponents is that they must be dealt with regardless of whether one wants to or not. No doubt populist leaders have good reasons to object to the disproportionate power of business in politics and to seek to reduce economic inequality, but by failing to engage business in a process of mutual adjustment, they drastically increase the risk of economic crisis.

President Trump's forays into protectionist tariffs might prove to be little different. Some worry that by unilaterally pursuing what he views to be commonsensical trade policy, he has provoked a reactionary trade war that may end up producing more harm than benefit.

In domestic policy, commonsensical ideas about criminality and punishment stymie intelligent explorations of alternative criminal justice approaches. Critics contend that "tough on crime" legislation is both costly and ineffective at reducing crime rates. Locking people up for life for three felonies or giving them exorbitant sentences over drug possession costs taxpayers more than $30,000 per inmate per year on average. Some even worry that incarceration is counterproductive. It not only deprives families of a parent in the short term but also harms a family's longer-term earning potential—job options and career pathways for former felons are rarely good. As a result, the underlying state of poverty, financial insecurity, and fragmentation of family and community life that gives rise to crime in the first place is reproduced generation after generation. Despite being "tougher on crime," the United States has a recidivism rate that remains one of the highest in the world.[44] Yet many conservatives embrace the belief that if only punishments were strict enough, then citizens would be sufficiently incentivized to clean up their act. So strong is the commonsense narrative of crime and punishment among some conservative citizens that Scandinavian-style rehabilitation—or even simply providing air-conditioning in the summer—is viewed as "coddling criminals" and a sure pathway to more rapes and murders.[45] As a result, myriad alternative systems that may better reduce the crime rate—perhaps focusing on only the least-violent and most-promising candidates at first—are rarely considered or tested.

An additional part of the problem lies in the fact that populist politics tends to evoke fanatical reactions. In the same way that passing laws to make antivaxxers feel like social outcasts can breed entrenchment and further exacerbate the perceived illegitimacy of mainstream medicine, populist policies can worsen political divisiveness. One thinks of the violent confrontations now occurring between supporters and opponents of Venezuela's president Nicolás Maduro. A similar, albeit less extreme, example is how President Trump's derogatory rhetoric regarding political opponents and his implementation of policies meant to appease supporters and/or punish his opposition—a ban on Muslim immigration, "zero-tolerance" policies that separate immigrant children from their parents, removal of the state income tax write-off, among others—has fomented levels of animosity rarely seen in American politics. Within liberal social media bubbles, memes and articles comparing President Trump to Hitler and other fascist leaders proliferate. By exaggerating how far the United States has strayed from democratic institutions, such rhetoric recasts opposition to Trump's policies as a fanatical battle between good and evil, thus exacerbating polarization and the perception that political institutions are illegitimate—both of which in turn further drive the popularity of populist candidates.[46]

The decline of cooperation and concession—that is, of mutual adjustment—has been occurring in United States for some time. Some of its roots can be traced to Newt Gingrich's "Republican Revolution" insistence on "no compromise." Yet the use of filibusters by Democratic members of Congress exploded during the second Bush presidency, while Bush's behavior itself reflected an abandonment of any pretense of bipartisanship. More recently, Tea Party Republicans justified their own obstructionism with outrageous claims that President Obama and fellow Democrats did not "love America" or were even national enemies.[47]

At the same time, worries about the growth of populism can themselves turn fanatical. The diagnostic style often cuts both ways. Those supporting populist leaders are accused of possessing an "authoritarian" personality type, which ostensibly renders them incapable of critical thought and therefore a threat to democracy.[48] Diagnosis of supporters of populist politicians as "emotional," "ignorant," or simply "racist" and "xenophobic" prevents a sober reevaluation of the reasons why previous political representatives have lost legitimacy. Nineteenth-century American populism, for instance, developed out of a movement of farmers who felt that their livelihoods were increasingly at the mercy of bankers and railroad companies and that the two major parties were doing little to ameliorate the situation.[49] When value consensus forms among political elites, ordinary people can feel left out—regardless of whether that consensus involves the rightness of certain economic policies or attitudes about diversity.

Elite-level consensus often turns into what is identified as a form of common sense in its own right, with predictable results. Consider Noah Rothman's denigration of citizens who turn toward populism because they see themselves as left behind by the globalized economy. With a bit of utilitarian logic, Rothman reasons that because the winners of liberalized trade seem to outnumber the losers, populist citizens should simply be "overwhelmed" and "defeated" rather than listened to because they are "dangerously wrong" and are a "dire threat to prosperity and liberty."[50] Even though Rothman and others make frequent mention of "democracy" in their writings, their argument that the interests of a minority group—one recognized to be on the losing end of current policy—are unworthy of political consideration is antithetical to democratic principles. Worst of all, this attitude prevents political actors from imagining creative solutions for producing far fewer economic losers.

Other leftists have rejected economic explanations for the recent uptick in populism.[51] As a result, they transform Trump supporters' perceived antagonism for increasing diversity in race, religion, gender presentation, and sexuality into a sin against leftists' commonsensical notions of justice. This antagonism is seen as mere ignorance of the established facts regarding racism, sexism, and other forms of structural inequality. Because Trump supporters' political commitments are depicted as inexorably rooted in racism and sexism, they become illegitimate by definition—turning Trump voters into the social justice equivalent of antivaxxers. To many leftists, it is unimaginable that "Trumpists" could have any positive contribution to make to policy. Yet defining Trump supporters as heretics acting contrary to economic and social truths prevents a deeper exploration of the motivations behind their politics.

That reactionary proselytizers such as Jordan Peterson have garnered a large following among disaffected white men may be simply because they offer a positive, albeit hierarchical and traditionalist, narrative for white men to understand their lives. Alt-right narratives promise a return to an era when Western men were more unapologetically masculine, heroic masters of their own destinies, and free from having to navigate the complexities of increasingly diverse societies. At the same time, the emerging leftist narrative on race and gender relations can end up framing white men as little more than the bearers of a kind of "original sin," namely benefitting from a legacy of racism and patriarchy. Writer Roland Merullo recounted how a former female student told him that he was not even allowed an opinion on women's rights or domestic abuse because it was now his and other men's "turn" to be silent.[52] An undergraduate student at my institution once lamented to me, "I wish we could have a conversation about race and gender where the starting point isn't that I'm evil because I'm a white guy."

No doubt some of my leftist colleagues would be quick to label such laments as rooted in several misunderstandings of antiracist and antisexist projects or to dismiss them as products of "white fragility." But to do so seems to repeat the error of political scientism and the diagnostic style of politics. One mistakes the dispute for a matter of objective facts and reason, privileging being *right* over doing effective politics. Contentious disputes center on what people care about rather than what they know. Most people deeply care about being able to see themselves as a good person, as someone who has a positive influence in the world rather than as an unwitting propagator of white supremacy and patriarchy. The urge to diagnose opponents rather than think carefully about the roots of conservative discomfort and disagreement with the Left's discourse about diversity prevents strategic thought about which narratives could spur *more mutual* adjustment toward a less racist and sexist world while preserving at least some of the cultural values that conservatives hold dear.

In conclusion, populism's appeal to democracy is disingenuous. At its core is an authoritarian form of identity politics: democracy for "the people," autocracy for everyone else. As Robert Dahl has commented, people who believe "that the public good is clear and self-evident" rarely exercise a "spirit of civility," instead seeing those who disagree as "fools or knaves."[53] This lack of civility leads to a recession of democracy, a reduction in the representation of the interests of a diversity of citizens. It undermines the intelligence of policy making as groups try to establish permanently their own version of common sense as society's foundational political framework. Even in cases such as the United States, where institutional checks and balances continue to function, the result is gridlock. This political logjam leaves most citizens without genuine political representation and reproduces the view that democratic government—and perhaps politics writ large—is inevitably dysfunctional. As is clear in Levitsky and Ziblatt's overview of different nations' slide into autocracy, the loss of faith in political processes, widespread polar-ization, and the framing of opponents as enemies of the people form a down-ward spiral. Fanatical populism begets a fanatical political response.[54] Citizens' chances of avoiding the polarizing spiral toward antidemocratic forms of pop-ulism depend on their collective ability to eschew the black-and-white view of common sense that undergirds it.

OTHER TRUTH NARRATIVES

"The facts" and "common sense" are not the only political narratives that undermine democratic discourse. Several others are also used to shut down and polarize disagreement. Everyday speech is rife with "indisputable" truths meant to obviate political conflict.

How do terms such as *nature, progress*, and *the economy* function like *the facts* and *common sense* to hinder productive political discussion regarding issues such as childrearing, driverless cars, and the fueling of growth through corporate tax breaks? All of these narratives lead political actors to diagnose opponents as cognitively unworthy of engagement, encourage fanatical policy, and prevent both the coalition building and partisan mutual adjustments necessary for intelligent decisions. That said, the goal of this chapter is not simply to reiterate that point but also to examine how these Truths with a capital T distort political disagreements in a more fundamental way. What is left out when public debates are dominated by appeals to the indisputability of nature, the economy, or progress?

NATURE VERSUS THE FACTS

In some online circles, the charge "That kills babies!" is all too common. It is difficult to imagine another area of life in which people are more invested than the well-being of their newborn children—or one fraught with more anxiety. Contention over childcare practices demonstrates people's reluctance to talk about what really matters to them and how they instead fall back on naturalistic metaphors or claim to stand on the side of science. The debate over whether infants can sleep safely in their parents' bed is emblematic of this situation.

Advocates of "safe sleep" contend that infants must only sleep on their backs, by themselves, and in a crib devoid of other objects. To them, safe sleep is simply "more scientific" or "evidence based." They point to recommendations by the American Academy of Pediatrics and the Center for Disease Control to dismiss alternative views, such as pediatrician Dr. Sears's advice on bed sharing, as "pseudoscientific piffle."[1]

Similar to other cases where science is claimed to settle a social debate, the facts in this issue are nowhere near complete or certain. Controlled study of sleep-related infant deaths would be impossible and unethical, so researchers must make considerable assumptions and piece together incomplete data on real-life incidents. As in research on environmental carcinogens, accounting for all the complicating factors in research on infants' sleep is extremely difficult. First, it is rare for infants to die in their parent's bed, with the odds for most babies being somewhere on the order of getting struck by lightning over their lifetime. Moreover, discerning whether an infant's death was ultimately caused by bed sharing rather than by its combination with inappropriate bedding material, a parent's alcohol consumption, or a congenital abnormality is rarely done and probably impossible much of the time. No one knows the risk of bed sharing for sure. In fact, some studies suggest that sleeping near parents helps babies regulate their own breathing.[2] And even if the evidence behind "safe sleep" were rock solid, many parents would still find its recommendations impractical, conflicting with the on-the-ground facts of parenthood or less conducive to infant–parent bonding. The National Institutes of Health's Safe to Sleep website, for instance, warns parents to avoid comforting or feeding their infant in an armchair when they are tired lest they fall asleep.[3] Those who have cared for newborns would likely note that there are no times during the day when they are *not* tired and that it is prohibitively expensive to replace all of their armchairs with suitably uncomfortable modern furnishings.

Yet in the minds of many safe-sleep advocates, reality cannot be more certain, nor can safe sleep be any more straightforward. Indeed, one prosecutor in Deschutes County, Oregon, threatened to charge parents with manslaughter if their infants happened to die while bed sharing. The Milwaukee Health Department even put out public-service announcements that compared sleeping with one's newborn to letting them slumber next to a butcher knife.[4]

Safe-sleep advocates almost never explicitly articulate the values underlying their position. In a rare moment of candor, one lawmaker arguing for stiff prison sentences for bed-sharing parents justified that position with

"I just don't want any baby to die."[5] Underlying the safe-sleep position is a utilitarian moral commitment to absolutely minimize the number of infant deaths, which means avoiding false negatives at all costs. That moral commitment makes anything outside of "safe sleep" dangerous by default and frames bedsharing as the cause of sudden infant death until proven otherwise.

Many bed-sharing advocates counter with the claim that bedsharing is more "natural," arguing that we should just "trust our evolutionary blueprint."[6] However, narratives like ones that advocate "the natural" can oversimplify complex issues just as much as "evidence-based" narratives can. Numerous health fads from the Paleo diet to minimalistic shoes meant to make runners mimic a barefoot running style get promoted through the appeal to nature.

Part of the trouble with evolutionary or naturalistic arguments is that they fail to account for changes to both humans and their societies since they lived in hunter-gatherer communities. Minimalistic shoes can lead to injuries for contemporary humans no longer living Paleo lifestyles, who largely occupy desk chairs during the day, carry considerable extra weight, and do not run on Paleo-era surfaces. Likewise, the naturalness of meat-heavy Paleo diets is questionable in light of how much the natural world would be depleted if a large chunk of the world's burgeoning population tried to follow it. Similarly, few people in Western nations sleep on Paleo-era beds. In fact, although it is not yet clear why reported sleep-related infant death rates in Asia are so low, despite high rates of bedsharing, some attribute it to the rarity of bulky Western-style bedding.[7] Moreover, the drive to make children sleep alone may have a lot to do with Industrial Age scheduling constraints and work demands. Families no longer live in Paleolithic societies supportive of childrearing but rather in nations where parents must raise children in isolated family groups and are still expected to get to work on time. The practicality and goodness of more "natural" practices are less certain once they are extracted from the web of technologies and cultures that originally supported them.

Further complicating "nature" as a political narrative is that it is unclear exactly what makes something more natural. When uttered in defense of certain diets, sexual relations, social structures, and other practices, the narrative is often tinged with the idolization of ancient humans. The natural is an instance of common sense, viewed as a kind of primeval knowledge that is corrupted by contemporary scientific expertise.

Yet people imagine the character of uncorrupted nature in drastically different ways. As Mike Hulme finds, there are no fewer than four views of nature in the debate over climate change.[8] Nature can be seen as fragile and unstable, something easily destroyed by human activity; others see it as resilient and malleable to efforts to manage it; some view the climate as capricious and beyond human control; and still others consider nature to be inherently benign with regard to humanity's needs. Recall that proponents and opponents of the pesticide DDT saw nature through similarly incompatible lenses. One side viewed nature as a threat to the survival of humanity and, hence, as something to be controlled. The other side saw nature as delicately balanced web of harmonious relationships upset by the use of industrial chemicals.

Some advocates of "natural" infant sleep embrace a frighteningly capricious view of nature. They refuse to follow American Academy of Pediatrics Guidelines, interpreting sleep-related infant deaths as the product of "fate."[9]

In any case, once armed with conflicting but assumed to be unquestionable framings of nature, political opponents on issues such as infant sleep and climate change largely talk past each other. Their appeals to "the natural" obscure the values and beliefs underlying their political disagreement as much as claims to be on the side of science do.

Lost in the debate over infant sleep practices are the realities of being a parent today, especially the considerable feelings of inadequacy that come with it. Contemporary parents live in an era of uncertainty regarding how best to raise a child. Previously taken-for-granted narratives about childrearing no longer hold the kind of sway they once did. Although increasingly freed from past truisms, parents must now bear the anxiety-inducing burden of no longer knowing if they are doing the "right thing"—not to mention the sting of online parent shaming.

Different childrearing approaches reflect divergent understandings of what is most valuable in life—and different ideas about whom to trust. The scientistic approach leverages statistical predictions of survival rates to enforce a particular moral commitment. Its primarily quantitative understanding of healthy infant sleep paves over parental concerns about obtaining sufficient rest for themselves, mothers' aspirations to make breastfeeding work, the hard-to-quantify joys of cosleeping, and the reality that imbuing fear and anxiety into every stage of parenthood tends to make raising children far less gratifying.

Yet the naturalistic approach can be equally short-sighted, overlooking the hidden biases in different conceptions of nature and failing to recognize that contemporary Western science can alert us to hidden risks in seemingly natural practices. Simple naturalistic myths obscure a more complex reality.[10] And any practice, however "natural," still needs technological, social, and expert support to work as advertised.

Rarely does any participant in the debate engage with the underlying value conflict: *Who* gets to decide *which* risks are worth taking when it comes to childrearing? Parents? Scientists? Politicians? Citizens as a whole? When political actors convince themselves that their view is rooted in science or in a respect for nature, they can easily forget that any approach to infant sleep is also built upon moral and political values, not just on scientific or natural facts.

PROGRESS AND ITS CRITICS

Anyone who has criticized an emerging technology has probably had the experience of being dismissed as a Luddite. In a society where *politics* is a dirty word, many citizens put their faith in technology to make our collective lives better. In fact, surveys find greater public confidence in Silicon Valley firms than in Congress, though trust in social media giants has recently shown some signs of deterioration.[11] But the idolization of technical progress makes democracy impossible, as it prevents us from seeing that whether technological change means human advancement depends quite a lot on a person's station in life and what they care about.

Consider driverless cars. The technology has no shortage of champions willing to prophesize fantastical futures of an environmentally friendly road system that is free of road fatalities—and often free of mass transit as well.[12] These visions are implied to be indisputable and unavoidable—if only opponents would stand aside. Under such assumptions, how can the pesky technological contrarian be anything but an "enemy of the future"?[13]

The narrative of technological progress overlaps with the narrative of "the facts": purveyors of both narratives generally claim to be on the "right side" of science. The association is more symbolic than actual, given that technological promises are often built upon a smattering of facts and a large dollop of faith. Advocates of nuclear energy predicted that reactors would be far safer and cheaper than they ended up being—they were supposed to produce energy "too cheap to meter"—because those advocates made their predictions using theoretical projections and generous assumptions rather than real-life performance data.[14] The purported safety of driverless cars is little different. Computer simulations can predict perfectly safe transportation systems, but actual performance is not going to be certain until, according to RAND Corporation researchers, driverless cars are driven billions of miles.[15] Moreover, humans are actually surprisingly good at driving, each one on average traveling some 94 million miles before being involved in a fatality. If one were to subtract incidents involving people driving under the influence, distracted, or fatigued, the fatality rate would likely be considerably lower. Critics charge that even the autopilot feature on Tesla automobiles— which takes over only the relatively simple task of highway driving—has not performed as well as flesh-and-blood drivers.[16] Because the consequences of technological change are even more uncertain than many scientific questions, the methods of science are even less well positioned to settle disagreements.

In any case, the presumed inevitability of driverless cars, repeated ad nauseum in "progress" narratives, stifles criticism and prevents a deep consideration of potential undesirable consequences and costs. Might a more effective means of reducing traffic fatalities be to add features to cars so that impaired, distracted, or fatigued drivers are prevented from using them? It would be similarly less complicated to provide adequate public-transit alternatives for the tired, drunk, and Instagram addicted. Suggesting those possibilities or highlighting the technology's risks, however, quickly gets a person labeled a fuddy duddy. When Robert Reich raised concerns about job losses, one commenter insisted that "this kind of anti-progress agitating is something that just sounds ignorant. Technology will not stop. Driverless cars will happen." Silicon Valley investor Sam Altman echoes the same sentiment, worrying that focusing on possible job losses means taking an "anti-progress angle."[17]

But what is "progress" anyway? *Progress* seems an even fuzzier and more "feel good" word than *nature*. It is usually not too difficult to read between the lines of seemingly objective pronouncements about technology to find the values undergirding them. The Koch brothers–funded lobby group Americans for Prosperity goes door to door in American cities to persuade citizens to defund transit projects, arguing that trains and buses are outdated technologies standing in the way of a driverless vehicle future. Bus and train technologies, however, can actually be just as technically sophisticated as an autonomous automobile. In light of their political positions, the Koch brothers' opposition is more likely because bus and trains are forms of *mass* transit offered by public entities rather than an individualized form of transportation owned by private businesses. At the same time, many citizens prefer visions of *carless* societies to *driverless* futures because the former means decreasing the role that large corporations play in providing transportation.[18] Still others care more about minimizing disruption to the millions of Americans who drive as a profession than realizing more technically sophisticated vehicles as quickly as possible. Progress means drastically different things to different people—and is rarely just about improving technical efficiencies. However, the word is nearly always uttered in complete obliviousness of those differences. In that sense, it too is a kind of common sense, a narrative built upon the illusion of harmony.

When progress is assumed to mean the same thing to everybody, dissenters become truth heretics. In chapter 2, I mentioned how powerful ideas about the future motivated the US federal government to waste billions of dollars on fanciful projects such as atomically powered jets. Critics of such projects were waved off as simply lacking sufficient "vision." For many people at the time, it seemed indisputable that the future would be nuclear, which entailed powering anything and everything with uranium.[19] Wide-eyed optimism about technological possibilities is ironically often a major factor in societies failing to make intelligent and beneficial use of new technical innovations.

A similarly fanatical commitment to an automated automobile future prevents the process of mutual adjustment among supporters and critics necessary to enable intelligent transportation decisions. Yet for many political actors the future is unavoidably automated and automobile based. Even if nations were restricted to only car-centric development—they are not—few acknowledge the possibility that automated cars may not ever work as promised or not without serious unintended consequences. Complex technologies, such as driverless automobile systems, are prone to cascading chains of error that can produce catastrophic accidents.[20] Moreover, humans have rarely proved capable of babysitting an automated technology and properly intervening in the rare cases where it fails. A number of plane crashes have occurred because the pilot was "out of the loop" and caught unaware when the autopilot failed or the pilot made an elementary error because routine use of autopilot had deskilled him or her. Shoshana Zuboff noted more than 30 years ago that computer technology could be used just as well to "informate" tasks as to "automate" them. It could be designed to make humans operators more informed and perform at higher levels of proficiency rather than to replace or deskill them.[21] But the idea that automation equals progress remains so strong that informated automobiles are almost never discussed as an alternative pathway.

Like the term *nature*, the word *progress* obscures people's reasons for disagreement more than it enlightens. When uttered with respect to new technologies, it is often colored with assumptions about "who" gets to drive progress—typically private industry. Indeed, some champions of market-driven technological disruption go so far as to argue that Silicon Valley firms should be allowed to innovate with abandon, that "asking the permission" of regulators or the potential victims of those innovations prevents the ushering in of "amazing, life-enriching change."[22] Yet that view outright denies that some people benefit more than others, that Silicon Valley investors and creative-class engineers are unequally enriched by some economic disruptions. They get to enjoy the spoils of progress, while those put out of a job can end up forced to make ends meet with menial, low-wage work on a "sharing platform" such as Uber or TaskRabbit or perhaps never find stable, gainful employment again. At its worst, the gentle tyranny of technological progressivism turns a society into what Neil Postman calls a *technopoly*, "a system in which technology of every kind is cheerfully granted sovereignty over social institutions and national life, and becomes self-justifying, self-perpetuating, and omnipresent."[23] That is, technologies themselves get assigned an almost unquestioned right to exist regardless of whose disproportionate power and say got them created in the first place and irrespective of the scale and distribution of their harms.

Because questions about "who exactly benefits" are obscured by the widespread idolization of progress, societies too rarely proceed intelligently. The question concerning how the benefits of these technologies could be realized with fewer of their downsides gets lost in the polarized battle between technological cheerleaders and skeptics. Nations could remain innovative without seeming to stumble half-blindly from one set of unintended technological consequences to another.[24] Indeed, if applied to technological change, the practice of democratic pluralism advocated by this book would help realize the kind of progress that technolibertarians mostly just give lip service to. Imagine if ride-share apps were partly developed and owned by cab drivers. Consumers could enjoy much the same conveniences as today but without the immense costs to workers. Given practicing cab drivers' unique knowledge of passenger service, input from them would probably help such apps function even better.

Critics of technological "progress" are typically not opposed to technical changes per se; neither were the historical Luddites. Rather, the problem is that large-scale technological changes tend to suffer from deficits in democratic intelligence. Yet so long as the myth of progress continues to fanaticize debates about technology, the prospects for more dynamic and democratic innovation look dim.

THE ECONOMY

Given the importance of jobs, credit, and other economic goods for citizens' financial well-being, it is unsurprising that the economy dominates political debates. Yet, as Chantal Mouffe notes, the economy is increasingly framed as outside the political realm. That is, the economy is a thing to be managed by technical experts rather than shaped by democratic politics. She quotes former British prime minister Tony Blair's insistence that "the choice is not between a left-wing economic policy and a right-wing one but between a good economic policy and a bad one."[25] Despite being an ostensibly leftist Labour politician, he gave tacit agreement to Margaret Thatcher's claim that "there is no alternative" to the neoliberal paradigm of actively weakening labor unions, ensuring the free movement of capital and goods, cutting social programs, and privatizing government services. Such changes are depicted as warranted by an objective economic reality rather than by subjective political preferences.

The level to which people treat their ideas about economic activity as unalloyed truth is further evidenced by their fanatical opposition to alternatives. The social critic Christopher Lasch long ago lamented that leftists had come to label everything to the right of liberalism as fascism, whereas conservatives saw liberal programs from the New Deal on as equivalent to communism.[26] Among Tea Party conservatives and some libertarians, any level of governmental intervention into the economy beyond the protection of property rights is a slippery slope to state-led socialism.

Even people whose rhetoric is not so polemical nevertheless act is if their own political position on the economy simply reflects a better understanding of the facts. One *Forbes* writer has insisted that liberals need to learn to accept certain economic "truths," including that sky-high CEO pay is not a problem, that income inequality does not affect the economy, and that government-provided goods inevitably end up being low quality—"truths" that suspiciously coincide with conservative/libertarian beliefs. It is easy to find others claiming that Democrats and even libertarians fail Econ 101 or—bizarrely in retrospect—are so economically ignorant that they cannot see that Obama's policies "have created . . . *complete economic collapse.*"[27]

Such rhetoric obscures the incredible diversity of economic thought. The economist Ha-Joon Chang points out that there are at least nine different schools of economic theory, each with its own blind spots and limitations.[28] It would be surprising if economists were not attracted to different schools of thought in part because of their own moral commitments. Those idolizing the spontaneous order produced by markets read Friedrich Hayek, whereas economics students who care more about inequality and the rights of workers are attracted to Karl Marx. Economists who believe that people are rational optimizers follow neoclassical economics, and those who see irrationality as unavoidable in human reasoning follow behavioralism. Studies show, predictably, that economists' political values shape the outcomes of their economic research.[29] As in scientific studies in general, a researcher's ideas, beliefs, and commitments often influence what he or she thinks are reasonable assumptions, proxies for detecting effects that are not directly observable, appropriate techniques for measuring a phenomenon, and theories for interpreting the results. This explains why two different groups have come up with diametrically opposed conclusions about the effects of Seattle's minimum-wage increase on employment numbers and hours worked—with each side claiming methodological superiority and casting the other as biased and ideologically motivated.[30] The scientific discussion ends up distracting from the crux of the debate: How can business owners' desires for autonomy or interests in keeping costs down be balanced against the demands of workers for a wage high enough to support a decent life?

The fanatical division of economic thought into truth and heresy prevents an appreciation for the complexities and contradictions of economic reality. Despite the fact that corporations are a part of the "free market," their internal structure is actually based in centralized planning, a feature they share with communist countries such as the former Soviet Union. Furthermore, the economic policies implemented by cities, regions, and nations are far more intricate and inconsistent, with far more interesting outcomes, than can be encompassed by any one model. Free-market advocates point to Singapore as an exemplar, yet most Singaporeans dwell in government housing, and a large percentage of national firms are state owned. Scandinavian-style social policies are supposed to render a country uncompetitive on the global stage, but Sweden has more start-ups per capita than any other country, with Stockholm second only to Silicon Valley in billion-dollar tech companies.[31]

Also shunted aside are innovative economic approaches that do not fit into today's black-and-white categories. *Economic democracy* works within a market system to create a more equal society. By fostering cooperative firms and public forms of finance as well as by breaking up monopolies and other barriers to entry, economic democracy achieves leftist goals—more equality and reduced corporate power—as well as right-wing ones—more opportunities for property ownership, increased competition, local forms of control, and entrepreneurial activity. Fanatical readings of the economic landscape obscure such innovations. Many people—especially those who think of themselves as "free marketers"—forget that market-advocate Adam Smith was also an egalitarian. He would have seen the corporations dominating contemporary capitalism as akin to feudal-era "private governments" (e.g., the manor and the guild) that reduced competition and limited laborers' economic liberties. In many ways, worker-owned firms and other "leftist" redesigns of the market system mark a return to Smith's ideal vision of capitalism as characterized by self-employment and wealth building rather than by wage labor.[32]

Worse for the prospects of intelligent pluralist democracy is the extent to which the ideas of some schools of economic thought are rarely contested. Mainstream liberal and conservative politicians disagree surprisingly little on many economic issues, apart from who is seen as deserving of the biggest tax cut. Neoliberal policy is for the most part considered common sense. President Bill Clinton reformed welfare along conservative lines. The Affordable Care Act, or "Obamacare," was modeled on Mitt Romney's market-oriented reforms as governor of Massachusetts. Recent attempts by the Democratic Party to discourage primary wins by economically progressive candidates—who often speak fondly of Scandinavian-style welfare policies—reflects that they have come to accept Thatcher's claim of there being no alternative, or at least no alternative when it comes to winning elections.[33]

Reflective of this convergence of thought is the belief that economic modeling can provide an objective perspective on policy changes such as battling climate change and using tax breaks to encourage development. As the economist Richard Denniss argues, economic modeling is often used to "limit the menu of democratic choices" rather than to "help explain the trade-offs." He has described how industries—such as mining—use economic modeling to present citizens with a Hobson's choice: let us do what we want or suffer the economic consequences. Thick, densely worded, and math-heavy reports are produced to dissuade opposition, sneaking in political values under the veneer of objective logic.[34]

Many of these models contain very questionable assumptions. An infamous World Bank memo by Larry Summers argued that the lives of people in developing nations were not worth as much as those in the developed world. He contended that because those populations earned lower wages, all pollution should be offshored to poor countries. Or consider how the multinational corporation Rio Tinto claimed that a new mine in New South Wales would produce 44,000 jobs. It arrived at this number only by designating a "job" to be a "person year" of employment, which allowed it to count a single long-term employee as 30 "jobs" and numerous short-term contracts as if they were permanent work. In light of these problematic practices, Denniss argues that economists often act as modern witch doctors, whose divine consultations of the "market" provide leaders with a means to legitimate otherwise unpopular policies, portraying those decisions as if they were ordained by the economic spirits.[35]

The biggest hurdle to economic thought becoming productive of democratic—rather than narrowly epistocratic or technocratic—decision making is the tendency for both advocates and critics of markets to see them as autonomous and amoral machines. The economist Julie Nelson has argued that the machine metaphor of the market is at the root of our inability to adequately address public problems. According to laissez-faire advocates, the market "*automatically* serves the common good," whereas skeptics see them as inevitably and irredeemably generative of naked self-interest and greed. This reasoning blinds people to how economic activity could be made to align with their broader ethical aspirations. Firms' activities are actually the result of their internal organizational culture and the broader sociopolitical system. The contemporary corporate form is nothing natural, nor is businesses' consideration of every other concern subordinate to profit making. The character of laws, rights, business schools, and prevailing culture determines what values get represented in economic activities.[36]

The recognition that economic tools and systems are *social* constructions rather than *natural* phenomena frees people's thinking to be far more creative and tolerant of what might seem to be wild ideas. I have already mentioned how instantiations of "economic democracy" could simultaneously satisfy leftists' demands for greater equality and right-wingers' moral aspirations regarding work incentives and property ownership. Heterodox approaches such as Modern Monetary Theory also upset traditional ideas about the economy. Modern monetarists build off the recognition that all money is created out of thin air by governments in order to argue that there is no limit to governmental spending apart from inflation. As long as that spending supports an equivalent amount of productive activity, then governments are in the clear. Worries about debt death spirals are, in this view, misguided because they are built upon the false equivalency of nations—which can print money—and households—which cannot. If this theory is correct, then financial hurdles to eliminating poverty or offering universal health care are less significant than is currently believed. No doubt Modern Monetary Theory and economic democracy may prove to have unrecognized downsides or to be unworkable, but overly rigid ideas about the makeup of the economy prevents even experimenting with them and other alternatives.[37]

The most fanaticizing aspect of "the market" is the belief that capitalism requires that all other concerns be less important than ensuring the dominance of capital and managers over labor, prioritizing economic growth, and protecting large national industries. For instance, "right-to-work" laws have been passed in several US states. It is claimed that these laws, by preventing unionized workplaces from requiring dues from all employees who benefit from labor negotiations, enhance the economic freedom of workers and increase economic growth. The veracity of such claims remains disputed, and critics contend that employees in right-to-work states have lower wages and enjoy fewer benefits.[38] At best, right-to-work advocacy suffers from the *illusion of harmony*, failing to dig deeply enough into the differences in values and distributions of harms and benefits as well as naturalizing one conception of labor rights. More importantly, these laws undercut unions' ability to fund themselves and decrease their ability to force management to make compromises and concessions. Such fanatical economic policy diminishes the level of democratic pluralism within the labor market and helps to ensure that management is so powerful relative to labor that it rarely has to make concessions. Whether intentionally or not, right-to-work laws function to destroy organized labor as a political enemy rather than to regard it as a political opponent.

Still other laws have been developed in order to quash economic dissent. Canada's C-51 bill, passed as the Anti-terrorism Act in 2015, has allowed for the monitoring of citizens whose activities can be construed to interfere with the country's "economic or financial stability." In fact, the Canadian Royal Mounted Police has already labeled the antipetroleum movement a "security threat"—probably because oil and gas constitute some 10 percent of Canada's gross domestic product.[39] Likewise, in the United States many states have attempted to make it more difficult to protest public policies by labeling such activities "economic terrorism" if protestors happen to block a street—with potential penalties of up to 25 months in prison.[40]

Food-disparagement laws prevent legitimate criticism of agricultural corporations by making critics open to lawsuits. The laws' wording puts the onus on critics to prove that no one can interpret their arguments as implying—falsely—that an agricultural product is unsafe. The Texas cattle industry famously took Oprah Winfrey to court, claiming $10 million in damages, because she stated that she stopped eating burgers after an outbreak of mad cow disease. Then Texas agriculture commissioner Rick Perry claimed that "the economic livelihood of our beef producers is at stake."[41] But, as we have seen, safety is not merely a matter of truth or falsity but of whom one is willing to trust and what risks one deems to be worth the benefits. In obscuring these concerns, disparagement laws leverage political scientism toward privileging the economic rights of large agricultural industries over their political opponents.

As in the use of the terms *nature* and *progress*, economic discourse tends to obscure or tries to sidestep the value concerns that are central to political disagreement. Too many citizens speak as if economic activity—whether nominally capitalistic or socialistic—has an immutable character. Talk about invariable economic realities not only prevents intelligent decision making, insofar as it hinders inclusion of diverse perspectives, but also forgets that markets are human inventions and as such can be designed to uphold any number of values. The gentle tyranny of thinking only in terms of the bottom line can be de-emphasized to fashion economic institutions supportive of equity, community, environmental resilience, better family life, or other human aspirations.

The move in the mid-twentieth century to focus almost solely on corporate shareholder value above all else was a shift in culture, not a necessity for capitalism—it actually depresses investment rather than spurs it. Activist hedge funds helped force the cultural shift by punishing non-shareholder-value-maximizing companies with corporate raids. They could have been stopped, and the economic world could still be revised. Policies such as Senator Elizabeth Warren's (D–MA) proposal to rewrite the conditions for awarding corporate charters aim to convert corporate capitalism into something that works for a greater portion of citizens, not just for shareholders.[42]

But the potential for reworking economic systems is also hidden by the leftist tendency to demonize markets. Market mechanisms remain a powerful and decentralized way to coordinate human activities, one difficult to replace. Consider how Bill Clinton boosted the recycled-paper industry by committing the federal government to make the switch. Governments can help steer nations toward achieving social and environmental goals through their power as buyers, not solely as regulators. Market activity can even be a vehicle for social change. One example is SodaStream, an Israeli company that has Jews and Arabs working side by side in its factories. Critics contend that the practice is just a public-relations move, whitewashing the fact that the company benefits from Israel's widely condemned settlement of Palestinian areas. Even if that is true, the case still illustrates how greater economic integration may help begin to resolve deep-seated distrust between different ethnic groups. The CEO David Birnbaum seems genuine when touting the friendships created on the factory floor. In any case, less polarization in economic policy may expand societies' collective imagination and open the door to policies that more strongly enable and reward corporations that balance the "bottom line" with larger social and environmental goals.[43]

No doubt, economic systems still have to be well designed with respect to human behavior and culture, as the failed Soviet experiment with central planning showed. But one should also recognize, contra laissez-faire ideologues, the poor design of today's "free" markets, which is evident in widespread environmental decline and rising inequality. Only when talk of markets or economic actors as having an objective character—along with the preoccupation with political purity that comes with a personal allegiance to some abstract economic "ism"—is dispensed with can partisans even begin thinking about how to incrementally step toward better economies. How might economies better balance rewarding individual ingenuity and hard work with the goal of sustaining goods such as community vibrancy and fulfilling forms of employment?

The point of these three short sections has been to illustrate how "truth" narratives too often undermine political deliberation about peoples' varied interests and values. Safe-sleep advocates fail to recognize that people weigh risks differently when they rhetorically bludgeon others with American Academy of Pediatrics recommendations. Their opponents obscure the deeper, more personal reasons for their attraction to attachment-based forms of childrearing with vague appeals to nature. Prophecies of autonomous-vehicle utopias tell people with different visions of America's transportation future that their preferences are irrelevant. Questionable claims that some policy or another must be followed to ward off economic catastrophe overstate the certainty of economic models at the same time that they prevent discussion of what kinds of economic lives people would like to have. When couching their political preferences in terms of "truth," people fail to talk about the values, experiences, and aspirations that underlie different positions and in this way become more intransigent.

Politics is not a matter of enshrining scientific truths in policy, decreeing the commonsensical will of an invented "people," or trying to appease the gods of nature, progress, or the market. Rather, it is fundamentally about adjudicating matters of care. People who value market-led economic growth often do so because it permits and encourages a competitive, entrepreneurial life that they find exciting. Those who extol progress care quite a bit about the wondrous possibilities certain technologies seem to offer in terms of enhanced mobility, profits, and consumer wonders. Advocates of safe sleep uphold the sanctity of infant lives so much that they believe that everyone else must make considerable sacrifices to secure babies' slumber. Their opponents worry that injunctions about safe infant sleep unduly shames parents who either value physical closeness or find safe-sleep practices impractical. Critics of Silicon Valley's vision of progress sympathize with the masses who work the low-wage, menial jobs that enable the investor class to buy multiple vacation homes. They see human progress in more tightly knit communities or in greater closeness to nature rather than in ever more sophisticated consumer products. If people are to realize a less pathological political culture, it will only be if they learn to see that politics is as much about caring as it is about knowing.

These various narratives appear to function similarly to "rights talk." Decades ago Mary Ann Glendon noted the tendency for people—Americans in particular—to reduce political disagreements to disputes over rights and argued that such a reduction impoverished public discourse.[44] In place of acknowledging the existence of varied concerns about how to achieve the good, opponents polarize around legal abstractions that they take to be absolute and unerring. Abortion, for instance, is framed as a stark conflict between the fetus's right to life and the mother's right to autonomy or privacy. One is *either* for women's ability to choose *or* for the fetus's right to life, full stop. To Glendon, that framing denies the obvious relationship between the mother and fetus and the still larger network of relationships to father, community, and state. She describes how European nations—less encumbered by a fanatical commitment to a language of individual rights— pair barriers to abortion with more generous state support. Germany, for instance, limits most abortions to the first trimester and requires a waiting period and a doctor's note classifying an abortion as medically necessary or not. Yet the nation's government also better supports both mothers and the adoption process, coupling losses in women's privacy rights with greater state responsibility. Glendon sees such policies as representative of the compromises that would be possible if "rights talk" were replaced with a more complex moral language. In the next chapter, I explore what that broader political language might include.

THE GHOST OF THOMAS HOBBES

Too much of contemporary political discourse seems preoccupied with the question "Who has the requisite knowledge to contribute to collective decisions?" Antivaxxers or climate denialists are to be shunned for their scientific illiteracy, while progressive college students cannot be trusted in the voting booth because of claimed deficiencies in common sense. As I have attempted to demonstrate in the previous chapters, the common refrain that some citizens' cognitive deficits constitute a "threat to democracy" is actually the bigger hurdle to productive democratic politics than whatever deficits may or may not exist. The refrain leads people to see opponents as unworthy of debate, compromise, and concession. The word *democracy* in such cases is uttered somewhat erroneously (if not disingenuously), not much differently than when it has come from the lips of American politicians rattling their sabers for some new war in the Middle East. Those singing funeral dirges for ostensible losses in the respect for facts or common sense pronounce a "threat to democracy" when what they really mean is a "threat to (their) truth." Anxieties regarding the fact that some people reason and interpret the world far differently do not have their roots in pro-democratic thinkers such as Thomas Jefferson. Rather, they can be traced to a conservative monarchist: Thomas Hobbes.

Hobbes lived through and wrote his most well-known work, *Leviathan* (1651), after the English Civil War (1642–1651), which pitted Royalists against supporters of parliamentary power. It was an era characterized by the dissolution of previous truths and the declining legitimacy of traditional authorities on knowledge, a time not too dissimilar to our own. Not only was the assumed naturalness of monarchial rule increasingly under attack, but the Protestant Reformation had given rise to a kind of spiritual individualism. Groups such as the Levellers were agitating for popular rule, and Protestants challenged the authority of the Catholic Church to provide "the right" biblical interpretation. In the midst of all this disruption of tradition, Robert Boyle was helping to lay the groundwork for what we would today call empirical science.[45] He developed an experimental apparatus, an air pump, to explore the properties of airless space, a vacuum, and submitted his observations to an audience of his peers to establish "matters of fact."

It is a complex and long story, but most pertinent to my argument is Hobbes's reaction to Boyle's experimental approach to knowledge production. He dismissed it as unworthy in comparison to philosophy and even denied that it merited being called "science," referring to it instead as "natural history." To Hobbes, geometry was the most fitting model for generating knowledge, for once one defined basic terms and followed logical processes, the result would be irrefutable.[46] When compared to the objective potential of logical deduction, Boyle's empiricism seemed unreliable: It depended on the human senses, which could be deceptive, and on private beliefs that could not be made visible to others.

Worst of all for Hobbes was that this form of producing knowledge permitted and even encouraged dissent. Different people could view the same experiment and come up with widely divergent interpretations. He viewed the legitimization of such private forms of judgment and individualistic claims to knowledge to be generative of social chaos.[47] He believed that the fragmentation of judgment and knowledge characterizing Boyle's empirical approach to science would ultimately lead to the fragmentation of authority, which in turn would undermine the absolutely sovereign ruler that Hobbes saw as the only means of assuring civil stability. For Hobbes, only through the right kind of philosophizing would unifying spiritual, political, and natural truths be established.

Contemporary rhetorical appeals to "the facts" and "common sense" echo Hobbes's fear of disagreement. If dissensus is viewed as a recipe for fragmentation and internecine strife, then the cure must lie in enshrining certain truths and modes of producing knowledge as unerring and unchallengeable. A person yearns for a populace that "respects facts" or "uses common sense" with the hope of sidestepping the messy, conflictual world of democratic politics. The simplistic view of "Truth" undergirding such hopes is misguided and drives political fanaticism. It is the refusal to see factions as an unavoidable, indelible feature of political life that fuels intransigence. Only when political actors refuse to tolerate differences in thinking does disagreement become dangerous. It is people's unwillingness to accept the legitimacy of other groups' understanding of the good society that results in deadlock, ever more uncivil debate, and the exclusion of minority factions. Followers of truth narratives risk ending up like Hobbes, justifying to themselves restraints on democracy in the pursuit of an indisputable Truth that will bring order and stability to society.

Worries about democracy and calls to limit its practice, however, stem from more than just a Hobbesian fear of factionalism: they also arise from anxieties that majority coalitions will oppress minority groups. As sound as such concerns seem in the abstract, evidence for the existence of tyrannical majorities is sparse. Greek philosophers of ancient Athens wrote a great deal about their fear of the tyranny of the majority, but Athenian democracy itself was effectively a tyranny by the landowning minority. Slavery and Jim Crow laws in the United States, post–Civil War legislation that limited Blacks' ability to participate in economic and political life, persisted via a similar pattern: oppressed groups are actively disenfranchised, not outvoted. It is often claimed by skeptics of majoritarian decision making that Hitler was democratically elected, but they forget that neither he nor his party ever earned a majority vote; he was appointed to the chancellorship, and the parliamentary decision to award him emergency powers occurred because Communist Party members and a fair number of Democratic Socialists were ousted from the Reichstag (German parliament) and because Nazi paramilitaries were present to intimidate the remaining members.[48]

Moreover, the term *tyranny of the majority* is very often used melodramatically to exaggerate the perceived injustice of a political loss. *Tyranny* means far more than just the minority not getting their way in a policy decision. Every political outcome involves someone gaining something at the expense of someone else's interests. Laws banning child labor or protecting workers' health and safety at the job have limited the economic liberties of store and factory owners. Only extreme libertarians would consider such legislation to be tyrannical, however. Genuinely oppressive governmental action goes further to deprive a group of citizens of essential political rights and powers, such as the ability to participate in and influence policy decisions. Such a move automatically renders a government undemocratic.

The tyranny of the majority is more a phantasm than a reality. Cases of tyranny in democratic nations are more often the result of the failure to ensure the practice of democracy than an outcome of democratic politics itself, and they are often instigated and exercised by a disproportionately powerful and fanatical minority at that.[49]

It is also unclear whether political bodies designed to protect citizens' liberties from the perceived excesses of democracy actually do so with any kind of regularity. Supreme courts are often seen as responsible for protecting against congressional majorities passing tyrannical legislation. Yet a careful review of the US Supreme Court's history undermines such a view. As the political scientist Robert Dahl long ago pointed out, the Supreme Court has referenced the Constitution in upholding the interests of privileged groups over oppressed ones—namely, slaveholders over slaves and whites over nonwhites. The civil rights amendments, developed to assure the civil and political liberties of Black Americans, became a mechanism to award personhood to corporations, yet the Supreme Court upheld poll taxes, segregation, and other Jim Crow laws for decades. The high court's judges denied Blacks equal citizenship. Even apparent exceptions such as the decision to desegregate schools in 1954 arrived just as a near majority of the public came to view racial integration favorably.[50] The protection of minority rights has not come from the supposedly superior and impartial reasoning of justices but rather has been a product of democratic amendments and shifts in judicial interpretations that reflected changing popular sentiments.

The limited degree to which the US Supreme Court actually functions in its liberal guardianship role is unsurprising when one remembers that justices are political appointees. They are selected largely because their understanding of constitutionality is found palatable to the president who has appointed them—and not too unpalatable to Congress. The myth of the Supreme Court as an impartial defender of the Constitution is sustained by the same kind of thinking behind "the facts" and "common sense" narratives. In reality, there is hardly a decision that is not disputed by some set of constitutional scholars or another, with many decisions—such as to treat corporations as if they were people or to equate political donations with free speech—seeming to run contrary to common sense. Even worse, the idea of judicial objectivity leads opponents on issues such as gun control, campaign financing, health care, and other contentious issues to forever debate the "truth" regarding abstract constitutional liberties rather than to discuss what really matters to them. In any case, logically deducing constitutionality or how the intent of the constitutional framers might play out for present problems is decidedly not as straightforward as geometry.

Moreover, nations that historically lacked judicial review of legislation, such as the United Kingdom and New Zealand, appear neither to have been less robust in their support of individual rights nor to have had a less nuanced public debate about contentious issues such as abortion.[51] Given the mixed results of constitutional courts and cases of democracies persisting without them, seemingly commonsensical arguments about their being necessary counters to the risks of democratic tyranny are unconvincing.

The fundamental concern with worries about tyrannical majorities does not seem to be about oppression but rather about whether majority coalitions will make the "wrong" decision. Recall that the Federalists' anxieties about direct democracy centered on the possibility that the landless majority would redistribute land or pass other pieces of legislation contrary to the interests of economic elites. And they presumed that the latter's preferences would better align with the interests of the nation as a whole. Hence, like "the facts" and "common sense," the "tyranny of the majority" is ultimately a truth narrative. It is assumed that citizens will fail to respect certain facts or to reason properly. Their failure to make the objectively "right" decision, in turn, necessitates the intervention of some semisovereign, elite body (e.g., the Supreme Court, the Electoral College, appointed legislative bodies) to act as a guardian of the democratic process. Such reasoning is positively Hobbesian in that it justifies restrictions on democracy by a desire to ensure the preeminence of certain kinds of truths or styles of political reasoning.

Yet many political scientists, such as Steven Levitsky and Daniel Ziblatt, insist that societies risk falling into autocracy without political parties acting as gatekeepers, standing between authoritarian personalities and the office of the president or prime minister.[52] They cite the barring of demagogues such as Henry Ford and Huey Long from entry to party conventions and the inability of the strictly democratic process of the Republican Party in 2016 to prevent Donald Trump's nomination as evidence of the importance of party gatekeeping.

But there is another, more pro-democratic, interpretation. The election of Donald Trump was as much a product of the democratic Republican primary as of the gatekeeping of the Democratic Party in its own primary. Democratic Party leadership made obvious efforts to sink the meteoric rise of Bernie Sanders. Moreover, the attractiveness of Trump to many voters can also be seen as a product of the growing sense of the illegitimacy of traditional "insider" politics. Political parties' gatekeeping breeds resentment and disillusionment with democracy as much as it bars entry to demagogues. In a sense, it helps sow the seeds of populist destabilization.

Moreover, the outcome of the 2016 election is as much a product of Republican Party elites choosing to stifle internal disagreement in order to win rather than to shield American democracy from a candidate with autocratic tendencies. The party's "enlightened" gatekeepers decided it was better to carry the presidency with Donald Trump than not at all. In fact, none of them encouraged right-leaning voters to pull the lever for Clinton.

Finally, the election of more authoritarian-leaning candidates does not invariably lead to the death of democracy. Without the compliance or acquiescence of politicians, police, the military, bureaucrats, and other political actors, constitutions cannot be rewritten to centralize power, supreme courts cannot get packed, and electoral processes cannot get distorted in response to crises. Therefore, it is the strength of a society's collective commitment to democracy rather than the guardianship of gatekeepers that is the ultimate assurance of democratic government.

To be fair, democratic majority coalitions can pass unfair legislation or elect potential tyrants. The real danger, however, does not stem from such coalitions occurring from time to time but from their becoming too cohesive and long-lasting—from their being protected from democratic disruptions. Jim Crow persisted in the American South and the American labor movement lagged in part because the "common sense" of Black inferiority—and the appeal of the advantages accruing to some whites as a result of that "common sense"—proved far too entrenched to be undone by the Civil War and passage of the Thirteenth Amendment. This common sense prevented poor white workers from recognizing that they often had far more in common with their African American brethren than with their affluent bosses and political elites. The stability of certain ideas about whiteness hindered the development of interracial class coalitions that could have agitated for the end of oppressive legislation.[53] A majority acting too consistently to the disfavor of a single group signals that pluralism has broken down, either by one group becoming too powerful or by others being too weak to demand compromise, or that certain ideas and beliefs have become sacrosanct. As a result, the solution is *more democracy, not less*. Intransigent and unjust majorities can be steered away from fanatical ends just as well by fostering disagreement as by replacing democratic decision making with elitist institutions.

But how exactly can democracy be fostered in this way? It is a challenging question that is tempting to avoid. Democracy is usually analyzed either as an ideal or in practice but only more rarely in terms of how its practice could be made more ideal. I will not get bogged down in further defending democracy in the abstract but instead focus on how citizens can improve the functioning of democratic societies. The next chapters approach democracy as an ecological process, a living thing. Democracies are a kind of political ecosystem: they are vibrant to the extent to which both the environmental niche—institutions, venues for debate, prevalent norms—and the "organisms" within it fit together. What kinds of political talk can help ensure a well-functioning pluralist democracy? How might societies and governments need to be redesigned so that people can be reasonably expected to act and think more democratically?

DEMOCRATIC POLITICAL TALK

The comedian George Carlin would ask his audience, "Have you ever noticed that anybody driving slower than you is an idiot and anyone going faster than you is a maniac?" Politics often seems little different: anybody believing something you think to be false is brainwashed, and anyone who doesn't believe what you know to be true is ignorant. Could the situation be otherwise, or are our political interactions destined to devolve into the rhetorical equivalent of road rage?

I have argued in the first half of this book that truth narratives such as "the facts" and "common sense" distort political discussions and undermine the pluralist process of negotiation at the heart of democracy. Yet what reason is there to believe that political disputes can be made any better? If "truth" should be de-emphasized, what should take its place?

TOWARD DEMOCRACY-ENHANCING DISCOURSE

If democratic political discourse needs to meet some minimal level of civility, what are its features? Hannah Arendt contended that politics should be defined by common sense, albeit a very different kind than was described in chapter 3. Her vision of common sense is one built up through a form of public life "that forces [citizens] to constantly weigh and consider things from the perspective of other people" rather than "a coercive attachment to abstract logic in which basic axioms seem to fit all situations without regard to real-world circumstances."[1] That is, politics should be rooted in consideration of a diversity of experiences rather than in supposedly eternal truths.

Others have pointed to the quality of interactions and the need to avoid appeals to outside authorities. Benjamin Barber defines deeply democratic political talk as involving "listening as well as speaking, feeling as well as thinking, and acting as well as reflecting."[2] By this, he means that such talk is a means for mutual exploration, not merely for a rational adjudication of competing rights or truth claims. No voice is unchallengeable by means of position or expertise, for the process must legitimate almost everyone's expressions. Robert Dahl advocates a similar kind of robust civility that demands mutual learning, hearing others out, and recognizing that disagreements are inevitable and almost never fully resolvable.[3] Charles Lindblom emphasizes the importance of reducing the impairments that lead to political intolerance and intransigence. The first step is for citizens to recognize their own impairments and to see their political values, interests, and aspirations not as dogma but as emergent out of an exploration of public issues alongside other people.[4]

That seems like a tall order. If citizens are to achieve anything like what Lindblom and others have recommended, they will somehow have to be pushed to dispense in part with their comforting belief systems, those inherited ideologies that depict the world as built out of simple, already known truths. Hence, a prerequisite to the kind of democratic talk described by Arendt, Barber, and Dahl appears to be that people must be capable of recognizing their own ignorance in the face of an almost overwhelmingly complex world.

In this chapter, I explore these various facets of democratic interactions: admitting uncertainty, sharing experiences, and tolerating and negotiating disagreement. What is pluralist "political talk" actually like? What are its limits?

THE BOUNDS OF KNOWLEDGE

It is understandable that most people are reluctant to admit uncertainty when it comes to contentious issues. Psychologists have long argued that the desire for certainty is a fundamental human drive. Indeed, I suspect that most readers have felt an almost "fight or flight" response to having their beliefs or knowledge challenged.[5] Being wrong does not feel good. In addition, political culture in the United States and elsewhere almost fetishizes certainty. A politician who changes his or her mind is often referred to as a "flip-flopper," someone whose perceived lack of conviction makes him or her untrustworthy. And citizens are constantly told that uncertainty regarding future political policies scares off investors and risks negative market consequences. Not knowing is frequently portrayed as a danger, something to be avoided.

Yet the desire for closure and the attraction to simplistic, single-cause explanations may be more destructive than uncertainty. Diego Gambetta and Steffen Hertog associate these tendencies with membership in terrorist groups—perhaps their most extreme manifestation. Gambetta and Hertog argue that the drive to understanding the world as clean, ordered, and made up of straightforward causal relationships explains why many extremists are attracted to both engineering and fanatical political movements. Indeed, radical Islamists tend to view both science and Islamic texts similarly as "fixed, indisputable truths, not as an open quest for knowledge."[6] People who see the world in totally certain terms, as if it were a simple engineering model, tend to fill the member rolls of violent, fanatical political movements. This may be why attempts to "correct" the post-truth age via the promotion of science literacy as "knowing the facts" do very little to reduce polarization.

If overestimating certainty breeds fanaticism, then highlighting ignorance should encourage its opposite. When psychologists have asked people to explain how a proposed political policy works, such as deploying sanctions on Iran or transitioning to single-payer health care, they have found that having to explain leads many study participants to be less unwavering in their support or opposition of the proposed policy. When subjects are brought to recognize that their understanding of an issue is not as good as they originally thought, they become less certain of the goodness of a given solution.[7] The same pattern has been found among policy experts as well. Political scientist Éric Montpetit's research has uncovered that "mindsets of compromise [about biotechnology] are most probable among actors with nuanced beliefs who tend to acknowledge some uncertainty"[8] People are more likely to behave pluralistically if they recognize that there are limits to what they actually know.

Therefore, scientific expertise can have a more positive role in politics by highlighting what we do not yet understand, not by claiming a consensus. Taking advantage of science's tendency to complexify and raise new questions, scientists might be used to provoke greater thoughtfulness rather than easy certainties, to push citizens and policy makers to consider seriously the "what if's?" that are easier to ignore when the spell of truth narratives is at play. For the case of the claimed link between vaccines and autism, that would mean highlighting the limits of our understanding of what causes autism in addition to poking holes in the assertions of antivaccine spokespersons. That is, one battles fanatical certainties not with equal and opposite certitudes but with skeptical questions made in good faith. At the same time, vaccine skeptics will be pushed to make compromises or concessions only if their opponents also ease up a little—for instance, if vaccine advocates negotiate as if they believe that some still unrecognized side effect of vaccination might indeed exist.

Emphasizing uncertainty runs against the dominant politically scientistic belief that certainty is a prerequisite to action. One sees this scientistic belief underlying the insistence that chemical regulations or climate policy not be instantiated until supported by "sound science." Such claims are more delaying tactics than smart policy. People simply will not know the scale of problems such as climate change until it is too late. Scientists cannot precisely predict how carcinogenic new industrial chemicals will be until citizens develop cancer at sufficiently unusual rates. And conflict is nearly always over potential risks rather than over known harms, which has real consequences for under- or overestimating the possibility of undesirable outcomes.

This is why many policy scholars recommend adopting the "precautionary principle" when it comes to risky technologies, chemicals, and acts of legislation. Lack of scientific certainty should not stop societies from taking preventative actions.[9] People routinely buy home insurance despite not knowing whether their house will ever catch fire, so nations should not hesitate to do at least something to mitigate uncertain risks such as climate change. In any case, acting precautiously does not mean preventing change from happening until interventions are proven harmless—or what the political scientist Aaron Wildavsky refers to as requiring "trials without errors."[10] Rather, it merely means recognizing that new innovations— whether technological or political—are uncertain and that reality is usually complex enough to escape complete human understanding. As a consequence, societies should proceed strategically and incrementally, leaving themselves capable of redesigning or abandoning innovations before their harms become too great.[11]

Proposals for more "intelligent trial and error" in the realms of technology and politics are not pro-stasis or anti-innovation but intend to make change more robust and broadly beneficial. With the recognition that all political (and technological) decisions are made under conditions of uncertainty, policy itself becomes a method for learning about the world. That is, the best policies are incrementally discovered and steered toward rather than chosen from the outset.

Recall the reason why nuclear energy in the United States remains in a state of arrested development: its champions proceeded in leaps and bounds and all but locked in use of the light water reactor design before fully understanding it. At times, GE and Westinghouse sold reactors more than three times larger than the ones they had previously constructed yet underestimated the increasing complexities of scale.[12] Those involved in the push toward nuclear power overestimated what they already knew and failed to recognize that they would only really understand nuclear technology through experience. If decision making about nuclear power had highlighted uncertainty by encouraging criticism rather than certainty based on an infatuation with the atomic dream, the US nuclear energy industry could have avoided embarrassing failures and maintained popular support far longer than it did. By putting people in the position of having to persuade, negotiate with, and strategize against opponents, democratic pluralism turns politics from a machine wherein groups battle only to ensure victory for their own narrow preferences into a more dynamic process where citizens' goals, beliefs, and aspirations evolve in response to their interactions. Policy becomes more intelligent and circumspect as a result.

In the same fashion, a more uncertainty-oriented approach to policies such as gun control, the establishment of a minimum wage, and climate-change mitigation would proceed via some combination of gradual scaling-up, pilot programs in smaller regions, and inclusion of mechanisms to slow down, change, or reverse course. The advantage of this approach is not just smarter, less haphazard policy but also change that can gain the assent of a greater portion of fence sitters. Giving skeptics a seat at the table for periodic policy revaluations would likely go a long way toward reducing polarization in politics. Bringing at least some of the members of opposing coalitions to the table will assuage fears that new policies can become slippery slopes or locked in.

Incrementalism, as a result, helps spur the development of trust between political actors, driving coalition building and more reliable movement toward substantial policy decisions. The political scientists Robert Keohane and David Victor offer the example of global free trade, which began in bilateral and other smaller agreements and was enshrined via organizations such as the World Trade Organization only after nations' leaders built up mutual trust and experience. Although some may argue that such changes have been in error, the changes at least demonstrate how fairly radical policy shifts happen. Climate policy might proceed more productively if it were to occur through bilateral, reciprocal agreements rather than via grand global protocols that are generally toothless, frequently ignored, and generative of considerable polarization.[13]

Another example of uncertainty-respecting incrementalist policy is the approach to planning the neighborhood of Quartier Vauban in Freiberg, Germany. In contrast to this development, most grandiose proposals for "green" or "new urbanist" neighborhoods end up being significantly watered down in practice. Plans for a carbon-neutral community on the site of Edmonton's old city-center airport have been plagued by delays, and many touted "green" features were eventually dropped because they were viewed as "too risky."[14] With millions of dollars invested and profits on the line, it is no wonder that developers get cold feet when it comes to uncertain housing innovations. Likewise, municipal planning offices are often resistant to signing off on what appear to be untested designs.

Today having one of the highest concentrations of homes in the world whose net energy use is practically zero, Quartier Vauban side-stepped these problems by splitting up the development into smaller parcels and selling them directly to future residents. Planners, developers, and residents were thereby enabled to learn as they went along. After gaining experience with—that is, coming to *trust*—energy-reducing design features, these groups felt comfortable imposing increasingly stringent requirements on future development phases. They even skirted requirements to cover much of the neighborhood with parking—which would have made homes more expensive and undermined environmental goals—by designating green spaces as "virtual" parking spaces. Those areas would remain undeveloped until residents decided that they needed more space to store automobiles, a move that increased flexibility and appeased would-be opponents in the city planning office.[15]

Cases such as Quartier Vauban highlight the advantages of taking uncertainty seriously. Incrementalism in such cases not only has helped participants better navigate disagreement but also has led to more radical change in the long run. Grand designs—whether in technology or politics—often look to be more effective, but the result typically involves taking two steps forward and one step back as unanticipated failures begin to mount. Such was the case, as described in chapter 2, when the United States gave hundreds of millions of dollars to NASA engineers to develop wind-turbine technology in the 1980s. NASA developed technically advanced and gargantuan but ultimately unsuccessful prototypes and was eventually outdone by small-scale Danish producers.[16]

Examples such as Vauban and Danish wind energy also highlight the next important feature of pluralist democracy: the importance of respecting *experience*. Whether one is pioneering new forms of energy or exploring social problems, people's experiences tend to challenge and complexify simplistic truth narratives. NASA engineers could have avoided their wind-turbine design problems by drawing upon the hands-on knowledge of craft builders. Neighborhood developers can ensure similar successes by letting residents' small-scale experiments shape planning requirements. And, as we will see, contentious social issues can be more productively navigated by encouraging people to reflect on their past.

THE IMPORTANCE OF EXPERIENCE

Many citizens have come to believe that politics ought to consist of logical defenses of philosophical positions and rational assessments of the public good. Perhaps this view comes from the tendency to idealize and idolize the American forefathers or the deliberations of ancient Athenian politicians as if they were more thoughtful and civil than they actually were.[17] In any case, one wonders about the practicality of proposals for rational political discussions. Consider the political philosopher Michael Sandel's call for a renewed national emphasis on civic virtue and a focus on deliberations concerning the common good. Although I make a similar argument here about moving political talk away from endless fact disputes and polarized shouting matches, Sandel sets his sights too high. His demonstrations of "reasoned public discourse" unfold like university philosophy seminars, with Sandel himself helping participants realize the fundamental premises that underlie their political positions.[18] Sandel's lecturing is no doubt a sight to behold, but it seems unreasonable to expect people in their everyday political disputes to be capable of calmly interrogating each other's logic.

Studies on political canvassing conversations suggest a more attainable pathway toward productive political discussions. In one example, a canvasser talks to a woman who expresses support for laws that bar transgender people from using public restrooms that match their chosen gender identity—mentioning concerns about child predation. Rather than cite statistics or engage her in a philosophical discussion about people's right to gender autonomy and privacy, he simply asks a series of questions: Do you know any transgender people? Have you ever felt discriminated against? She admits to having a transgender nephew and to refraining from talking to him about it because of how uncomfortable it makes her feel. At the same time, she can recall moments when she felt excluded because of her identity. Finally, the canvasser shares his experiences of facing discrimination because of his sexual orientation, and the interaction ends with the women reconsidering her earlier position.[19] Such canvassing efforts are productive because their goal is not to inform but rather to connect.

Taking on another person's perspective—whether fostered through face-to-face interactions, the reading of first-person narratives, or virtual-reality simulations—has been shown to produce durable and long-lasting increases in tolerance and understanding of people of different gender, sexuality, race, and personal circumstance. More importantly, perspective taking has proven more effective than fact-based interventions; the latter often lead people to become more entrenched in their views and express doubts about the fact-providing expert's credentials.[20] Perspective taking, in contrast, provokes the recognition of shared experiences. The war of words regarding childhood vaccinations, for instance, would be more productively fought if parents communicated, at least some of the time, in the shared terrain of feeling powerless with respect to their children's health. The anxiety that an antivaxxer parent feels in the face of an apparent and mysterious growth in autism is similar to that felt by a parent who worries her child will needlessly contract whooping cough or measles. By focusing on what people *care about* rather than on red-herring claims about who respects science more, experience-based deliberations can more quickly get to the heart of disagreements.

The importance of experience is well known to scholars who study how the public perceives risky science and technology. In the controversy over fracking, fossil-fuel industry spokespersons used to claim that contamination of aquifers by fracking wells was impossible, at least according to their models. The industry's political scientism thus obscured the underlying drivers of controversy. Pollution concerns and high levels of mistrust of the industry were often a product of citizens' history of negative experiences with oil and gas development.[21] If firms had focused less on attempting to "inform" the public and more on the experiential roots of the public's distrust, a far more productive debate about fracking could have occurred.

Paying more attention to people's diverse experiences enhances policy making in the same way emphasizing uncertainty does. Recognizing the limitations of human knowledge leads to a more incremental and intentionally experimental policy process; appreciating experience leads to including a greater diversity of people in political decisions.

One well-known example is the case of participatory budgeting. Cities in Brazil have experimented over the past 20 years with allowing ordinary citizens to negotiate and vote on municipal expenditures. The local residents' participation has led to far more reales being spent to help the poorest residents via sanitation infrastructure and health care than in other Brazilian municipalities, resulting in far lower rates of infant mortality. Studies even find that local participation in politics rises when cities let residents, not just experts or politicians or officials, contribute to budgeting decisions.[22] Participatory budgeting reflects the recognition that the people who directly experience city services have important expertise to contribute to choices about municipal allocations.

Should there be limits on the role of experience in political discourse? On the one hand, most—if not all—political issues have some experiential element to them; otherwise, people would not care about them. Controversy over governmentally provided health care, for instance, is not just a matter for constitutional law. Many Americans have faced medically induced bankruptcy, the anxiety of mounting bills, and frustration with insurance companies, or they at least know people who cannot get affordable care. The dispute over personal firearms hinges on people's differing experiences of safety, often rooted in their having been the victim of crime or affected by gun violence. Although focusing on those experiences rather than on abstract statistics or political philosophy is no guarantee of a greater willingness to compromise, it at least makes deliberation more tractable. It is one thing to denigrate another person's interpretation of the Second Amendment, quite another to dispute the veracity or relevance of his or her *experiences*. Conservatives would probably sway more liberals to listen to their complaints about governmental red tape if instead of decrying "creeping socialism," they discussed how bureaucracies have made them jump through too many hoops when running a small business. Some of those same conservatives may more often then hear in response about what

it is actually like to live on welfare and to deal with equally onerous bureaucratic struggles.

On the other hand, perspective taking may not be possible in certain
cases, or ideological commitments may prevent people from finding commonality. Many upper-class citizens have simply had no experience with
being poor or with butting up against structural barriers to economic or
academic opportunity. Or they are adept at interpreting their own frus-
trated aspirations as being stymied by structural barriers while seeing
everyone else's unrealized ambitions as caused by indolence or stupidity.
A relatively well-off relative of mine once asked me in all seriousness why
poor people could not just move to a city that offered better employment
prospects. Having never experienced struggling to pay for two months'
rent upfront, a security deposit, and transportation and never having been
deemed unworthy of affordable credit, many middle- to upper-class citizens often presume that the poor stay put simply out of a lack of initiative.

Similarly, most advocates of "tough" prison conditions have never experienced life locked in a cell. They can let their ideology drive their imaginations about life "on the inside." In contrast, consider how former Tea Party
politician Kent Sorenson made an about-face on incarceration policy after
serving a 15-month stretch in federal prison.[23] Moreover, most middle-
to upper-class Americans of European descent have never feared for their
lives in the presence of police. Many men have never feared being sexual
assaulted, a worry that most women live with on a daily basis. In such cases,
discouraging fanatical, uncompromising positions will depend on cultivating a greater willingness to understand the lives of others.

Even though more respect for experience would do a great deal to
defanaticize politics, couldn't it also become a kind of fanatical truthism?
According to some critics, "identity politics" is just that. The political scientist Sonia Kruks characterizes identity politics as groups advocating for
political recognition on the basis of their identities—the intersection of
gender, race, sexuality, and class—and in light of the unique experiences
that people accrue because of those identities.[24] It is not really about who
is "more oppressed" but rather about recognizing that ordinary people are
quasi-experts regarding their own station in society. Identity politics pos-
its that women hold a privileged position in evaluating the experiences of
mothering a child because biological men cannot do so; because structural

racism is something whites cannot experience in the United States, they ought to pay attention when people of color tell them about it.

To the psychologist Steven Pinker, however, identity politics is a "syndrome" that is "the enemy of reason" because it establishes separate truths for different groups. Pinker's and others' opposition stems in part from their perception that identity politics tribalizes the public sphere and thus prevents solidarity or unity across diverse groups.[25] If people's experiences are so identity based and largely incommensurable, then the liberal project of progress via universalistic notions of rights and a common human interest falls apart. Classical liberalism is no longer an objective good but just one partisan notion of the public good among many.

From the view of democratic pluralism, the fragmenting of political beliefs along identitarian lines is not actually a problem but the very stuff of politics. In this view, attempts to construct universalistic, "reason-based" notions of the good society—like Pinker's—are the real fanatical threats to the democratic process, however well meaning they might be. That said, if identity politics does truly lead to people's experiences being seen as incommensurable or toward sanctioning people from the "wrong" identity group for expressing their opinions about public problems, it does pose difficulties for pluralism. Treating a person's political interests or perspective as sacrosanct by dint of their identity chops up the public sphere into ever smaller and feebler factions. Absent efforts to build coalitions across identities, politics risks devolving into an unproductive morass of competing claims for recognition. If identity politics seems to slide in this direction, it seems to do so only in reaction to the fanatical liberal universalism favored by Pinker and others. The insistence on an idealized politics that is blind to identity and limited to a rational debate of big ideas and "objective" facts denies the relevance of people's lived experiences. It is no wonder that some political identitarians dig in their heels. Fanaticism begets fanaticism.

Rather than try to reclaim lost political unity or insist upon a purely rational debate, a better response is to admit the legitimacy of people's unique experiences while ensuring that identity politics is not just about asserting competing claims for recognition but also about finding commonalities. Conservatives' uneasiness with some practices of identity politics alerts us to something important. When such practices are focused exclusively on detailing all the ways in which white people, males, or cis-gendered persons *on average* enjoy special privileges or unconsciously reproduce inequality, people within these demographics can get the message that their only role within an increasing diverse country is that of a privileged oppressor. Some white identitarians, rightly or wrongly, see the alt-right movement as a "safe space" in an identity-politics-driven society that no longer has a place for them.[26]

That interpretation is both unfortunate and inaccurate because there is considerable diversity among people who happen to be white. Although Caucasian and male demographics tend to enjoy a range of privileges as a statistical class, many individuals within those groups have experienced discrimination, prejudice, or trauma. Many white men have been sexually assaulted as children or adults, have suffered domestic abuse, or have been brutalized by police officers; some fathers face a disproportionately uphill battle in child-custody disputes or are expected to provide alimony to an exwife who has a high-earning job; a portion of males have faced bullying for their sexuality or for being perceived as insufficiently masculine or for acting too nerdy; others have experienced discrimination for being "poor white trash" or for pursuing traditionally feminine callings such as nursing and stay-at-home parenting; and some have received glimpses—albeit partial and voluntary—of life without their standard privileges when living in a non-English-speaking country.[27]

Although these experiences aren't exactly like those of people who are female, trans, and/or nonwhite—because larger structural biases in favor of maleness or whiteness remain present—they deserve recognition, if only to encourage empathic understanding. Anti-oppression activists may be *technically* or *morally correct* to argue that white men should more often be quiet and listen to people from more marginalized groups.[28] Yet given the research about perspective taking discussed earlier, identity politics is likely at its most productive when political actors *draw upon* and *validate* the similar negative or traumatic experiences of others—even if they seem significantly less oppressive.[29] Doing so softens identity barriers and sows the seeds of understanding and empathy. People are better prepared to explore their differences in nonpolarizing ways by first being brought to acknowledge their commonalities. This strategy overlaps with the next feature of productive pluralist talk: being able to disagree in ways that are more likely to resonate with potential allies and probable opponents.

BETTER NAVIGATING VALUE DISAGREEMENT

Perhaps the largest barrier to more pluralistic, less fanatical political interactions is that disagreement itself is talked about as if it were unproductive,
dangerous, and inevitably polarizing. Political scientist Éric Montpetit has
found that when newspapers cover contentious issues, they usually portray disagreement negatively. Cloning policy, for instance, is "hostage to
stalemate"; opposing sides are "fundamentalists" falling prey to "dogma"
or concerned only about profits; and "progress" is likely only when people
respect science. Montpetit argues that readers are "likely to be left with the
impression . . . that disagreement over biotechnology policy is harmful and
that solutions to avoid disagreement should be sought."[30] Until journalists,
teachers, politicians, and others who influence public thought more often
frame disagreement as the pathway to better knowledge and sounder decisions, citizens are likely to continue to fall prey to populism or fanatical
scientism.

In the absence of such changes, there is still a great deal people can do to
have more productive political discussions. The political psychologist Jonathon Haidt's research provides one pathway.[31] Haidt argues that a person's
reasoning with regard to contentious issues is shaped by some combination
of moral intuitions about right and wrong: care/harm, fairness/cheating,
loyalty/betrayal, authority/subversion, purity/contamination, and liberty/
oppression. When people are asked about perceived moral transgressions,
psychologists find that these intuitions usually come first and that people
develop rationales to justify them after the fact. That is, few people, if anyone, think about contentious issues in a perfectly rational way but instead
feel their way through them. When presented a story about two siblings
having protected and consensual sex, many people will say that the act is
wrong even though no one has been hurt—largely because of their intui-
tive feelings about the purity of familial relationships.

Political or ideological commitments are similarly underdetermined
by evidence and reason. Despite the depiction of libertarianism as rooted
in rationality—its main magazine is arrogantly named *Reason* after all—
libertarians' love of markets is based more in privileging the moral intuition
of individual liberty than in demonstrating superior reasoning skills. Like
every political worldview, libertarianism is founded in several unprovable
axioms, which adherents must simply accept. Libertarians define liberty as

a negative—a freedom from external constraints—and as individualistic, often focused narrowly on the right of people to do what they so choose with their dollars or property. To nonlibertarians, this definition seems arbitrary or even harmful because it leaves out positive freedoms—whether people actually have the means to realize opportunities—and still higher-level freedoms available only via collective relationships.

Consider unions. Although they can compel workers to contribute dues—thereby lessening an individual freedom—the gains in negotiating power with management give workers greater economic liberties as a collective. This negotiating power also comes at the expense of management's freedom to set unilaterally working conditions. A unionized autoworker in a non-right-to-work state loses a chunk of her paycheck whether she likes it or not, but she gains freedoms in voting rights and advantages through the ability to collectively negotiate pay rates and benefits. Whether the worker finds this arrangement to be desirable or undesirable is rarely due to a lifetime of careful and impartial study of the evidence but to her political allegiances, which, in turn, come from her intuitions about what is right. The world is simply too complex and human reasoning too limited for there to be an iron-clad empirical or logical defense of any one view of freedom. Hence, Haidt's work helps uncover the moral commitments that fill in the gaps in rationality and evidence, explaining the deeper reasons why people subscribe to a given political ideology.

Recognizing that opponents are guided by different moral foundations allows people to better understand and navigate disagreement; it helps shift discussion away from endlessly disputing truth claims and toward uncovering and appealing to underlying moral motivations. Leftists, for instance, too frequently dig in their heels when facing conservative reticence over slogans like "defund the police" or "Black lives matter." They insist on informing skeptics of those phrases' supposedly objective meanings. They would be better off looking for rallying cries that both describe their goals and resonate with a few nonleftists.

In the case of vaccine refusal, research has found that the moral intuitions of purity and freedom resonate the most with antivaxxer parents. Arguments about herd immunity and protecting vulnerable populations fall flat because they have their roots in the intuitions of fairness and harm. Vaccine advocates should instead focus on the ways in which vaccines are "natural"—they provoke the body's innate process for creating antibodies—or how vaccine hesitancy takes away other people's freedom to choose.[32] Facts *can* help sway antivaxxers. But such rhetoric is most persuasive when it focuses on the evidence that resonates with the underlying moral motivations of vaccine-hesitant citizens.

Yet mere rhetorical changes would seem to be insufficient. Mainstream medicine often feels oppressive, especially when doctors are too old-fashioned, busy, or overly confident to listen to patients' concerns. Not evoking the liberty/oppression moral intuition takes more than just talk—actual experience should be taken seriously. Doctor–patient interactions could be made less paternalistic, and offices and procedure rooms could be made to feel less sterile and artificial, both without sacrificing quality of care. Integrating more holistic health-care practices within traditional doctors' offices would help bring at least some vaccine skeptics into the fold. Not only would doing so better recognize the considerable evidence that procedures otherwise thought to be "mere" placebos do have the power to heal,[33] but it would also create environments that help people feel more comfortable.

This approach could be fruitful for a multitude of other cases. Efforts to universalize health-care coverage in the United States have faltered in part because of the perception that universalization taints the purity of market-based health care with governmental intervention, and such intervention threatens citizens' freedom to make health-care choices. Responding to this perception with fact-oriented rhetoric—for instance, claiming that private insurance raises costs and creates inefficiencies or that universal health care requires a relatively small expansion of already existing governmental programs—does little to persuasively address the moral intuition underlying disagreement. Referencing how particular groups are disproportionately disadvantaged by a private health-care system is equally ineffective, given that many conservatives are not swayed by moral intuitions of harm or social justice. They can reply that the un- or underinsured should simply work harder for a better job. Compromise and concession with conservatives would be more likely to result by pointing out that a privatized health-care system gives corporations disproportionate say over people's health decisions, discourages entrepreneurial activity, harms small businesses, undermines children's equality of opportunity, and makes societies less stable. One could emphasis that private insurance lets people "cheat," allowing them to wait to buy coverage until they are older and more prone to disease or encouraging the use of the emergency room in lieu of a primary-care physician—which results in the uninsured rarely paying their fair share.[34] It is hard enough to elicit concessions out of opponents, but expecting them to both compromise and embrace one's own preferred moral framing is unrealistic.

Further measures would need to ensure that governmental intervention is not experienced as a "corrupting" influence on health care. Correctives might include redesigning health-care proposals to give patients greater legal rights or to create a body of citizen overseers that contests health-care decisions made at the federal level. Or there could be ways of rolling out universal health care so that individual states manage its provisioning, bringing the level of control closer to the reach of average citizens rather than leaving it with distant Washington bureaucrats. There is no reason the federal government cannot just require that state governments ensure universal coverage and leave states to choose exactly how to do so. If a market-based universal system is actually feasible, then the onus would be on conservative states to develop and implement it. In any case, the unease provoked by governmentally managed health care may be a result of negative bureaucratic experiences (or at least a perceived lack of positive ones). As such, advocates of universal health care need to do more than emphasize the cases where governmental initiatives do work well; they should design policy to ensure that bureaucracies provide citizens with a greater number of positive, trust-building interactions. The moral intuitions and experiences that motivate conservative citizens' reticence can be a driver to better health-care policy, not simply a barrier. Conservatives' greater sensitivity to the risk of federal oversteps and administrative failings is a critical corrective to leftists' bureaucratic optimism. Again, diversity is at the core of the democratic pluralist theory of good political decision making.

For their part, conservatives could disrupt "commonsensical" framings of gun control on the left by highlighting the potentially unequitable consequences of firearm laws. Given that the criminal justice system already disproportionately arrests and imprisons poorer and nonwhite Americans, stricter gun regulations are likely to come down far harder on those groups. A greater portion of them would stand to lose access to self-protection via a personal firearm and be put in prison for violations. By emphasizing the ways in which gun control could threaten leftists' underlying commitments to preventing harm to less-privileged groups, rather than by extoling conservatives' supposedly more objective understanding of the Second

Amendment, gun-control opponents can motivate the other side to be more circumspect and targeted in their policy proposals.[35]

A similar tool is the "broker frame."[36] Like moral-foundation theory, the concept of the broker frame recognizes that polarized opponents speak different languages. One notable example is in the issue of climate change. The roots of many conservatives' opposition to trying to avert or mitigate the climatic effects of human carbon emissions lies in their distrust of government-driven regulations. Recall the comic described in chapter 3, in which the cost of drinking the climate-change "Kool-Aid" is the US "free-market economy."[37] Because the majority of climate scientists and activists are on the left wing, they rarely frame climate policy to be, at least in part, compatible with conservatives' values. Meeting climate change head on can just as easily mean enabling new forms of entrepreneurship, creating a more competitive economy, or—as the US military sees it—ensuring national security. And consider that many rural conservatives in Germany have learned to love renewable power and have embraced community ownership of green energy as a lifeline for their small towns and way of life.[38] Most importantly, a pluralist process would ensure that climate-change policies actually deliver some of these entrepreneurial goals.

Progressive prison reform in the deeply conservative state of North Dakota has been helped by reform advocates' ability to tap into different value systems. When speaking to legislators, they frame "tough on crime" legislation as a bad investment and not fiscally responsible. Yet they also use right-wing values to justify Scandinavian-style practices. Giving prisoners greater responsibilities and focusing on developing healthy relationships among prisoners and staff rather than emphasizing punitiveness, with the aim of more quickly and reliably integrating prisoners back into society, fit not only into the liberal frame of harm reduction or social justice but also into conservative aspirations about neighborliness and the cultivation of self-reliance.[39]

At the same time, studies find that conservatives could elicit compromises from leftists on issues such as military spending or making English the official language of the United States by appealing to fairness and harm. Military service is a path to the middle class for many poor citizens and recent immigrants—although many on the left would just as well frame recruiters as preying on vulnerable populations. Likewise, matching the de facto status of English as the official language with de jure policy—and one assumes increased governmental support for language classes—can improve immigrants' job prospects and reduce the likelihood of their facing discrimination. No doubt there are leftist rejoinders to these framings, but these narratives at least open the door to compromise. Last, as Peter Beinart has noted, conservatives could elicit more cooperation from leftists just by being sensitive to the disproportionate harms of their policies on different racial groups and income levels. For instance, conservatives more rarely rail against the dependence of farmers, mining operators, and other large corporate businesses on generous governmental subsidies or against middle-class whites' home mortgage write-offs than they do against food stamps and public housing. If they were more careful and consistent in the application of their moral framework, they might convince at least some on the left that their concern is really the social production of dependency rather than the maintenance of racial or class-based inequalities.[40]

The utility of such approaches leads to the recognition that no issue is wholly determined by the facts or common sense. Rather, every issue is multifaceted enough to sustain multiple moral framings. Guided by that recognition, one sees that politics is more about the story that gets told about a problem as well as about how that story fits into people's own personal narratives.

The psychologist Timothy Wilson illustrates the power of stories in his book *Redirect*. Contrary to popular belief, immediate psychological interventions after a traumatic incident causes higher rates of post-traumatic stress disorder, and "scared-straight" approaches to discourage juvenile delinquency do the opposite of what is intended. Holding psychological debriefings too soon after an accident can be excessively painful, reinforcing the story of an incident as traumatic and senseless. Giving people time before prompting them to explore their feelings helps them "edit" the story so as to not relive the event so traumatically. Likewise, scared-straight interventions inadvertently tell youth that they are "bad," thus evoking a "troublemaker" narrative rather than the story of a "good" kid who simply made a mistake.[41]

Acting in ignorance of the power of stories often leads to perverse outcomes, but well-designed narratives can be incredibly positive. In one case, giving college students a thirty-minute presentation that portrayed the typical academic experience to be one of struggling at first but eventually getting the hang of things had a larger impact on grades than explicitly teaching study skills.[42]

The power of storytelling explains why narrative composes one of the three N's of deradicalizing jihadis or neo-Nazis—*narrative*, *need*, and *network*.[43] Violent fundamentalists are not swayed by contrary facts or theological argument but by narratives that recognize their need to feel significant and deserving of respect. For example, an outreach poster telling neo-Nazis that "if [they're] tired of living in the darkness of a hate-filled life, there's a way out" is unlikely to work because it begins by shaming them rather than portraying deradicalization as a challenge or heroic journey. The process is not complete, moreover, unless fundamentalists can be provided a nonviolent, alternative means for feeling respected or significant. For some, fulfilling work or family life can meet that need. For others, dedicating oneself to a larger cause, such as deradicalizing other extremists, can do so. What matters is that their new story is as compelling as the old one and that it is backed up with a new and supportive social network.

The importance of social relationships in reducing polarization cannot be overstated. The sociologist Robert Putnam has found considerable evidence that people who are engaged in community organizations and civic groups are more tolerant of dissent and difference. Putnam more generally argues that vibrant networks of social reciprocity help to maintain a healthy democracy, in part by encouraging collective action and discouraging free riding, opportunism, and other forms of hypertrophied self-interest.[44] Is it any surprise, then, that the inflection point for increasing polarization in Congress aligns with the moment representatives started no longer moving their families to the capital and began to check out of Washington's social scene? Lacking underlying social relationships—not to mention bonds between their spouses and children—politicians can more easily wage far more vicious rhetorical and political attacks on each other.[45]

Social capital building plays a valuable role not only in discouraging the polarization of political rhetoric but also in helping partisans move past apparent impasses. The journalist John Fleck describes how this process unfolded when Colorado River stakeholders sought to devise solutions to some of the river basin's problems: risks of shortages, insufficient flows to sustain important wetlands, and declining water quality—especially for deliveries to Mexico. The Yuma Desalter Working Group—developed out of an informal rafting trip among members of the opposing sides—gave participants a chance to more informally discuss their ideas, better understand each other's perspectives, and propose numerous alternatives through nonbinding conversations. Over time, this "cheap talk" eventually made way for official policy and better cooperation between the disparate groups. The development of social capital helped lead not only to an historic agreement between the United States and Mexico to release environmentally important flows of water on the Colorado but also to pilot-test a contentious desalting plant in order to learn about its performance and costs. If the various stakeholders had seen each other only on opposite sides of public hearings, such compromises would have been less than forthcoming.[46]

Even in cases where suitable broker frames cannot be found or opportunities for developing social capital are not available, there are still ways to reduce the risk of political polarization. The political scientists David Braybrooke and Charles Lindblom argued in the early 1960s that focusing political questions on incremental policy changes meant to correct in part an undesirable status quo can garner considerable more agreement than debates of people's ultimate values.[47] The Affordable Care Act is just such an example of incremental policy—being founded upon market-based health-care reform ideas developed by Republicans decades earlier. Although the act employed Braybrooke and Lindblom's strategy, it failed to achieve bipartisan agreement mainly because it was introduced at a time of already extreme levels of political polarization. Senate Republican leader Mitch McConnell strategized to ensure that the bill had practically no bipartisan support, despite its content, lest it became legitimized in the eyes of the public.[48] So although incrementalist proposals remain a potent strategy for eliciting compromise, it seems they stop working beyond a certain threshold of polarization. How social and political arrangements could be changed to better keep political interactions below this threshold is a question I take up in the next chapter.

A final way in which political talk might become less fanatical is by complexifying simplistic framings. Many contentious issues end up being polarized into two distinct factions rather than reflecting the diversity of perspectives that actually exist. The insistence that we split the controversy over childhood vaccinations into antivaxxer and pro-vaccine camps prevents a more detailed evaluation of the benefits and risks of different vaccines. For example, immunization for Hepatitis B—a blood-borne disease spread mostly by sexual activity and needle sharing—is given to all newborns in the United States, whereas other countries do not require it for years. The reason for early immunization in the United States is not that American babies are especially prone to engage in high-risk behaviors but rather that prenatal care is so unequal that a sizable portion of mothers are not screened for the disease, increasing the risk that they pass it on to their offspring. And it is not clear that earlier vaccination is a better strategy than improving prenatal screening because the vaccination is more effective when given closer to the age of probable exposure to Hepatitis B.[49] Yet by treating hesitancy about any and every vaccine as just a manifestation of antiscientific ignorance, vaccine advocates give up an opportunity to be more effective partisans. Even though a law permitting conscientious objection lowered vaccination rates for smallpox in early twentieth-century England, it also effectively emptied the member rolls of the National Anti-Vaccination League.[50] By allowing a percentage of parents to delay or refuse certain vaccinations when it is reasonably safe to do so, vaccine advocates could be more effective in achieving their political goals.

The lesson for politics writ large is to discourage binary framings of debates and instead seek to elicit the full range of stakeholder interests. Only then can a productive form of problem solving take place, wherein diverse alternatives can be proposed, discussed, and redesigned so as to mobilize a sufficiently large multipartisan coalition. Quite the opposite is the case for many issues, such as America's firearm laws. Part of the reason for this is that opponents rarely understand each other. Simplistic narratives fill the vacuum. On the one side, gun advocates are depicted as preferring a violent society where children are put at risk so that gun owners can feel empowered. On the other side, the gun-control crowd is seen as attempting to create an unarmed population that would live at the mercy of vicious criminals or a growing police state or both. The more complex reality between these two strawman depictions cannot be explored without efforts to encourage far more democratic political talk.

WHAT DEMOCRATIC POLITICAL TALK IS NOT

We should not idealize people's political interactions. Politics is inevitably messy, emotional, and contentious. Attempts to reform it into something rational and harmonious are bound to fail. For instance, efforts to include nonscientists in decisions about controversial science and technology, such as GE crops, have often been biased by the idea that participants should come in without strong convictions, as if their minds are infinitely open to any possible decision and that such openness will result in more "rational" choices that are representative of the public good.[51]

This line of thinking errs by believing that rationality lies within the minds of individuals rather than via pluralistic interactions. Citizens who have no stake in an issue will be partly blind to and less motivated to address the differential harms produced by a policy—and thus likely to fall prey to the illusion of harmony. A forum composed of only "open-minded" citizens on GE crops would exclude organic farmers who risk losing their certification due to nearby GE fields or those people who are strongly worried about collateral damage to other insect species or those who strongly favor GE crops.

Even worse, ideas about civility and openness can turn into inflexible and arbitrary rules of decorum. Insistences on maintaining civility can be a cover for excluding opponents—traditionally women, the poor, and other groups whose rhetoric may fail to meet a gentlemanly standard of rational political discourse. Moreover, an inappropriate sense of "political etiquette" keeps many Americans from talking about their political views in public and leads them to couch their dissent in self-interested rhetoric focusing on property values, children, and tax bills.[52] Therefore, it is important for the strategies described earlier to be used not as covers for idolizing consensus or stifling conflict and contention but rather as means for maintaining productive, publicly spirited dissent.

Moreover, fanaticism is too often equated with the ends of the political spectrum. Although centrists serve an important role in pluralists societies by ensuring that novel, untested policies are implemented more gradually, moderation per se is not always a virtue. Surveys find that a greater percentage of self-declared moderates in the United States and Europe are skeptical of democracy and free elections and, in many cases, are more likely to support autocratic, "strongman" leaders.[53] Centrism can be as fanatical as the political extremes. Furthermore, overly idealizing centrism undermines support for diversity, making political decisions less intelligent. The assumption that the truth lies in the exact middle between opposing sides is not guaranteed to be wiser than any other partisan position. It is difficult to see the wisdom in an unyielding allegiance to moderation for political questions such as slavery and women's right to vote.

The same mistake is made by a widely circulated infographic on news bias, which practically equates a media outlet's having a partisan leaning with its being a low-quality news source. The V-shaped Media Bias Chart idolizes "centrist" outlets, portraying them as being uniquely in the business of "fact finding." *Bloomberg News*, for instance, rates considerably higher than the *Huffington Post* or the *Washington Times*.[54] Yet centrist outlets are just as limited in their perspective as other news sources. Democratic socialists read *The Jacobin* because it presents political considerations that would never be represented in *Bloomberg*. But inherited myths about moderation lead many people to fail to recognize that centrist outlets' status quo bias is also a partisan position. In the same way that celebrating moderation as a virtue can easily become another undemocratic form of fanaticism, championing supposedly unbiased fact reporting risks the exclusion of important partisan analyses and perspectives.

Careful readers may have detected a potential contradiction at this point in my argument. Pluralist politics promise that compromise and concession will produce incremental changes that partly satisfy most partisan groups' demands, right? Doesn't that imply a moderate outcome? The intelligence of democracy, however, is a product of the *process* of mutual adjustment between partisans. Believing that "moderation" will be able to divine the "right" outcome prior to the political process is the same kind of mistake as believing that science or common sense will.

Some Hillary Clinton supporters leveraged fanatically moderate rhetoric after the primary in 2016, demurring efforts by Bernie Sanders and "Bernie Bro's" to push the Democratic platform leftward to include a $15 minimum wage and universal health care. Such rhetoric labeled the attempt to force Clinton to partially adopt progressive policies or lessen her dependence on corporate donations as "childish" and as ignoring the necessity of compromise in the "real world."[55] However, moderating one's position before engaging with opponents is only something shrewd partisans do strategically; otherwise, they are just undercutting their own political aspirations.[56] The claim that moderation is a higher form of cognition, like other truth narratives we have seen, undermines pluralism. Whether an intentional strategy or not, moderation rhetoric in this election situation shamed the progressive wing of Democratic voters into dropping their demands for compromise and concession and to toe the party line. Democratic Party leaders wanted to have it all, to capture both the elusive "centrist voter" and progressives without actually negotiating.

A corollary of avoiding the veneration of moderation is eschewing the idolization of consensus. Just like "the facts," consensus is tentative and not guaranteed to be a perfect representation of political truth. Consensus in one era is frequently overturned in the next, something most obvious for issues such as civil rights but also true for most areas of policy. Inherited agreement often becomes a *governing mentality*: "a tacit and often ill-considered pattern of assumptions that fundamentally shapes political relationships, interactions, and dialogue."[57] Consider how it used to be unthinkable to question the authority of royalty. The assumed correctness of the "divine right of kings" crippled most people's thinking, and the idea was eventually rejected once it became acceptable to dispute it.

Without more diversity in political thought, governing mentalities in many areas of life remain unchallengeable. The ideas, assumptions, and beliefs that make up the core of the mainstream, centrist Democratic platform, for instance, ought to be questioned by leftists who see themselves as nonliberals: Marxists, anarchists, and communitarians. Radicals in the wings are more likely to notice biases and blind spots than the moderates in the chorus. Likewise, absent the activism of people such as Rachel Carson and interest groups such as the Environmental Working Group, the easy assumption that the ubiquity of toxic chemicals is simply the cost of living in a "modern" society would too easily rule over us as if it were divinely decreed.[58]

The appropriate response to the existence of human bias is not to seek out objectivity. The idea that a single person or perspective can fully represent reality is a destructive myth. As mentioned in chapter 2, even science functions *intersubjectively*, creating more reliable knowledge through the contestation of ideas by people with often wildly differing perspectives. If all scientists were encultured with the exact same moderate view on the state of knowledge in their fields, new theories would rarely get developed or would be dropped too quickly by overly meek researchers.[59] What democracy needs is not objective truth—if that were even possible for most political issues—but a proliferation of multipartisan perspectives. The celebration of cognitive diversity recognizes that democracy is a kind of *distributed cognition*, a form of rationality that emerges from group interactions. It is little different from markets in this regard. Even Marxists recognize the amazing feats of social coordination achieved by the market system. One pops into Starbucks for a coffee without giving a single thought to the intricate web of relationships through which beans, machinery, paper cups, labor, and other inputs coalesce into a cup of joe—all accomplished without a central planner or plan. Democratic pluralism achieves similar cognitive feats for political problems. As Christopher Lasch puts it, democracy is defensible "not as the most efficient but as the most educational form of government."[60]

Although pluralism upholds the value of dissensus over agreement and encourages skepticism of the idea of objectivity, it is not the same as relativism. The point of recognizing that everyone has an invariably partial and biased understanding of the world is not to argue that truth does not exist or that all perspectives are equally right.[61] Rather, it merely means that human beings face considerable challenges in distinguishing truth from spurious beliefs. That does not mean that there is no point in trying. Shrugging one's shoulders and taking a relativistic view on important issues would be self-stultifying. Pluralism functions by political actors advocating strongly for their vision of the good. It lies between an intransigent fanaticism and an indifferent relativism.

This is why I have argued that it is better to focus on only the minimal capabilities that enable agonistic—rather than antagonistic—interactions, what Teresa Bejan refers to as "mere civility." Mere civility is a form of toleration that does not demand that political participants respect or even like one another, only that they "learn to make the most" of being stuck in a society with other people who believe things that seem outrageous. Cultivating empathy, respect, deep listening, and social capital are helpful in this regard, but we should not turn those strategies for more effective pluralism into grounds for excluding those who fail to practice them adequately. Dissenting groups should be included irrespective of their level of disagreeableness, for without their inclusion there is little hope of eventually realizing compromises and concessions with them. To call for civility as such is not to pine for some underlying harmonious consensus or form of polite decorum that will minimize political contention but rather to make the effort to navigate disagreements in ways that maintain our "unmurderous coexistence."[62] As Benjamin Barber has argued, the point of democratic political talk is to create "a sense of commonality, not of unity."[63]

The goal of emphasizing uncertainty, experience, and a modicum of civility is to ensure dynamism in coalition building, a constant fracturing and reforming of alliances along various lines for different issues. It is fine for politics to be a team sport and for people to have strong convictions. What matters is that they are willing to work with opponents, build new political "teams" for unrelated issues, and hear people out. Left-leaning environmentalists too often neglect hunters and fishers as potential allies, failing to temper their gun-control aspirations in order to emphasize their shared interests in protecting natural spaces—to take one example. Such cross-cutting coalitions are the very stuff of democratic politics, helping to prevent the entrenchment of friend–enemy distinctions that give rise to exclusionary or even violent policy. Good politics is a lively process of building understanding and making temporary compromises. As Charles Lindblom argues, "Ever-shifting alliances and voting patterns . . . hold out to citizens expectations of future victories on the issue on which they for the moment suffer defeat."[64] What matters for sustaining the demo-cratic process is keeping an open-ended and dynamic democratic process going.

WHEN IS FANATICISM APPROPRIATE?

There is much to be said about the greater intelligence, representativeness, and productiveness of incremental changes that occur through democratic pluralism. Yet there are issues where incrementalism appears to be neither wise nor just and where certain groups and ideas seem to be unworthy of even "mere civility."

I consider prosperity gospel to be just such an unworthy idea. Prosper-ity churches preach that godliness brings not only spiritual salvation but also financial success and physical well-being. Simply put, religious faith unequivocally provides for a comfortable life on earth. But prosperity the-ology also makes the converse true: poverty and illness are signs of per-sonal spiritual failure. The theology scholar Kate Bowler describes how one megachurch attendee who was stricken with cancer was told to stop com-ing to the altar for prayer. The church leaders told him, "You have to heal yourself."[65]

I find it difficult to see anything of value in prosperity theology. Pros-perity preachers such as Joel Osteen and Creflo Dollar in my view are char-latans peddling a distorted, victim-shaming theology. They take what little extra money poor people have in their pockets in order to build tax-exempt fortunes for themselves, while claiming that the whole process is driven by piety rather than by avarice. On my more pessimistic days and despite my usual spiritual agnosticism, I hope that hell exists so that prosperity gospel preachers can have a place within its inner circle.

Yet part of the appeal of prosperity gospel is that it provides a sense of empowerment, something that people who have not been dealt a very good hand by society may struggle to find elsewhere.[66] Leftists' failure to recognize this leads them to endlessly lament how poorer Americans vote "against their own interests"—as some progressives condescendingly put it—rather than to develop better approaches to the issue. Followers of prosperity gospel reject the "victim narrative" that so often founds leftist rhetoric. As much as I despise prosperity gospel, its existence alerts me to how I could be a more effective political partisan. Rather than pointlessly decry prosperity gospel preachers, I should be advocating for policies that address inequality while providing recipients more control over their own lives, policies that do not frame them as nothing more than downtrodden victims.

Perhaps that example is too easy. What about cases such as slavery and white supremacy? Is fanaticism *always* antidemocratic, or can an argument be made for sometimes taking an uncompromising position on an unjust status quo? The term *fanatic*, as the political scientist Joel Olson observes, is treated as a pejorative by laypersons and philosophers alike. The zealot is viewed as always dangerously irrational and intolerant in his or her politics, someone open to terrorism and other forms of political repression.[67] So far this book has been little different in its view of fanaticism, although it has not celebrated moderation or consensus as an antidote to tribalism or polarization.

Olson challenges the too easy equation of zealotry with violent, antidemocratic fundamentalism by pointing to the case of slavery abolitionism. Prominent abolitionists were immovable in their commitment to end slavery. Yet they made no effort to stifle free speech—allowing pro-slavery views to be aired at their meetings—and neither did they shun debate. Fanaticism was a consciously chosen political strategy in response to the reluctance of Congress and other important institutions to meet the issue head on. Rather than being driven to emotional unreason by their beliefs, they developed their fanaticism out of the view that differing perspectives on the issue were incommensurable, inexorably separated by fundamentally divergent ethical views. Once one sees slavery to be an abomination, morally just compromises are no longer possible. Fanatical strategy works by emphasizing these moral divisions, starkly splitting up the populace into friends and foes with the aim of pushing fence sitters to choose a side. Fanatical discourse is meant to shock the audience into action. Fanatical abolitionists did just that by arguing that political moderation was complicit in the injustices of slavery.[68]

Such sentiments were also reflected in Martin Luther King Jr.'s "Letter from a Birmingham Jail" a century later, in which King concluded that "white moderates" were a bigger barrier to freedom than the Ku Klux Klan; their devotion to maintaining "order" led them to resist King's protests and activism as too disruptive to the social fabric or as pushing for too much change too soon.[69] King and his fellow activists, like the pre–Civil War abolitionists, were striving against political opponents who were already fanatically resolute in their opposition. Calls for moderation in such circumstances hardly seem to be in good faith, for they stack the deck in favor of an unjust status quo. Grossly oppressive practices can end only when the oppressors lose; the other side must eventually stop giving concessions.

Political fanaticism for cases such as civil rights and slavery can be seen as democratic insofar as it seeks to shock citizens out of their complacency and to create disagreement where stale convergences of thought stand. Agitation by persons with strong convictions helps break the gentle tyranny of an insufficiently challenged status quo.

Yet how can we make sure that fanatical politics remain democratic? Olson notes that abolitionists refrained from dehumanizing slaveholders, instead painting the collective system of slavery as an evil to be destroyed and their political enemies as potential brethren. They consciously ensured that the conversion of individuals remained a strategy for attacking the institution of slavery. When an Arkansas slaveholder showed up at the abolitionist Wendell Phillips's doorstep in Boston, he was politely given a tour of the city.[70] Abolitionists' policy recommendations, furthermore, were far from antidemocratic. Rather than advocate the freeing of slaves by force, William Lloyd Garrison called for the North to voluntarily secede from the Union. He believed that withdrawing the North's economic and military support (e.g., slave patrols) would drive the collapse of slavery. Although John Brown on the morning of his execution expressed his certainty that slavery would end only through bloodshed, other abolitionists did not see violence as necessary. Hence, fanaticism seems most democratic when tempered by minimally civil commitments—namely, extending toleration to opponents and advocating for policies that are not violent or actively oppressive, even though they may explicitly aim to undermine opponents' way of life.

Yet the actual resolution of the slavery question was a civil war that claimed the lives of some three-quarters of a million Americans and maimed countless others—though one could argue that the war was due more to a fanatical attachment to preserving the Union rather than to defeating slavery per se. It is impossible to know whether strategies such as Northern secession or incremental but more morally uncomfortable approaches, such as financially compensating slaveholders for emancipation, could have worked.[71] Southern states were as fanatically committed to keeping slaves in bondage as abolitionists were to agitating for their freedom. But it is clear that the eventual resolution to the fanatical division of the nation over slavery was incredibly costly for both sides. Apart from the toll on human bodies, it also had a psychocultural cost. Political polarization in the United States remained intense throughout Reconstruction. Even today the geography of political divisiveness in this country continues to mirror in part the split between Union and Confederate areas—even in states such as New Mexico.

Polarization did lessen for a period in the United States, but only because Republicans looked the other way as Southern states established Jim Crow laws.[72] For all the blood spilled in the Civil War, emancipation still ended up being compromised. Former slaves were de jure free but continued to have their liberties constrained in practice. This outcome signals one of the difficulties of political fanaticism, especially when it results in violent or otherwise antidemocratic policy: How do we go back to democratic pluralism after the fanatical moment has concluded? The outcome of the Civil War can be read in at least two different ways: either it was not conducted fanatically enough—the North should have deslaved the South in a process similar to the denazification of post–World War II Germany—or too little was done to prevent the slide into a costly and ultimately ineffective form of violent zealotry.

Democratic fanaticism can be characterized as a form of intransigence that does not seek to constrain debate or demonize individuals, whether opponents or moderates, but to attack systems. Its practitioners employ a fierce—albeit minimally civil—relentlessness in their demands for justice. Yet the decision to move from incrementalist pluralism to democratic fanaticism is not one that should be made lightly. Although fanaticism is often an appropriate response to an equally zealous opponent, fanatical political battles come with potentially high costs. Democratic fanaticism can very easily transform into a dehumanizing form of fundamentalism that spurs the repression of political rights and even encourages outright violence.

Because of the risks associated with fanatical politics, I have advocated a range of discursive strategies that can help political talk stay within the realm of democratic pluralism. Rather than claim to have all the facts, political actors should focus on uncertainty. Doing so motivates a more incremental approach to policy, which is less likely to alienate opponents. As Susan Matthews has put it, "Curiosity is . . . one of the first casualties of polarization."[73] Maintaining a sense of openness and willingness to experiment with public policy, conversely, can be an effective strategy to avoid entrenchment. Politics should not be about realizing the "correct" policy immediately but instead about adopting flexible political interventions and adjusting them over time, which prevents the implementation of undercooked "grand plans" and helps build trust among skeptics.

Emphasizing the diversity of experience helps challenge the illusion of harmony that underlies appeals to common sense. Getting opponents to pay attention and to take those differing experiences seriously, however, is not always easy. Studies suggest that people are more likely to take on the perspective of another person when they are pushed to find commonalities within their own personal history. Making experience a productive component of political talk means walking a fine line, emphasizing similarities while avoiding the illusion of harmony, highlighting differences without implying that people have absolutely no hope of understanding the experiences of someone from a different race, gender, class, or position in society.

Tenacious disagreements can be better navigated by recognizing that people are motivated and inspired by very different values and framings. Eliciting compromises out of political opponents or converting some of them is difficult enough; to expect them to do so while also embracing the other side's value commitments and preferred moral language is naive. Shaming citizens who do not accept "the truth" fails because it ignores how people are also narrative beings. Political actors' effectiveness in building successful coalitions is rooted in their ability to advocate for their preferred policies while also tapping into people's broader aspirations such as the desire to feel respected or self-reliant. Such coalitions will only prove effective, however, if policies actually deliver some of those goals. Understanding the values and narratives that motivate political opponents is made easier by socializing with them. Building social capital, moreover, helps people and decision makers better weather the storm of disagreement and conflict. Even absent these strategies, contention can be made more bearable by focusing on strategy rather than on the final goals of policy as well as by recognizing the diverse range of interests at stake. Simplistic strawman portrayals of opponents make democratic politics impossible. If citizens shift the debate away from all-encompassing visions of the ultimate makeup of society, they open the door to reformed coalitions and negotiated agreements that different sides can "live with," at least in the short-term.

Most importantly, by recognizing the multifaceted roots of disagreement, people are likely to become humbler. Citizens can come to recognize that their own acceptance of "the facts" or "common sense" is based in their experiences, relationships, and moral intuitions—not on their intelligence. It is far easier for people to accept mainstream medicine's view of vaccine safety when the moral framework of care dominates their thinking or if they already trust the Food and Drug Administration to undertake adequate levels of safety testing. Few people are literate in the complexities of the underlying science. Guided by that humility, vaccine advocates will find it easier to see antivaxxers as human beings rather than as mere dupes.

The point of these strategies is not to seek to erase conflict but rather to channel it toward action. Disagreement is what drives democracy forward. Attempts to temper contention by idolizing consensus, moderation, or civility risk expunging viewpoints from the public sphere. As the example of slavery abolitionism shows, fanatics of one era are often vindicated by history. Even in less-clear cases, extremists provide insight into underlying aspirations and concerns that are inadequately represented within mainstream politics. Without zealots agitating for change, stale convergences of thought act as a form of gentle tyranny on the minds of more moderately minded citizens. Even when those zealots advocate something immoral or distasteful, they provide useful information about their underlying motivations. Careful attention to their words can uncover their values and aspirations, which opposing groups can use to talk to and possibly convert some of the less-extreme members of a fanatical group.

Yet I do not want to depict the challenge of productively incorporating or diffusing fanatical sentiments as if it were easy. The strategies mentioned earlier are probably insufficient on their own, for people's ability to act is constrained by the broader world around them. Contemporary citizens fall prey to fanatical truth narratives and are poorly adept at political talk because of broader processes of socialization and enculturation. How might American society, government, technology, and culture be reconstructed to be better compatible with the practice of democratic pluralism?

RECONSTRUCTING DEMOCRACY

People will not become more "merely civil" in their disagreements just because someone with a PhD has written a book arguing that they should. Citizens will be inclined to do so only if societies are appropriately redesigned. Attempts to reform society are often portrayed as utopian or out of touch with "human nature." But the diversity of human history and culture shows that people's ability to disagree productively has changed appreciably over time. Contemporary citizens have come a long way from the medieval Norse, whose disputes on the Greenland colony often ended with opponents lying dead from ax wounds.[1] Anyone who has spent considerable time abroad, moreover, has likely experienced differences in the acceptability of disagreement. I will never forget my astonishment at how positively a German supervisor responded to my public contradiction of him after a research talk. Yet when I was teaching English overseas, I would have made my Taiwanese coworkers very uncomfortable if I had disagreed with them so openly.

Such diversity highlights possibilities for gradual cultural change, potentialities that could be supported and accelerated. How might citizens be socialized or otherwise prepared to be adept disagreers? What alterations to political systems, technologies, and major institutions would help support the kinds of dispositions and interactions compatible with democratic pluralism?

MAKING POLICY MAKING MORE PLURAL

As discussed earlier, the political design of the United States was rooted in a distrust of democracy. Revolutionary-era thinkers such as James Madison and Alexander Hamilton feared, albeit largely without evidence, that democratic decision making would become mob rule. Places where mobs seemed to rule, such as postrevolution Reign of Terror France, were often as absolutist and autocratic as the regimes they replaced—courting the passions of particular populations more than enabling dissent. They were not really cases of functioning democracies. And demagogues' pathways to power are usually paved by the manipulation and assent of powerful decision makers and other elites, not only by swaying the masses. Populists become dictators because other political actors cooperate with the dismantling of checks on executive power—very rarely because of a popular plebiscite. Even in cases where a majority or winning plurality of active voters choose a candidate with authoritarian tendencies, such a vote can be seen as a symptom of an already dying democracy rather than as the cause of political decline.

Consider how populism in the United States and Australia has been presaged by record low rates of trust in politics. The vast majority of Americans agree with the statement "Public officials don't care much what people like me think." Is it any wonder that climate-change skepticism and conspiratorial thinking abound? Indeed, as I write this in the midst of the COVID-19 pandemic in early 2020, both countries are being rocked by antilockdown protests by citizens claiming that the pandemic is "all a hoax." Insofar as democracies actually do devolve into unintelligent mob rule, it appears to be a response to the perceived unresponsiveness and illegitimacy of political representation.[2]

But erring on the side of epistocracy and designating appropriately credentialed people to serve as political guardians does not necessarily prevent authoritarianism—or unintelligent policy for that matter. I have argued that it is instead the intolerance of disagreement, which affects elites no less than laypeople, that really drives fanatical politics and thoughtless policy, not an excess of democracy. Although it is tempting to hold out hope that the right kind of vetting system might put highly intelligent and unbiased stewards of the public good into the highest offices, I prefer to ask a different question: How can political systems discourage intransigence and better foster productive disagreement among invariably biased and partisan individuals?

Democracy is too often equated with elections. Such thinking conflates the policy process, which is the procedure for developing and establishing laws, rules, and regulations, with arrangements for selecting political officials. It obscures how electoral systems can actually make a country less democratic. The political scientists Amy Gutmann and Dennis Thompson, for instance, argue that the American system itself selects *against* the personal characteristics of an effective policy maker. Although an openness to compromise aids the policy-making process, it makes for a weak campaign platform. Voters are swayed by candidates who stand firm on principles and attack their opponents at every turn, not ones who seem willing to make concessions or negotiate with political enemies. This approach would not be so damaging to the US political process if officeholders were not locked into a "permanent campaign," wherein preparations for the next election cycle effectively begin the day after taking office. Politicians end up trapped in a nonproductive and uncompromising principle-based style of policy making, carrying the mutual distrust and Machiavellianism of the political campaign into public office. For instance, it was patently obvious that Republicans' unwillingness to hammer out a bipartisan health-care compromise with President Obama had more to do with permanent campaigning than with the actual merits and flaws of the proposed policy. One conservative representative put it baldly, "If we're able to stop Obama on this, it will be his Waterloo. It will break him."[3]

A few incremental steps toward a less-polarized political world would entail small tweaks to the electoral system, though many steps would require amending nations' constitutions. At least in the United States, some combination of term limits, longer terms for representatives (who currently serve a mere two years), and rules limiting the length of the campaign season would lessen the dominance of electioneering on the minds of representatives. Such measures are not unheard of. In Mexico, Canada, Israel, and the United Kingdom, the election season is explicitly limited. The latest Canadian parliamentary election was considered a "marathon" when it lasted a mere two and half months. In any case, insulating politicians from the constant pressure of campaigning can open the door to more thoughtful policy making—at least in theory.[4]

Other changes to the way citizens elect politicians could foster a greater openness to compromise among policy makers. One promising strategy is proportional representation. Proportional systems award the fraction of seats in state or federal legislatures to different parties in accordance to the percentage of the vote they receive rather than having "winner-take-all" districts. The perversity of the latter—along with the effects of gerrymandered districts—is demonstrated by the fact that Republicans won the House in 2012 despite receiving 1.4 million fewer votes than Democrats.[5]

Proportional representation already exists in numerous countries around the world, with some using a mixed system where voters directly choose a representative and a party representative. Proportional representation tends to increase the number of parties represented and to reduce the odds that any one party enjoys a simple majority. Moreover, they increase the diversity of potential legislation and debate, opening the door for not only socialists and greens but also libertarians. As a result, ruling regimes and most policy decisions are more likely to be the product of compromises among multi-party coalitions—though that is not necessarily guaranteed to happen.

According to Arend Lijphart, proportional representation leads to a "kinder, gentler democracy." Nations employing proportional systems tend to have fewer violent internal conflicts and less economic inequality, better protect civil liberties, be far more representative of women, support higher levels of political participation, and rate higher in terms of governmental functioning.[6] For example, Josep Colomer credits Spain's embrace of proportional representation for the relative stability of its post-Franco democracy. Although the country's implementation of proportional representation is not as inclusive as that of other nations, it has so far prevented the reemergence of the highly polarized two-party system that preceded the outbreak of civil war in 1936.[7]

A more radical possibility would be to do away with elections in part. This proposal might seem farfetched at first, but it appears at least worthy of consideration if one takes a look at the flaws of representative democracy. There is little conclusive evidence that electing representatives to steward the "public good" results in democratic outcomes. One, albeit disputed, longitudinal study of congressional decisions has found that policy outcomes correlate far stronger with the preferences of economic elites and business interest groups than with the preferences of average citizens; its authors conclude that the "majority does *not* rule" in the United States.[8] Even worse, representative power tends to corrupt, especially when legislators' decisions affect the economically powerful or when legislative bodies themselves are made up mainly of people from the highest echelons of a society. Most legislative bodies across the globe skew toward dominant groups in race, gender, and class. High levels of corruption by the political establishment seems to be behind Brazilian voters turning out for right-wing populist Jair Bolsonaro.[9] Although there are no doubt significant challenges to doing democracy without elections, one should not weigh them against idealized visions of electoral politics but rather against the chronic deficits in democratic participation and the routine decision-making failures that characterize real-life representative systems.

Even more cynicism inducing are the myriad problems with citizens' voting practices. In an overview of survey evidence, the political scientists Christopher Achen and Larry Bartels find that citizens' voting patterns are more a product of group identity than of their policy preferences or underlying ideology. That is, citizens often vote out of loyalty to a "political team" or for candidates whose identity matches their own, not according to a discerning understanding of a politician's platform or actual accomplishments. In fact, people's beliefs about changes in the budget deficit—for which data are readily available and rarely disputed—are colored by their party affiliation. Many Republicans in the 1990s mistakenly believed that the Clinton administration's budgets raised the nation's deficit. Similarly, party affiliation predicted whether people believed that the economy after 2016 was thriving and whether President Trump deserved any credit for it. Citizens do vote against previous allegiances, of course, but even this switch is too often a myopic response to changes in their income level, a recent drought or flood, or numerous other things largely out of public officials' control. In light of the failure of elections to translate citizens' values and interests into substantive changes in the ruling regime, Achen and Bartels conclude that "election outcomes are essentially random choices . . . [that] simply put a different elite coalition in charge."[10] Once one recognizes how low a democratic bar is set by electoral politics, other selection systems start to look more attractive.

One alternative mechanism is demarchy: randomly selecting a representative sample of citizens to serve as legislators. Although this proposal might seem absurd, it was in fact practiced in ancient Athens. The Greek philosopher Aristotle even argued that demarchy was more democratic than elections, given that representative democracies are prone to devolve into a quasi-aristocracy.[11] Democracy by lot has several advantages. It frees policy makers from the destructive effects of campaigning and overly developed allegiances to parties as "political teams." Second, it diminishes the role of fanatical populism. An elite interpreter of the "will of the people" is no longer necessary when a random sample of the people does the actual legislating. Moreover, such a population sample would better represent women, racial minorities, and the working class, allowing them to bring their varied experiences, knowledge, and values to bear on public issues. As Hélène Landemore has pointed out, random selection increases the cognitive diversity of a legislative body more so than traditional elections do.[12]

The latter advantage is important because it addresses the concern about competence—though that objection arguably overestimates the competency of current officeholders and the effectiveness of elections in selecting for intelligence or ability. As examples such as the institution of science and the organization of safety on an aircraft carrier illustrate, the intelligence of decision making is more a product of proposals being subjected to critique from diverse perspectives than of the individual participants' IQ. In fact, one recent study found that ideologically diverse teams writing Wikipedia entries engaged in longer, more constructive, and more focused debates than groups made up of like-minded individuals, thus producing higher-quality entries as a result. In short, demarchy takes advantage of what we have learned regarding how to accomplish complex tasks intelligently.[13]

In any case, worries about grossly incompetent or irresponsible participants could be addressed by providing preliminary training, access to quality information, and information sessions with relevant experts—or perhaps through a recall process. But there is good reason to believe that lay citizens would be considerably more thoughtful in a demarchal legislature than they are in the voting booth. Scholars who study similarly randomly selected "citizen assemblies" have noted that "it was hard not to be impressed with the capacity of citizens to learn, absorb, and understand the intricacies of a subject to which most had given little, if any, prior thought."[14] I can think of no reason why the lawyers and businesspeople currently overrepresented in most legislatures are necessarily any more competent than the scientists, public-school teachers, engineers, and blue-collar workers who would take their places. Certainly, the former know more about legal minutiae, payroll taxes, and other issues, but they are likely to be considerably less informed about science and technology, the educational system, and the daily struggles of the modal citizen. Nevertheless, there is something to be said for the expertise developed by multiterm representatives in navigating disagreement and the policy process. Perhaps citizen legislators who garner positive reviews from both their peers and their constituents could gain an increased likelihood of being reselected. Similarly, sagging approval ratings or the failure to pass a budget might spark a snap reselection, similar to the "no-confidence" procedure used in parliamentary systems. Barring that, a staff of legislative experts could provide advice to citizen legislators, although there would need to be protections against such staffs of experts being captured by elite interest groups.

One objection is more difficult to counter. A national demarchal legislature would not be responsive to any particular set of geographical constituents. Many local concerns—such as important infrastructure projects beyond the means of individual municipalities—might slip through the cracks. One solution would be to develop nested demarchal legislatures. A hundred or so people could be selected to explore and debate policy issues for each—nongerrymandered and equally proportioned—representational district. Those districts would then select some number of participants to move on to represent the district's interests within a national house of representatives. Similar state-level demarchal bodies could select federal senators.

Even if legislative bodies themselves were not based on random selection, the method could still be used to democratize the regulatory process. Most nations are beholden to the demands of global economic bureaucracies. For instance, Greece was threatened with bankruptcy and ejection from the Eurozone unless its leaders capitulated to the European Union's demands, mainly the requirement to implement austerity measures that were highly disruptive to the lives of average Greeks. Even domestic decisions are increasingly made by unelected bureaucracies. The Federal Communications Commission gets to decide the extent to which "net-neutrality" principles govern the US internet independently of what citizens think.[15] And the growing perception that governmental bureaucracies are technocratic, unresponsive, and/or corrupt drives the attraction to populism.

Scholars who study the postcrisis behavior of private companies, bureaucrats, and politicians contend that openness and inclusion are the most reliable ways to gain public trust and legitimate contentious decisions. MetEd's failure to answer difficult questions and their attempts to conceal information after the Three Mile Island near disaster cost the firm its legitimacy and strengthened the leftist populist narrative that nuclear energy companies are not to be trusted.[16] If obstinate opponents of the construction of new nuclear reactors or of new rules on the purchase and sale of firearms are to trust the process, it will only be if they are given a seat at the table. Otherwise, it is too easy for them to suspect that they are being hoodwinked by dishonest corporations or politicians. Complex regulatory decisions do not have to be made so bureaucratically—and it is probably best that they are not.

Although greater citizen involvement in and oversight of governance is a commonly cited antidote to technocratic unresponsiveness, some forms of public participation are not helpful. As Claudia Chwalisz has pointed out, referenda have questionable democratic credentials. In fact, direct popular voting is probably one of the least desirable ways of involving the public because little to no deliberation or political negotiation actually takes place. It is difficult to imagine intelligent decision making resulting from the reduction of incredibly complex and multifaceted issues into binary "yes or no" choices, especially when the public is then subjected to big-money political advertising. Average people are rarely involved in deciding which exact question is put to voters in a referendum. And the process is initiated and driven mostly by political elites—unsurprisingly given that average citizens generally have neither the time nor the means to be so politically entrepreneurial. The fact that only a small minority of the British popula-tion felt well informed prior to the referendum on European Union mem-bership and that Google searches for "What is the EU?" spiked *after* the vote inspires little confidence in the potential intelligence of plebiscites.[17]

The demarchal corrective to bureaucratic rule and the limitations of referenda is the long-form deliberative body in which randomly selected collections of citizens spend months learning about and deliberating a con-tentious issue. These bodies function similarly to an extended jury: average people interface with experts and discuss challenges amongst themselves in order to render policy recommendations. Far from being a mere academic exercise, deliberative bodies have been practiced in Canada, Australia, and other countries for quite some time, examining issues such as condomin-ium policy, transportation infrastructure planning, mental health, obesity, and their nation's nuclear-fuel cycle.

In contrast to dour assessments of the typical voter's cognitive capabili-ties, studies find that long-form deliberative bodies render decisions that are thoughtful and garner greater public legitimacy than choices made behind closed doors by governmental bureaucracies. Deliberation spurs thought-fulness. People become less polarized and more nuanced in their positions when they learn that an already known political opponent will hold them accountable for their views. Consider an experiment where psycholo-gists had people with opposing stances meet and then attempt to describe each other's political positions. Because the psychologists told participants that their partner in the conversation would evaluate the accuracy of the description, they became much less polarized in their assessment of their opponents' beliefs. Insofar as deliberative environments force participants to take opponents' political views seriously, make them get to know their opposition, and empower rival sides to hold each other accountable, they discourage political fanaticism.[18]

Polarization is also lessened by increasing the diversity of legislators and other policy makers. The political scientists Christopher Hare and Keith Poole have observed that the American two-party system tends to become more polarized whenever the parties themselves are no longer divided internally by various regional and other concerns.[19] That is, when political groupings become unidimensional rather than constantly negotiated coalitions, party platforms too easily become dogma. Hence, expanded participation and encouraged dissensus provide an alternative to liberal guardian institutions, letting disagreement among partisans work to decentralize power rather than relying on the supposed beneficence and wisdom of unelected guardians.

Nevertheless, it is understandable why many people would be hesitant to expand democracy, especially when it gives their opponents more say. The prospect of deliberating alongside white nationalists is not something that I would expect many citizens to relish, and some Christian conservatives probably shudder at the idea of sharing a table with an advocate of legalized abortion. This sense of aversion is not simply because of differences in values but because political policies have real consequences for people and their loved ones. I cannot help but think of my friends with diabetes or multiple sclerosis when conservatives oppose legislation to improve access to health care. At stake in many issues is not just differing theoretical understandings of the Constitution, human rights, and the proper role of government but actual human suffering. When "tough on crime" advocates demand stricter and more punitive policing practices, their improved sense of security comes at a cost paid by other people, whose bodies are on the line if police receive more discretion to target them with random searches or in their ability to use deadly force. Bolstering democracy can sometimes mean expanding the potential for one's political opponents to do one harm.

Yet it is not obvious that explicitly excluding certain viewpoints, candidates, and parties actually makes their ideas or influence disappear, though it can keep more extreme policy proposals off the table. Trying to shame certain views out of existence leads them to be hidden behind dogwhistle terms and risks the exacerbation of political polarization. Consider how racialized politics in America continued to be after the civil rights era in the language of "welfare queens" and the "undeserving poor." Policies that arguably undermine African Americans' economic opportunities have proliferated, while the conscious avoidance of now politically incorrect racialized language makes it more difficult to recognize—perhaps even to supporters of these policies—that something discriminatory is happening.[20]

At the same time, when citizens rarely interact with people who hold antithetical beliefs, they can too easily learn to see political opponents as unalloyed monsters. Legal scholar Ian Haney López tells of how his experience hitchhiking around and listening to racists in apartheid-era South Africa led him to recognize how they could still be "good people," even while having distasteful racial beliefs. Human beings are complex and contradictory in their capacity for both generosity and harm.[21] Recognizing the kernel of human decency that exists among whomever one considers to be a political enemy provides an opening for democratic interaction.

All of the possibilities for changing the political system listed up to this point should be explored carefully and implemented incrementally. For all the potential merits of these changes, unintended consequences or perverse outcomes may result from them, especially if they are applied haphazardly. At the same, they also cannot be expected to fix American politics on their own. For instance, when New Zealand moved to proportional representation, politics remained nearly as polarized and unproductive as what preceded it, at least until a deeper cultural shift gradually occurred.[22] Unless the broader technological, social, and cultural environment fosters thoughtfulness, altered political processes will be woefully insufficient.

A LESS ANTAGONISTIC MEDIA LANDSCAPE

It has become very clear that digital technologies and the media can have a pernicious effect on political behavior. Early internet proponents, however, dreamed that the World Wide Web would become a kind of global village. Democracy would be rejuvenated through the virtual public sphere, which would empower ordinary people to voice their opinions and free them from control by dictators and media moguls.[23] Facebook CEO Mark Zuckerberg believed, at least as late as 2012, that his platform would create a more "open culture" by exposing people to diverse views and experiences.[24] Although considerable disagreement exists regarding the precise balance of benefits and harms of the contemporary media landscape on politics, a vibrantly democratic and tolerant global society has clearly not come to pass. Which features of our media system appear to be the most stifling of democracy?

The media can undermine pluralism by setting the stage for fanatical truthism. Studies find that citizens become more polarized in their political views when they deliberate with only likeminded people.[25] When left liberals talk politics only with other leftists and consume a narrow range of leftist news sources, the lack of exposure to criticism supports an overinflated sense of certainty in their political ideas. Back in 2011, Eli Pariser sounded the alarm that digital technologies could exacerbate ideological segregation, noting how the efforts by search engines and social networks to curate search results and news feeds steer users into echo-chamber-like "filter bubbles."[26]

Even worse for contemporary internet users, the process is no longer only demand driven. Political campaigns have purchased ad services—notably from Facebook in the election of 2016—in order to target citizens more precisely with pandering messages and disinformation or with narratives meant to discourage them from voting at all. Political action committees supporting Trump targeted conservative voters with ads claiming the Clintons participated in organized crime and that Hillary was on drugs.[27] People working for the Russian Internet Research Agency further targeted right-wing Americans with messages meant to inflame them and stoke their anger, describing Hillary Clinton as "pure evil" or spreading a doctored image of her shaking hands with Osama bin Laden. These messages were further legitimated when the targeted users shared them with friends and family, obscuring their original source.[28] As such, ad-curation technology not only risks the development of echo chambers but also helps fanatics drive polarization to new extremes.

In some cases, however, citizens do become more circumspect by hearing extreme positions. Research finds that exposure to radical views can lead people to reconsider tightly held beliefs. One Israeli study crafted videos that presented the Palestinian conflict as a positive contributor to Israeli Jewish identity, implying that the continuation of it helped Israel have a powerful army and a just society. Exposure to this almost cartoonish version of the pro-militaristic viewpoint led some participants to reconsider and moderate their previously hawkish position.[29] So it appears that the problem with digital filter bubbles is not simply that they insulate leftists and conservatives from each other's views but that people may also be less often exposed to diverse positions within the left or right. Seeing more extreme perspectives challenges citizens to reevaluate inherited "status quo" ideas, especially when those perspectives show a shared but unquestioned assumption or value in an exaggerated form.

The problem with a polarized media landscape, then, is not so much that different outlets have disparate views on political issues and events but that citizens can too easily limit themselves to a narrow range of perspectives. The extent to which people can entrench themselves in or be nudged by algorithms toward a world of self-reinforcing information and argument is the problem, not the biases of different perspectives per se.

Legal scholars have suggested that large digital media firms such as Facebook and Google should be classified as "information fiduciaries."[30] So classified, these tech companies would be held accountable to certain fair-information standards. Perhaps Facebook would not be allowed to sell user data to political campaigns at all—or only under very strict conditions. Nor would such firms be permitted to target specific groups with potentially manipulative political messages. Citizens might gain the right to opt out of different kinds of filtering in their searches or news feeds, thus ensuring that they see updates from their closest friends without blocking out diverse political messages or news items.

A more pluralistic media system would go further to ensure the representation of and debate between diverse partisan views. Among the barriers to such a system are inherited beliefs about what the news should be. Because most people are steeped in the mythology of nonpartisan American journalism, it is too easy for them to confuse multipartisan diversity with polarized echo chambers. As a result, they pine for journalism that is "objective," as if news writers could somehow succeed in completely disassociating their values from the work and meet a standard of objectivity that even scientists do not live up to. This view misunderstands the goal of democracy as well as journalism's place within it. The role of journalists and opinion writers in a democracy is not to be arbiters of fact but to help citizens better navigate their disagreements. Reliable knowledge for policy making, as for science more generally, is to be found through quality interactions between differently partisan media actors, not within any given journalist's assessment.

During the nascent stages in the spread of the World Wide Web, it was hoped that it would enhance journalistic pluralism by lowering the barriers to entry to the "marketplace of ideas." These hopes failed to recognize how the underlying political economy of media and the internet would drive centralization.[31] Practically speaking, most states treat freedom of the press as a negative liberty, a freedom from constraint. Only the subset of citizens capable of owning or acquiring access to a printing machine, news channel, or radio station have been able to practice it. Digital media seem to have lessened the financial burden of speech—opening it up to people with the means to purchase web-hosting services and to access a computer. But the practical constraints on citizens' ability to fully exercise their speech rights were more transformed than eliminated. *Producing speech* was now relatively easy, but *being heard* was another matter. As a consequence, the distributors of information gained considerable power over producers. Search engines, blog aggregators, and already popular outlets have become the new gate-keepers. They have benefitted from the network effects that drive the inter-net: certain platforms and websites become more desirable as more people use them. Because Google searches improve and Facebook grows only more useful with size, there is intense economic pressure toward monopolization. As a result, most people consume their political news from a handful of the top newspapers, magazines, and blogs—the dozen or so that are popular enough to dominate social media and the first page of Google searches.[32]

Guidance for making incremental steps toward a more pluralistic media system can be found by looking to countries in northern Europe, which have historically been characterized by a proliferation of partisan news sources. Despite the appearance of ethnic homogeneity, northern Euro-pean nations are full of various political, religious, and linguistic cleavages. A plethora of newspapers have traditionally catered to disparate groups: Catholics and Protestants, union workers and factory owners, competing political parties, and citizens whose mother tongue is, say, Flemish rather than French. Despite this diversity, these nations' media systems do not demonstrate the levels of polarization found in other European countries such as France and Italy. Northern European nations support this level of relatively unpolarized diversity by maintaining high levels of both journal-istic professionalism and public support.[33]

Although the path to establishing a less-polarized media system is hardly clear, borrowing features from these nations is at least worthy of experimentation. Multiple public radio and television outlets could be developed to represent a range of perspectives not generally found in mainstream media, including conservative ones. Or funds could be used to directly subsidize economically weak newspapers that give voice to minor political parties or underrepresented groups. And public-broadcasting time could be divided among differing sociopolitical classes. Funding could also be dependent on such outlets' inclusion of dissenting voices in a step back toward the "fairness doctrine" that used to ensure that multiple perspectives were represented by media outlets. High professional standards could be maintained by press councils, who would have the power to sanction these public media outlets for spreading outright falsehoods or violating other publicly agreed-upon journalistic expectations. Combining high standards with greater diversity is vital. The spread of misinformation is not simply caused by inadequate fact-checking. When a media system lacks diversity because of market centralization or widespread editorial preferences for "moderate" perspectives, more questionable outlets can too easily portray themselves as battling a corrupt journalistic elite.

The watchword for such a system would be *thoughtful partisanship*.[34] Journalists would still be expected to treat evidence fairly and make arguments in good faith but without the impossible pretension of "objectivity" or value neutrality. They would be upfront about their commitments and interests when criticizing policies, proposing alternatives, finding contradictions or gaps in knowledge, and discerning areas for common ground or opportunities for incremental experimentation. No news story affects everyone equally. Therefore, thoughtful partisanship would require greater honesty on the part of media producers regarding who exactly does and does not benefit from their reporting and analysis. The idea that there is one unambiguous value, desire, interest, opinion, or experience that defines all of a nation's citizens would be recognized for what it is: nonsense. Journalists would see themselves as tasked with provoking people to think more critically and incisively about public issues rather than "informing" them, which will require highlighting areas of disagreement rather than downplaying them or depicting contention as a barrier to action.[35] Moreover, news hosts and columnists should be expected to exemplify the kind of democratic political talk described in chapter 5: to emphasize the legitimacy of a diversity of opinions, attempt to show how an issue is seen by different stakeholders with differing backgrounds, highlight uncertainty in scientific knowledge, and explore the varied moral values driving disagreements.

A further constraint on the pluralism of the media system is posed by the lack of diversity within politics itself. The media scholar Robert McChesney argues that excessive agreement among political elites stifles good journalism because critical or dissenting journalists can be uniformly refused access. He cites how journalists in the 1960s were largely complicit in the drive toward the Vietnam War.[36] Because most officials agreed with the need for intervention, journalists had to parrot the state's arguments in order for decision makers to be willing to talk to them. Hence, the success of alterations to the media system is dependent on diversifying governance more generally.

The relative incivility of online discussion is another long-suspected detriment to thoughtful democracy. Most readers have no doubt experienced forum trolls, surprisingly vicious political discussions with great aunts on Facebook, the raging dumpster fire that is the political side of Twitter, and the noxious comments-section discourse of online news articles or YouTube videos. An argument can be made that some degree of incivility has a place in politics and that occasionally heated rhetoric about contentious issues is important for challenging stale assumptions. However, it depends on whether arguments are made in good faith. Uncivil speech is largely counterproductive if it unduly targets individuals who hold certain beliefs rather than the belief itself or the policies and systems that enact those beliefs. Recall that radical abolitionists focused their ire more on the inhumanity of the slavery system than on slaveholders themselves.

In any case, research suggests that echo-chamber-like polarization can be tempered or avoided by instituting deliberative rules through a facilitator who encourages participants to listen to each other, weigh alternatives more openly, and justify their opinions with clear reasons. Furthermore, the comment sections in some venues, namely newspapers, tend to be more respectful than others, such as political blogs. This greater civility is due in part to the differing standards of discourse: newspaper writers typically shy away from demeaning and overly inflammatory language, which reinforces the importance of journalistic standards in that media rhetoric sets the tone for citizens more broadly.[37]

The movement to "no-platform" contentious speakers on college campuses—that is, to deny such speakers a platform—via protests, heckling, and acts of civil disobedience is emblematic of the failure to maintain journalistic standards. One should not equate no-platforming with censorship. Pundits who have been no-platformed, such as Ann Coulter, Ben Shapiro, and Milo Yiannopoulos, make fairly questionable contributions to the public debate. The rhetoric they use—calling liberals "traitors," "idiots," or "snowflakes" who need their arguments "destroyed"—sets a poor standard for audience members.[38] Again, although democracy is enhanced by citizens being vocal about their convictions, these pundits move too far from "mere civility" by intentionally inflaming and insulting individuals. Activism aimed at shutting down controversial talks seems justified when speakers' polemics are mainly opportunistic strategies to sell more books and gain Twitter followers rather than good-faith attempts to improve popular thinking about political conflicts. The problem is not so much with these speakers' political commitments but with their intent to polarize the public for personal gain.

The predominance of denigrating and dismissive rhetoric online is further reflected and reinforced in other media forms. As noted earlier, web podcasts such as *Louder with Crowder* and television shows such as *Last Week Tonight* present starkly partisan views of current issues. The issue is not the partisanship of those programs but rather the fact that opponents are depicted as fools to be mocked or scorned and thus as undeserving of understanding. In this way, internet practices have become what the media scholar Neil Postman saw television becoming in the 1980s: "the background radiation of the social and intellectual universe."[39] As people's expectations are ever more conditioned by their online experiences, previous media forms have been reshaped to reflect the characteristics of internet media. People who came of age with an internet dominated by cynical speech, sarcasm, and trolling no longer bat an eye when such rhetoric comes to define media more generally.

The overarching problem is that few of the thousands of people who played a role in developing and advancing internet platforms gave much, if any, consideration to how its design might exacerbate people's worst tendencies. Given that the content most likely to go viral is either inane or inflammatory rather than thought provoking, there are clear incompatibilities between the underlying design of social media networks and democratic politics.[40] It is difficult to imagine exactly what a better net might look like, but a reasonable first step would be to hold information distributors to the same standards we would want information producers to abide by.

News aggregators and social media sites should be forced to protect against outright fraudulent claims and libelous speech and perhaps be incentivized or encouraged to prioritize material from multipartisan public media.

Yet there is reason to be skeptical that a reformed internet, alongside changes to political institutions, would be enough of a nudge toward thoughtful democracy. It is unfair to blame actors only on the supply side of the equation for the state of American democracy. Citizens themselves vote for populist leaders and choose to click on social media disinformation. Without attention to the underlying drivers of people's proclivities toward fanatical truthism, a more vibrant and pluralistic democracy will remain a utopian daydream.

TOWARD A MORE PLURALISTIC PUBLIC SPHERE

There are few words in the English language that seem to be spoken with as much disgust or hopelessness as *politics*. One can almost see the awful taste that some people get in their mouths when they lament how some decision or another was "political." Surveys and focus-group data reflect this common perception, finding that the only thing many American citizens want from the political process is "to be left alone."[41] Of course, most people also complain about undemocratic governance, especially when elites seem to be using their privileges to enrich themselves. The form of government that would resolve this apparent contradiction is "stealth democracy," a process by which people's values and interests would somehow be accurately represented without their actually having to do anything. Citizens seem to yearn for a means to sidestep the messiness of political conflict, a way for the "right" policy to be almost automatically implemented.

It is certainly true that politics can be exhausting. Oscar Wilde's quip that "the trouble with socialism is that it takes too many evenings" applies equally well to democracy. But one should not take widespread longing for democracy by stealth at face value. People's desires are not simple expressions of their authentic selves but complex mixtures of ideas inherited from family, broader culture, and their experiences with the world. It is hardly surprising that Americans have little patience or desire for political discussion and democratic participation when they have grown up having little substantive experience with it. One would not interview born and bred New Yorkers about the prospect of becoming farmers and conclude from

their negative assessments that there is little hope for getting people to participate in agriculture. What such perspectives do show, however, is the
magnitude of the cultural barriers to realizing a more vibrantly democratic
society.

No doubt there is reason to be pessimistic about people's receptiveness to
democratic participation. The wondrous conveniences of new technological innovations can make the relative slowness of politics and governmental
bureaucracy feel intolerable. In light of that contrast, it is unsurprising that
many Americans have come to expect that humanity's problems will be
solved apolitically through new technological marvels and scientific truths
rather than through intelligent policy.[42] But the desire for stealth democracy too easily transforms into an attraction to authoritarianism. Growing dissatisfaction with representative democracy, especially among young
people, has led many to yearn for "strongman" forms of government.[43] Of
course, young Americans' skepticism of democracy may have much to do
with a lack of personal experience with what it is actually like to live under
an authoritarian government. One hopes that attitudes about democracy
can change without people having to experience authoritarianism firsthand.

Perhaps citizens could be reenchanted with democratic politics through
experience with proportional representation or forms of public participation—
after a period of cultural lag. But I am tempted to write off many contemporary adults as lost causes, given that it takes most people considerable effort to
unburden themselves of specious truths embraced in their formative years. For
pluralism to blossom, the next generation may need to be brought up within
a democratic civic religion.

I use the word *religion* intentionally. The psychologist Jonathon Haidt
argues that strongly binding beliefs that confer a sense of belonging (i.e., religion) are powerful psychic resources that enable the religious to make more
easily those collective commitments that can entail considerable sacrifice.[44]
Consider how followers of orthodox sects of Judaism, Islam, and Chris-
tianity follow through on commitments to tithe, dress in particular ways,
and follow restrictive diets. Furthermore, studies of religious communes
find that they are often only strengthened by the presence of demanding
sacrifices—within reason. Therefore, the demands that a strong democracy
would place upon citizens are not intrinsically onerous but rather become
so in the absence of a foundational democratic civic religion. Getting people to embrace better political tenets—acknowledge uncertainty, respect

experience, and recognize an opponent's values—will require the development of places both to celebrate our collective commitment to them and to
put them into practice.

Much of American life, however, works against the development of a
democratic personality. The political scientist Eric Oliver found that the
makeup of contemporary suburbia actively discourages political involvement.[45] Part of the problem is homogenization. When the rich and poor
are segregated, the potential for political conflict is depressed. Residents
with diverse interests are no longer forced to debate each other and hammer
out solutions that "work" well enough for most of them. Instead, the rich
move to neighborhoods that give them what they want, while the poor try
to make do with underfunded city services. Moreover, the design of most
suburbs is biased toward an isolated and individualistic mode of existence.
The absence of collective gathering spaces such as front porches and neighborhood pubs and cafes— and the isolating effects of an automobile-based
society prevent spontaneous interactions between citizens. Such design features explain why sprawling cities in Arizona and Florida have much lower
rates of civic engagement. The typical results of suburban living, as M. P.
Baumgartner found in her sociological studies, are a visceral fear of conflict
and weak, transient relationships.[46] Suburban residents would sooner move
than work out disagreements and will more readily endure chronic psychological distress than confront others for misdeeds. They would rather
uproot themselves or suffer in silence than risk the stresses inherent in
working through disputes.

The retrenchment of a culture of conflict avoidance, however, means
that reforming urban spaces may be insufficient to evoke a more substantive democratic spirit. Housing cooperatives, for instance, are supposed
to function more democratically than condominium boards and homeowners' associations. Whereas the latter try to prevent conflicts from ever
arising through highly restrictive and punitive contracts and covenants,
cooperative arrangements are built upon written requirements for democratic governance and group deliberation. Moreover, members of a housing cooperative buy a share in a collectively owned building rather than
buying a private unit, which emphasizes the cooperative's communal character. Yet studies find that members of cooperatives often act little differently than condominium owners, avoiding the possibility of conflict by
minimizing social ties with neighbors, resolving disputes by appealing to

the cooperative's board to act as a police officer, and rarely participating in the building's governance.[47] Therefore, interventions into supporting the vibrancy of democratic pluralism must go deeper than simply increasing the opportunities for adult citizens to participate.

The roots of many people's extreme trepidation regarding conflict and disagreement begin much earlier in life. Apart from trivial experiences such as taking a classroom vote over what movie to watch or the popularity contest of choosing a class president, children have almost no opportunity to experience or learn how to practice democracy. The classroom setting even directly cultivates and rewards a disposition antithetical to democratic politics. Kids are generally rewarded for their docility and for being efficient at providing the "right" answer to an authority figure.[48] No doubt there are well-meaning teachers who do their best to make schooling more than that by creating small openings for open-ended critical thinking, but even they are often hamstrung by mandatory state exams that strangle the creativity out of lesson plans and student work.[49] In any case, one should not be surprised that people are attracted to simplistic truth narratives and anxiously avoid the murkiness of political controversy when they have spent their early years being taught that all that matters is knowing the "right" answer and obediently following instructions.[50]

Students could spend considerably more classroom time deliberating and exploring uncertainty and the multifaceted roots of disagreements. School districts in the United States, for example, could do far better than the token US government class required of most high schoolers. And social studies classes could more often demand tasks beyond the rote memorization of historical events, peoples, and dates. The challenge lies in rethinking the current obsession with quantitative "assessment."[51] The attempt to turn any and every aspect of student learning into something measurable means that instructors end up teaching material that is not very useful—and, even worse, incredibly boring—but that can be easily assessed quantitatively. It is less obvious how to assign a numerical grade to a student's effort to take on the perspective or experiences of someone very different to him or her, to reframe a policy change to appeal to a hypothetical political opponent, or to point out the uncertainties regarding the causes of and solutions to a contentious issue. However, such activities are more generative of democratic thinking than scantron-form regurgitation or other easily assessable assignments. How can we expect citizens to engage effectively in democratic politics when schooling does not help them acknowledge the formidable complexity of the world or the legitimacy of people's diverse perspectives regarding reality?

Engineering education is a prime example of this problem. Recall the study uncovering a correlation between studying engineering and belonging to a violent terrorist organization mentioned earlier. Because pedagogy for people who build things too often depicts "the right answer" in stark black-and-white terms, it seems to attract people who view truth fanatically—and perhaps even reinforces that view.[52] No doubt professional engineers need to be confident of their calculations when building bridges or designing the navigational system on a Boeing jet, but traditional engineering education almost venerates mathematical calculation—subtly teaching the lesson that little else matters. Engineers take relatively few courses on communication, critical thinking and reasoning, or the social and economic contexts of technology, despite evidence that those skills are used considerably more frequently on the job than information on topics such as thermodynamics.[53] But quantitative calculations are easier to grade and are believed to impart something called "rigor."

The trouble is that most of the twenty-first-century problems faced by humanity will demand far more from technical professionals than abstract calculation and modeling. Some of the oft-cited "grand challenges for engineering," such as better managing the nitrogen cycle or improving access to clean water, require an understanding of culture, economics, and politics almost completely absent from science and engineering degree programs. These problems cannot be solved without navigating difficult disagreements regarding which approaches are appropriate. For instance, should water access be improved through large reservoir dams, which often inundate people's homes or come with a host of environmental problems? Or through filtering technology, which can be expensive or can fail because replacement parts or suitably trained repairmen are rare in less developed regions? Who pays? Who decides?

Engineers are rarely taught to recognize that developing and deploying a technology is a political act.[54] Whether we choose to resolve the immense environmental and human costs of the automobile via autonomous vehicles rather than mass transit, we advantage some groups and not others. In the first case, people who desire urban spaces conducive to walking—and all the benefits that come with them—lose out, while exurban residents win.[55] Choosing to solve malnutrition-driven blindness in African children through GE rice neglects the broader social, political, and technical reasons why some Africans are too poor to eat anything other than rice in the first place—thus risking the further entrenchment of an unjust situation.

The limitations of engineering education are largely representative of schooling as a whole. So long as the pedagogical process privileges the memorization of facts, rote calculation, problem solving without attention to context, and other narrow "one right answer" stand-ins for critical thought, adults are unlikely to appreciate the complexities of reality, the importance of disagreement, and the value of trying to see things from other people's perspectives. Educational policy makers, instructors, and school superintendents will need to be pushed toward very different pedagogical paradigms, ones that value educational experiences and open-ended hands-on assignments over numerical assessment. Parents, students, and workplaces should demand it.

A broader barrier to developing a more democratic citizenry is that most of life is not democratically organized. Much of people's daily existence is little different from schooling: authority figures have nearly sole discretion in adjudicating disputes. Consider how many American children's previously unstructured play time, such as sandlot baseball and pick-up basketball, has been replaced by Little League, swim meets, and piano lessons. Situations where kids would be developing their own goals, settling disagreements, and varying the rules based on circumstances—such as the inclusion of littler siblings—have been replaced with ever more time spent pleasing grown-up authority figures.[56] Why would we expect adults to be capable of collectively working through disagreements when they never had to do so as children? The cost of quasi-professionalizing youth sports is the inadvertent lesson that conflicts are solved by appealing to all-powerful truth arbiters (i.e., referees and umpires) rather than by talking to each other. Filling children's time with *structured* activities gives them no time to practice *structuring* their own lives, something they need experience with so that they can negotiate political disputes later in life.

These democratic deficits continue as people enter the work world. It appears strange upon reflection that many Americans will openly decry bureaucratic forms or taxes as intolerable and unjust burdens but nevertheless tolerate workplaces that are run like miniature communist dictatorships.

Blue-collar Americans still toil in sweatshoplike conditions in garment plants, poultry factories, and Amazon warehouses—deprived of bathroom breaks and pushed to work at a pace that leaves them exhausted and at risk of chronic injury. Bosses are permitted to read employees' emails, monitor their diet in setting health-care premiums, subject them to drug testing without cause, and impose sanctions almost without limit—at least for classes of workers who cannot afford to hire a labor lawyer.[57] Management at many firms is a form of *private* government and with the demise of the American union an increasingly authoritarian one at that. Workers are left with few options. Those with the means and sufficiently marketable skills to move to better jobs do so; the rest suffer in silence. Whatever the merits of such a system for maximizing returns to distant shareholders, the system nevertheless prevents workers from developing into fully fledged citizens.

If more Americans are to be capable of pluralistic democracy, schools, workplaces, and other institutions will need to be organized around democratic principles. These alternative institutions do exist, albeit in small numbers. There are schools, such as ones that follow the Sudbury model, where students join faculty and staff in setting rules and designing the curricula—and whose students end up being no less successful in life than youth attending traditional places of learning.[58] Democratic, employee-owned firms—which include New Belgium Brewing and the makers of Gore-Tex—are no less competitive than authoritarian ones. Some reviewers have argued that they are even more efficient. Nondemocratic companies have to pay midlevel managers to surveil, sanction, and cajole workers into working hard for measly wages. In democratic firms, workers own a share of the enterprise, which provides an automatic incentive to work for the good of the company.[59] By making workers partial owners, firms can save considerably on payroll costs. Moreover, employees usually end up being more satisfied with their jobs and more interested in streamlining work processes.

The barrier to more democratic schools and workplaces, therefore, is not that they cannot compete with traditional ones but rather that they deviate so strongly from the status quo. High schools and business courses do not provide workers with the skills to develop and run cooperative firms. Only the most progressive owners choose to open the door to employee ownership rather than cashing out via an IPO or selling to a large conglomerate. Access to financing becomes an issue simply because bankers look askance at alternative ownership models regardless of the company's underlying merits. Finally, many highly skilled workers have little incentive to join with their blue-collar brethren in cooperative ownership. Given that they can move to a firm that will remunerate them well—perhaps providing, in addition to better pay, plenty of bean-bag chairs, free snacks, and comfortable break-out rooms in an open-concept office—they have little incentive to rock the boat and every reason to daydream about climbing the corporate ladder. Insofar as white-collar workers do so, they are little different from the well-positioned Soviet citizens who chose to hope for a better position within the Communist Party rather than to advocate for a freer society.

Broader opportunities for increasing the amount of democracy in people's lives lie in rediscovering how to provision goods and services more collectively. The United States was once dotted with all sorts of cooperative organizations that provided health insurance, sporting activities, belonging, and so on.[60] But the decades of increased affluence after World War II enabled many citizens to amass private collections of consumer goods and services. People's garages, for instance, now contain an array of tools that mostly collect dust between relatively rare home projects. Even opportunities to practice civil disagreement in the domestic sphere is hindered by the proliferation of private consumer goods. Families no longer have to argue about what to watch because each member now has his or her own pocketsize personal entertainment device. Like suburbanization, consumer society promises to render people into isolated, self-reliant islands, thus diminishing reasons and opportunities for sharing and cooperation.

Supporting alternatives to consumerism, therefore, would offer greener pastures for growing democratic community. Some citizens already participate in clubs dedicated to helping one another fix broken appliances, plan home-improvement projects, or run tool libraries.[61] But those alternatives are rarely seriously considered by most citizens—and perhaps understandably so. When most people work far too many hours and spend too much time commuting, the easy distractions provided by binge-watching streaming television and scrolling through social media at the end of the day become incredibly alluring.[62]

American society almost appears as if it was explicitly designed to prevent or discourage a citizen-led democracy. The media scholars John Nichols and Robert McChesney outline an array of sociocultural changes that have led to the domination of American politics by economic elites: the concentration of media power, the de facto "veto power" of the investor class, and so on.[63] They root these changes, in part, to a conscious effort to combat what some saw in the 1970s as "an excess of democracy." Contributors to the Trilateral Commission report *The Crisis of Democracy* in 1975 contended that public agitation for governmental solutions to problems relating to pollution, civil rights, and other public issues threatened to overload the political system with "unrealistic" demands. The solution, in the authors' view, was to cultivate a culture of political apathy and noninvolvement, which would protect the autonomy of the traditional political authorities: bureaucrats, representatives, and business elites.[64] Whether via conscious effort or mere sleepwalking, we seem to have arrived at the world that the Trilateral Commission hoped for.

Inequality in time and money—along with the sense of powerlessness that comes with that inequality—is perhaps the largest contributor to citizen apathy. As the political scientists Achen and Bartels argue, "The most powerful players in the policy game are the educated, the wealthy, and the well-connected."[65] The sheer cost of running for office or managing a social movement keeps politics out of reach for most citizens. The pluralist ideal ends up underrealized because of the "upper-class accent" of political participation.[66] The democratic deficits of inequality are rarely considered deeply. They are obscured in most people's minds by the myth that equates democracy with voting. Yet the connection between economic and political power has not been lost on political scientists. Robert Dahl once asked, "If income, wealth, and economic position are . . . political resources, and if they are distributed unequally, then how can citizens be political equals? And if citizens cannot be political equals, how is democracy to exist?"[67]

Most societies, however, are caught in a catch-22. Ever-increasing economic inequality undermines democracy, but without a strong democracy people are less able to push for policies to mitigate economic inequality. No doubt, campaign-finance reform in nations such as the United States could do much to reduce disparities, such as reversing the *Citizens United* Supreme Court decision that removed the cap on corporate spending on political advertising and other activities.[68] But that does not seem to go far enough.

One underexplored change would be to make adjustments to how political groups receive tax exemptions. Rather than give every group the same exemption, political organizations could either pay taxes or not at all based on a sliding scale of "eliteness." A relatively simple proxy for eliteness would be to divide the total donations the group receives in a year by the number of donators. A more "elite-driven" political action committee or lobby group might average around $10,000 per donator, whereas the mean for a grassroots movement would be more on the order of $30. A more democratically pluralistic political system would tax donations to—or perhaps spending by—elite political organizations or campaigns, say at 10 to 20 percent, and redistribute the funds equally to citizens. People could make yearly donations at tax time to their preferred interest groups—whether Planned Parenthood or the Republican Liberty Caucus—with their share of the fund.

The effect of such a change could be substantial. A very small fraction of the population donates more than a few hundred dollars to any given organization or campaign, and large donors constitute the largest source of funding—some 84 percent of the dollars behind the congressional election of 2010.[69] Not only would differentially taxing political donations provide average citizens with more money to donate to their preferred causes, but it would also incentivize political groups to engage with and be more responsive to the desires of small-dollar donors. If 80 percent of the roughly $6.5 billion spent on the election in 2016 had been taxed at 15 percent under this scheme, approximately $780 million would have been available to Americans to donate the following year.

Alternatively, taxing donations to or spending by elite-driven political organizations could be used to fund publicly financed campaigns, in which acceptance of private donations is strictly limited. In either case, the point is to level the playing field between haves and have-nots regarding the funding of candidates and political interest groups.

At the same time that economic inequities limit the ability of the less empowered to participate in democracy, they may also hinder the capacity of the more empowered to think and act democratically. Studies suggest that people who occupy positions of power disproportionately struggle to see issues from other people's viewpoints and are more likely to act impulsively and unsympathetically as a result.[70] This finding is unsurprising to students of history, who know how the hubris of absolutist leaders from Napoleon to Hitler and of corporate heads from Enron to Lehman Brothers led to their respective downfalls. Or one might think of Justice Brett Kavanaugh's angry, almost contemptuous statements at his confirmation hearing, in which he seemed oblivious to the need to maintain the degree of civility expected from a prospective member of the Supreme Court. Likewise, many Americans' intuition that their bosses are "sociopaths" may not be far off the mark—one study claimed to find that nearly one-fifth of high-level corporate professionals exhibit psychopathic traits.[71] No doubt it is difficult to know exactly to what degree either positions of power render people less empathic or the less empathic are more likely to seize positions of power. Either case provides justification for limiting the number of positions within society that lack democratic accountability.

WHITENESS AND OTHER RACIAL "TRUTHS"

The elephant in the room when discussing political polarization in the United States is race. Populism is driven not only by perceptions of corruption but also by the sense that "the people" are being deprived in order to favor newcomers (immigrants) and other groups that are seen to be "undeserving." Right-wing populists fear that rapid ethnic and cultural changes will lead to the "destruction" of a valued cultural identity.[72] For some observers, Donald Trump's success in 2016 was a "whitelash" among people who felt that they were losing their dominant racial status in America. Many Trump voters described feeling as if they were becoming "strangers in their own countries," arguing that other groups—women, immigrants, and minorities—were unfairly getting ahead of them.[73] Regardless of whether one believes the concerns of Trump voters are valid or not, it is uncontroversial to observe that recent political conflicts have been shaped by ideas about race and ethnicity.

There has always been a racial dimension to American politics. Recall how the intense polarization after the Civil War was mitigated in part by a racial compromise: Republicans became less radical and abandoned federal interventions that would have helped ensure the full citizenship of freed slaves. In essence, they looked the other way as Southern Democrats instituted Jim Crow in the ensuing decades. Leaving emancipation incomplete was a means to reduce contention and return Congress to a state of relative "civility." To some degree, current political polarization is similarly based on race. To hear some conservatives tell it, Democrats and progressives are waging a war against white people.[74] The question for contemporary Americans is how to cool the current fanatical moment without making the same kind of compromise as post–Civil War Republicans.

As I argued in previous chapters, polarization is the product of political coalitions ceasing to evolve. Something jams the gears of democratic pluralism, lessening its dynamism. The way out of racially driven polarization is therefore to upset entrenched ideas about race: to disrupt whiteness. By "whiteness," I do not mean merely having white skin. Whiteness is a social category that includes only some fair-pigmented people. White-skinned persons of mixed heritage or from the Middle East or South America would still be considered "nonwhite" by many Americans. Whiteness in the United States follows an unwritten "one-drop rule"—that is, any amount of non-European ancestry can lead people to see a person as nonwhite. Moreover, in the United States, people from Ireland, Italy, and eastern Europe were historically considered to be less than fully white and had to earn their racial privileges over time by intermixing with and eventually being accepted by Americans of higher-status European heritages. Along the way, people from these groups sometimes acted even more vehemently racist against Blacks and other minority groups than traditional whites did in order to "prove" their whiteness.[75]

It is better to think of whiteness as a coalition wherein a narrow set of ethnic and physical traits is seen as representative of the national body (i.e., culturally "normal"), whereas others retain the perception of foreignness no matter how long their families have lived in the United States. To call whiteness a "coalition," however, is not to say that it was self-consciously developed. Ethnic and racial discrimination is so tenacious in part because it is constantly and invisibly reinforced by structural disadvantages. Because barriers posed by poverty and other limitations make it harder for members of some nonwhite groups to succeed, negative cultural stereotypes about lack of initiative or any number of failings are too easily reinforced. Growing up poor has a range of deleterious effects on children's ability to succeed in the classroom and beyond, affecting their language development and mental health. Moreover, poor children often lack access to career networks, credit, and familial wealth that give higher-class kids a head start.[76] The fact that people from impoverished regions do not achieve the same level of success and come to rely more on illicit activities or government programs is taken by some relatively privileged citizens to be evidence that the former are "undeserving," which ends up justifying cuts to programs that could help remedy the underlying causes of poverty.

Some people hold out hope that demographic changes will automatically reduce the extent to which the cultural construction of whiteness dominates American politics. While increases in immigration from Hispanic countries and elsewhere may lead to the United States becoming a minority-majority nation, such an outcome will occur if some currently nonwhite groups do not become "white" in the interim. The same kind of politicoracial coalition building that made Irish and Italian immigrants white could happen again. Indeed, a growing portion of people with Latino ancestry consider themselves white and are treated as such by other citizens.[77] I have heard plenty of people named Chavez or Quintana make disparaging comments about "Mexicans" and then go on to insist that their own roots are Spanish rather than Mestizo. Also consider how the shooter of an unarmed Black teenager named Trayvon Martin in 2012, George Zimmerman, became a symbol of white supremacy among some left-leaning Americans despite having an Afro-Peruvian mother.

Ian Haney López has argued that racial polarization can be reduced by building multiracial, multiethnic coalitions around issues such as economic justice. According to Haney López, citizens need to directly target "dog whistle" language, which leverages unconscious racial stereotypes to maintain classist policies. Such language frames federal programs such as food stamps as "handouts" given disproportionately to "welfare queens," while attaching little opprobrium to subsidies to wealthy and often absentee farm owners. Section 8 housing is seen as giving money to the undeserving, even though far more dollars are spent on upper-class Americans through the tax deduction on mortgage interest.[78] More could be done to highlight how lower- and middle-class whites have much more in common with other ethnic groups at a similar socioeconomic standing than with the wealthy.

Yet I worry that Haney López's suggestion relies too much on an implicit leftist framing. The journalist Chris Ladd points out that many people vote Republican in full recognition that they could lose access to welfare programs because they believe—rightly or wrongly—that conservative candidates will help create jobs that deliver them out of poverty.[79] Rather than hope that these citizens' distaste for welfare programs will disappear, more fruitful proposals would seek to achieve racially diverse coalitions through policies that also resonate with conservative values. Recall the earlier discussion of employee-owned firms and other kinds of "economic democracy,"

which promise to achieve leftist outcomes without heavy-handed governmental invention. More thought could be given to binding currently economically disenfranchised whites and nonwhites together around the idea
of a "good job" in a cooperative or self-owned firm rather than via a federal
paycheck.

Another strategy would be to emphasize ethnic diversity within the category of "white." Many Americans' ties to their ethnic roots have waned
throughout the twentieth and the twenty-first centuries. One study of
Brooklynites in the 1970s found that they still saw themselves far more
as members of specific ethnic groups than "as abstract whites," a category
they felt was foisted upon them by bureaucratic forms.[80] Yet today the German American clubs, Italian American clubs, and other ethnic-based fra-
ternal organizations that used to dominate community life look like the
average church: either already shuttered or full of retirees and teetering on
the edge of insolvency.

One very small step in the right direction is the plan to include more specific European ethnic choices on census forms,[81] such as German or Italian,
which dilutes the idea of a unified white identity. A further step would be
to take a lesson from Canadians regarding how to support multiculturalism.
For instance, while everyone is expected to—and generally does—learn
one of Canada's official languages, English or French, support for other languages is ample. A person can send her children to a bilingual *public* school
in Edmonton that features Arabic, Chinese, French, German, Hebrew, or
Spanish. The Catholic school system adds Ukrainian and Polish to these
options. The Canadian Broadcast Corporation even supports the broadcast
of *Hockey Night in Canada* in Punjabi. Such moves are distinct from American visions of multiculturalism. Canada eschews the "melting pot" metaphor, preferring to support a cultural mosaic of groups that maintain their
languages and ethnic practices. Although disagreements and conflicts still
develop between people of different backgrounds—and no doubt some
Canadian citizens still harbor negative views of immigrant groups—the
Canadian approach to multiculturalism weakens the idea of a unitary ethnic or racial national identity that fuels binary us–them distinctions.

Moreover, I suspect that if at least some citizens were to dig into their
family's past, they would come to see themselves as having more in common with more recent immigrant groups than not. My family's own

history leads me to feel more solidarity with nonnative English-speaking immigrants than with irate citizens who demand that immigrants "talk American." Relatives on my mother's side spoke German at home for generations after coming to the United States, ceasing only once government agents began intimidating them during World War I. Although this family history is in no way comparable in magnitude to what the descendants of slaves or Native Americans have gone through, knowing it still helps evoke a stronger feeling of empathic solidarity with them. I am sure that many other citizens share similar stories from when part of their family tree was not yet fully "white" or "American." Yet such narratives are mostly absent in conflicts over immigrant groups and arguments about assimilation. That is unfortunate, for they offer Caucasians something that leftist narratives about race rarely provide: the potential for a positive narrative about their own ethnic roots rather than one in which they are reduced to being empty vessels for white supremacy.

This strategy might prove useful in other nations. For instance, Germany's apparent homogeneity belies considerable diversity within the nation, even apart from its sizable Turkish minority. A unified German identity and a standardized language were nineteenth-century inventions that paved over significant linguistic, religious, and cultural differences between regions. The counternarrative to the xenophobia of right-wing populist movements such as the Alternative for Germany is not limited to the cosmopolitan globalism to which leftists traditionally ascribe but could also include a kind of open-minded pride in one's own particular heritage and family migration history.

Realizing more dynamic conversations about race will likely require disrupting "woke" leftist narratives as well. Acronyms such as POC (people of color) and, more recently, BIPOC (Black, Indigenous, and people of color) may only further gridlock America's racial politics. These multiracial populist neologisms help prop up the fanatical binary between white and nonwhite and reinforce the association of whiteness with skin pigmentation. By fortifying the idea of race as a biological endowment, it is more difficult to recognize that race is sociopolitically foisted upon a person. Race is a social creation, brought into being not by people's genes but by specific policies and cultural practices that lead to discrimination and unequal outcomes for people with particular ethnic backgrounds and appearances. People with

African ancestry become racially "Black" not exactly because of the darkness of their skin but because landlords more frequently reject their rental applications, because their schools are more often inadequately funded and staffed, and because prominent think tank researchers publish books claiming that the inheritance of African genetic material represses intellectual development. Citizens with parents from Southeast Asia become nonwhite insofar as they get asked, "Where are you really from?" or have stereotypes applied to them.

Terms like POC and BIPOC, moreover, lump together diverse groups, obscuring their very significant differences. An affluent Hindu American, the child of a Hmong refugee, a member of the Lakota Sioux, a person belonging to Miami's Cuban community, and the descendent of an American slave would all be POC, despite their varied interests. In fact, a few of them might even have voted for Donald Trump or hold prejudiced beliefs about different minority or immigrant groups.[82] Americans' quest to end racism will prove unsuccessful so long as both racist and antiracist narratives trade in supposedly indisputable racialized generalizations. Whether in the form of nasty stereotypes or well-meaning categorizations of oppression, they end up obscuring the complexities of racialized inequity.

As helpful as alternative narratives about economic justice and ethnic background could prove to be, I do not blame readers if they remain unconvinced. Even though Canada's model of multiculturalism seems inspirational compared to the focus on assimilation in the United States, the country still falls short when it comes to long-marginalized populations. Indeed, Canada's Indigenous groups have not been substantially better treated than Native Americans or African Americans in the United States. Nor would highlighting differences be guaranteed to destabilize the idea of whiteness. Race in America is a wicked problem. If I had a good answer about how to fix the racial dimensions of political polarization in the United States, I would have written that book instead of this one.

In any case, the point of this chapter has been to provoke serious thought about how things could be otherwise. My suggestions might sound infeasible or like pie-in-the-sky social engineering to some readers, but I would encourage them to reject that fatalistic interpretation. Who would have anticipated major historical upheavals—such as the Civil Rights Act of 1964 or the forty-hour workweek—a decade or two prior to their occurrence? The tricky thing about social change is that it is a largely self-reinforcing or self-fulfilling process. As long as people throw up their hands at the seemingly overwhelming barriers to change, social transformation cannot happen. In many ways, the hindrances are more psychocultural. The Constitution could be amended to enable any number of political goals and ideals if enough citizens were to get over their learned helplessness.

I would also reject the charge of social engineering. Societies are constantly in the process of being designed and redesigned, albeit frequently in aimless and poorly coordinated ways. In a little more than a century, citizens across the globe have been conditioned to become people who favor buying over belonging, who see themselves as consumers first and citizens second. And such changes were in part intentional. Early twentieth-century managers of financial firms and other companies began to worry about overproduction as industrial manufacturing met more and more of people's basic needs. They found a solution through dramatic paradigm shifts in the fields of marketing and advertisement, whose practitioners helped nudge people's priorities toward materialism and self-focused consumption. Add to these shifts the myriad changes to peoples' expectations, beliefs, and personalities in moving from societies rooted in sharing and mutual aid toward ones based on markets. Consider what one Lehman Brothers banker argued in 1927: "We must shift America from a needs- to a desires-culture. People must be trained to desire, to want new things, even before the old have been entirely consumed. . . . Man's desires must overshadow his needs."[83]

One could also reflect upon the dramatic changes in the design of American homes, neighborhoods, childrearing approaches, and other social technologies. These changes have been tantamount to political legislations. For instance, although it is not illegal for Americans to walk to their neighborhood pub, it is essentially outlawed because such places are prevented from existing in the first place. Almost no one has gotten to choose what forms of community life are available to them.[84] Although many of the design changes to American society that ended up stifling local social relationships were not intentionally made to constrain people's life options, that unintentionality does not make them any less acts of social engineering. They just happened to be the product of collective thoughtlessness instead of explicit planning.

Yet for some reason widespread technological and economic changes that constrain the life options of ordinary Americans are not called "social engineering."[85] That pejorative label is saved for efforts by governments, whether democratic or not. There is no reason why privately led efforts to spur sociocultural change are any less deserving of the label; it is just that governments have notoriously been very bad at fostering social evolution. The urban historian Howard Gillette has outlined a few examples, from the City Beautiful movement to the designers of mid-twentieth-century housing projects, both products of municipal governments' belief that simply altering the design of urban neighborhoods would produce a more civil populace or erase the pathologies of poverty.[86] Such governmental efforts have been ineffective, but mainly because they have been top-down affairs that do not incorporate trial-and-error learning. They have not made use of the better features of competitive markets, features that make markets good mechanisms for coordinating the existence of cups of coffee at Starbucks. Nor have governmental efforts been instances of pluralistic democracy, being more enacted upon citizens than alongside them. Successful policy-making processes, as argued earlier, include the people who might be affected, discern the smallest possible unit size for testing out novel changes, effectively monitor for unexpected outcomes or unanticipated sources of interference, and adapt interventions accordingly. If previous governments had not overestimated their knowledge and proceeded more democratically, we might have a very different view of "social engineering" efforts today.[87]

As such, conservative thinkers such as Friedrich Hayek have been largely correct when they have decried the conceit of leftist advocates of central planning; the latter have too often believed that they understand society well enough to alter it in predictable ways.[88] But Hayek and his contemporaries erred when they assumed that only the market can coordinate the knowledge that is diffused throughout a society into reliable collective action. They overlooked the potential intelligence of democracy. Realizing just such an intelligent democratic system, however, will require the same scale of social transformations as the ones that cemented the market as a core feature of contemporary nations.

Yet the barriers are considerable. Most significant are the hinderances to more open thinking and imagining, psychocultural limitations that make current institutions, technologies, systems, and organizations seem unalterable. Different political arrangements, media systems, educational institutions, and work environments are out there for citizens to realize if they start to believe that different societies are possible. Yet conversations among experts and average citizens alike are rife with thought-stopping clichés to the effect that people cannot "stop progress" or that interventions that interfere with market "decisions" are doomed to failure. Unless people dispense with such simplistic heuristics and realize that humanity's capacity to choose is far greater than what many of us have been taught to believe, I have little hope that republics can avoid endlessly vacillating between the quasi-authoritarian rule of epistocratic political elites and populist demagoguery.

THE DEMOCRATIC SOCIETY AND ITS ENEMIES

The mid-twentieth-century deployment of American and Japanese troops to the South Pacific Melanesian islands led to some surprising unintended consequences. The culture of these islands centered on "big men," whose status hinged largely on their generosity. Their ability to create and give away surplus food and goods earned them their higher status and authority. That ability, in turn, depended not only on the big men's skill in using their social talents to siphon off excess goods from others but also on the caprice of nature—such as lucking onto a good fishing spot or having particularly fertile pigs. Religious activity, unsurprisingly, focused on humanity's relationship with nature and on pleasing the capricious gods in control of it.[1]

The arrival of foreign troops brought surpluses of manufactured goods to the islands. The soldiers gave candy bars and tools to the locals, a bounty that upended preexisting sociological—and, in turn, cosmological—relationships. As the troops eventually left, the cargo supply dried up. The islanders responded to this change with new and unusual religious activities. "Cargo cults" built replica runways, planes, and even control towers, hoping to entice new inflows of goods. Lacking the underlying sociological and technological mechanisms to restore the previous bounty, locals fell back on already-existing religious patterns.[2]

Democratic politics in the United States—as well as in many other places across the globe—is increasingly like a cargo cult. Facets of democracy remain highly visible. Elections are held. Representatives express their opinions on policies in legislatives halls. Laws are voted on. But the relative weakness of the underlying sociological bases for democracy means that such practices are more and more like the replica planes and control towers built by the Melanesians. Democratic appearances draw attention away from the reality that politics is dominated by a small number of elite coalitions. Rule is traded between epistocrats who champion their expertise on the facts of sound political policy and populists who claim to channel the will of "the people." However convincing the facade of democratic institutions may be, the internal mechanisms needed to make them function properly are ever more difficult to find.

Cultish behavior fills the void left by the absence of well-functioning democratic machinery. For many citizens, truth is their cargo. They pray for it to be delivered by priestly classes of scientists, economists, down-to-earth politicians, or some other group thought to have direct access to certitude. Democratic activities become more religious rituals thought to magically summon veracity rather than mechanisms for resolving conflicts through intelligent policy.

That is not to say that people should not have a strong faith in their own beliefs and political goals and an equally hefty level of skepticism of everyone else's. Most of us would say that slavery abolitionists were right. It does not hinder the practice of democratic pluralism if a person believes she is more likely correct than her opponents. But dividing the world into rational truth seers and ignorant heretics makes the practice of democracy nearly impossible. Partisan groups are more like cults, waging war against apostates, rather than collections of people negotiating, deliberating, and strategizing to get part of their political aspirations turned into law. Public debate changes. As Nathan Pippenger writes, public discourse too often "seems driven by an urge to deny the legitimacy of one's ideological opponents, to portray their views as not just mistaken, but totally out of bounds."[3]

Leaving behind the political cult of truth will require restoring more functional machinery into American democratic institutions, providing a sociological basis for democracy as a civic religion. First and foremost, the foundational interactions between citizens must change. People need to disagree better, not because doing so would create a nicer or more polite society but rather because the gears of democracy grind to a halt in the absence of constructive disagreement. Not only do disagreements need to be seen as legitimate and productive rather than as barriers to progress, but citizens must also have opportunities to practice better navigating them.

The idea that politics delivers Truth writ large throws a wrench into the gears of compromise and concession. Truth fanaticism turns opponents into enemies to be destroyed, making it impossible to elicit thoughtful deliberations about people's experiences, interests, and values. Politics becomes less a dynamic and ongoing coalescing and fracturing of coalitions and more a trench warfare between what and who are perceived to be good and evil.

Truth narratives create a false sense of certainty, preventing political actors from pursuing incremental policies—which in turn makes it harder to learn the merits, downsides, and inequalities resulting from political changes. Realizing better democracies will require learning to embrace the sociological reality of endlessly evolving pluralistic conflict. For all the anxiety regarding widespread ignorance, misinformation, and cognitive biases, it is far more damaging to democracy for a person to refuse to accept that otherwise reasonable people can legitimately maintain beliefs that he or she deems outrageous.

But cultural change is both difficult and slow. And it would be unwise to neglect the deep-seated psychological underpinnings of fanatical truthism. Whatever one's opinion of postmodernism, its fundamental recognition that various truths—whether scientific facts or commonsensical ideas about family structure or gender identity—are increasingly disputed today is difficult to deny. Whereas some see the blurring of traditional categories or the declining hold of previously undeniable truths as liberating, others find it intensely anxiety inducing. I do not blame citizens for reaching for "the facts" or other supposed forms of unerring knowledge in order to shore up their worldviews. They just want to believe that their political commitments are founded on something firmer than sand.

This underlying need for order may be why so many of us have come to see disagreement as frightening, for conflict reminds us that reasonable people think differently than we do. It forces us to consider that much of what we hold dear may be merely personal preference or social convention, that we might not actually know the "Truth." But the solution is neither to dig in our heels nor to abandon the notion of veracity entirely. Democratic pluralism offers a way to navigate between fanatical truthism and nihilism. In contrast to the common tendency to equate democracy with consensus, democratic pluralism is built upon the necessity of dissent. Disagreement in turn relies upon citizens having strong views and convictions. People should not abandon wholesale their cherished ideas about reality and the good society. They only need to admit the possibility that they may be wrong about some of those ideas and recognize the right of opponents to try to realize some part of their own cherished ideals. There is even room for zealotry, so long as it contributes to rather than disavows democratic processes.

A number of broader changes to political institutions, media systems, and the organization of play, schooling, work, and the rest of life will be necessary if citizens are to be better prepared for the challenges of doing democracy. Most people have been implicitly taught from a young age that the most important thing is getting the "right" answer, that conflicts are settled by appealing to authority figures or the law, and that good politicians stay the course no matter what the cost. Learning to recognize the benefits of tolerating and even encouraging disagreement, to be adept at collectively working through disputes, and to see give-and-take as the stuff of politics would help scaffold a vibrantly democratic society. Political systems could be arranged to elicit and reward compromise and concession rather than intransigence and to help citizens work through complex public issues together and to develop more intelligent policies collectively. Economic and educational policies could put democratic firms and schools on a level playing field with today's more authoritarian institutions. Journalism and media could uphold higher professional standards by demanding that writers and pundits acknowledge uncertainty and highlight the legitimate reasons behind public disagreements. If enough citizens demand it, the myriad acts of social engineering over the past decades that have made many nations' cultures and peoples ill suited to democracy could be countered.

ADVANCEMENTS

This book has provided a very different perspective on what has been called the "post-truth era." First, I have rejected the idea that there is anything especially post-truth about the present. As I discussed in the introduction, it is not clear if there was ever a "truth era." If a historical period has existed when politicians put aside their divergent interests and did whatever experts told them they had to do—a time when a respect for veracity defined politics—I cannot find it. Equally dubious is the belief in a mythical age when Americans (or citizens of any other nation) purportedly shared a common identity or a near complete consensus about important issues. Every historical period is characterized by its own seemingly intractable political conflicts. Writers who try to locate some golden age of American bipartisan comradery in the mid-twentieth century have seemingly forgotten McCarthyism and the Red Scare, the populism of Richard Nixon, large-scale and polarizing protests against the Vietnam War, race riots and considerable violence against Black Americans, and widespread disputes about sexual mores and other cultural conventions. It takes considerable short-sightedness to see any epoch as a time of bucolic political togetherness.

Second, I have avoided daydreaming about a future when most everyone learns to respect facts and reasons objectively. The reality is that both ordinary citizens and experts fall prey to innumerable personal and cultural biases. This is something societies must cope with, not overcome. At the same time, I have eschewed naive relativism. Recognizing that facts and other kinds of truths cannot end political disagreement does not mean facts do not exist or that all points of view are equal. Rather, the lesson is that societies must learn to resolve conflicts in ways that do not rely on Truth. Expertise can take its rightful place—alerting citizens and decision makers of potential problems, evaluating the likely trade-offs for possible solutions, developing future scenarios, and challenging inherited or unquestioned ways of thinking—only when it is not expected to do our politics for us. Science ceases to enhance debate when it becomes a means to bludgeon political opponents and exclude their value concerns. Democratic decision making can probably approximate truth, but only if participants do not try too hard to aim for it—only as long as democratic processes and outcomes remain the goal of politics.

This model of democratic politics, as a result, takes doing to be as important as talking. Metaphors such as "the marketplace of ideas" and even well-meaning arguments for the value of deliberation can give the impression that a kind of political truth is liable to emerge out of rational communication between citizens. They fool us into believing that the objectively "right" policy will inevitably rise to the top, be recognized as such by nearly everyone, and immediately dominate the debate. This way of thinking about democracy falls prey to the same mistake as arguments for epistocratic or expert-led decision making: it believes that truth can be discovered by a process that is independent of actually doing politics. At the end of the day, policies are invariably the imperfect products of ongoing compromise and negotiation. They are never really "right" but rather a result that most partisan political groups can live with in the short term, and we are inevitably reliant on the test of time and on collective experience to see and understand the effects of any given policy.

I have also parted ways with the view of democracy as somehow undermined by too much disagreement, as if it were a fragile system that must be protected from contention and discord. My motivation for arguing against such a portrayal is a practical one. Simply put, the view that democracy is destabilized by conflict is incoherent. The entire point of a political system is to settle disputes. If democracy is so fragile that citizens' stark, fundamental, and proliferating disagreements threaten to undermine its foundations, then it is not worth having. Any political system that is destabilized by the very thing that it is supposed to resolve is doomed to fail.[4] In contrast, I have argued that democratic pluralism—with the right supporting institutions and practices—channels disagreement into more intelligent policy, greater trust of political institutions, and more productive politics in general.[5]

Purveyors of the fragile model of democracy have in any case been mistaken in their anxieties. They have not really been lamenting the potential demise of democracy when bemoaning the decay of truth or the death of expertise; rather, they have been complaining about the decline of epistocracy. Growing populist ferment signals the potential death of the Madisonian state, a state built upon a fundamental distrust of the average citizen and privileging the reasoning of an elite class of political guardians. According to the fragile-democracy thesis, we are at risk of abandoning the idea that certain individuals, by dint of their education, upbringing, or personality, have an inherently better understanding of citizens' "natural" rights or the public interest. I say, "Good riddance."

In contrast to fragile models of democracy, pluralism thrives on and is improved by dissent. Democracy generally outperforms epistocratic organizations because of the epistemological advantage of decentralized disagreement. Consider spectacular failures such as twentieth-century nuclear energy, where a small cadre of experts or bureaucrats decided almost unilaterally on its production. Pluralistic success stories such as aircraft carriers and Danish wind-turbine development are suggestive of what democracy could accomplish if more widely practiced across societies. Additionally, the more disagreement drives political decision making, the more legitimate public choices become. Democratic pluralism channels nearly every citizen's simmering frustrations into the policy process, preventing them from boiling over into full-blown populism. Even though citizens are invariably angry when they lose a policy battle, losing in a pluralist process in which they are valued participants breeds far less distrust than not being consulted or listened to at all.

Although I celebrate the potential decline of the Madisonian paradigm of governance and its equivalent elsewhere in the world, I do not mean to understate the magnitude of the challenges ahead. Its demise does not necessarily imply the rise of a democratically plural state. There is no reason why the United States and other contemporary "democracies" cannot decline into Hugo Chávez–style populist dictatorships. Thus, the future of democracy depends on citizens doing the work to avoid the polarization death spiral.

I have also embraced a far broader understanding of politics. When many observers talk about the problems facing democracies, they tend to discuss things such as low voter turnout rather than the way citizens fail to talk through disputes.[6] But life cannot be so easily partitioned into private and public or into political and nonpolitical. Politics exists everywhere that conflict can be found. How citizens resolve disagreements at the dinner table, at school, in the workplace, and elsewhere is just as relevant to the vibrancy of a democratic society as what they do in the voting booth. How can one expect people to be adept democrats in public when they are either petty tyrants or docile subjects in much of their private lives?

But achieving more democratic and conflict-adept societies will not be easy. This goal asks that citizens hope for nothing more than the opportunity to hash things out with one another in productive and minimally civil ways and that they tolerate both having differences in opinion and occasionally being on the losing side of the battle. Even if such a vision seems obvious or uncontroversial in the abstract, it can be profoundly discomforting to put into practice. It became eminently clear to me as I wrote this book that embracing disagreement as an irreducible feature of social and political life is very difficult for most people—at least for the moment. My attempts over the past few years to engage in tough conversations with friends, family, students, and online strangers about tenacious public problems has demonstrated to me as much. It would be so much easier if facts or common sense could just settle people's disagreements. But the sooner citizens dispense with such fanciful ideas and begin to learn how to talk democratically, the better off they will be.

Persistent clichés about democracy being threatened by a lack of reasoning skills or knowledge have the problem backward. Editorial writers and other social commentators cite the simple-mindedness of many citizens' political viewpoints as evidence that democracy is unworkable—or will be in the near future. I do not dispute that people's knowledge about public issues can be frighteningly simplistic or seemingly wrongheaded—visits to older relatives or surfing websites that host insular and extreme ideological groups make for a quick refresher of that state of affairs. But rather than entertain the belief that particular groups of people are immune to simplemindedness, I have contended that the antidote lies in more democracy—not less. Citizens are primed to uncritically regurgitate sound bites from cable news or internet pundits because their lives are weakly democratic, if at all. The places where they live or the spaces in which they socialize do not expose them to disagreement or the need to contend with diverse experiences. And most people's relative exclusion from policy making means that they are never forced to think carefully about the complexity of public problems and the limits of their own knowledge. Contrary to advocates of epistocracy and populism, I have argued that citizens' ability to reason well about public issues is a *consequence* of democracy rather than a *prerequisite* for it.

Finally, I have described what could be done about the problems that I have outlined. It is tragically rare to find sociological or political research that dedicates as much time to solutions as it does to characterizing problems. I would not dare compare such work to fiddling while Rome burns but rather prefer to compare it to charting wind patterns and documenting the firefighting response as a conflagration grows. In any case, the last thing people need is another book telling them that the world is going to hell while not providing even the first steps toward a more desirable future. It is no wonder why political fatalism is so rampant. If the social and political sciences are to be much help to people without PhDs, researchers in these fields need to rethink the purpose of their vocation. Far too much scholarship is aimed at impressing other academics with the clever coinage of new concepts or with how many hours the researcher endured doing research in a historical archive, interviewing subjects, or exhaustively surveying the literature. What if scholars saw people outside of academia as stakeholders in their work—or even as clients? I suspect that a number of lines of scholarship would have to be abandoned if the researchers pursuing them were required to convincingly demonstrate that their work provides a clear benefit to somebody.

Exploring the potential pathways toward a more desirable society is too often brushed off as utopian thinking.[7] But utopians generally envision some ideal end state, an Eden, that must be realized either in its entirety or not at all. Grand visions of Edenic alternatives to the present are usually not amenable to practical policy suggestions. My approach has instead been to describe starting points, small steps worthy of incremental experimentation. My recommendations have been all-encompassing, running the gamut from political institutions and electoral processes to the media system, schooling, and the organization of work. But such comprehensiveness has not been an attempt to paint an image of a perfectly ideal society but rather to recognize the multifaceted nature of social change. Efforts to deviate from the status quo, no matter how incremental or piecemeal, invariably butt up against barriers. Taken-for-granted ways of doing things persist because patterns of thought, laws and regulations, technologies, and organizations tend to be self-reinforcing. They are like strands in a giant web that collectively resist efforts to reposition any one of them. A little bit of careful thinking, however, can help anticipate the probable hurdles to small social changes and provide guidance for how to design multifaceted policy interventions. Political changes gain momentum only if they provide helpful feedback for future iterations, not when they fail to get traction at all. In any case, I hope that this book—like my first one, *Technically Together*—can serve as a model of how *reconstructivist* research can provide diagnoses of social problems as well as prescriptions for how such problems can be feasibly targeted.[8]

LIMITATIONS

As helpful as the recommendations given in this chapter and the previous ones may prove to be, most of them would take some time to be effective. Even if people were immediately to begin striving to have more productive disagreements with friends, family, acquaintances, and strangers by highlighting uncertainty, emphasizing experience, and being sensitive to the moral frameworks and values underlying disputes, wholesale cultural change takes a generation. My own experiences with practicing more democratic talk have confirmed my suspicions about how difficult it is to undo years or decades of enculturation. Getting people to admit the uncertainties and complexities of social and political reality is not easy.

At a minimum, the strategies that I have recommended can help prevent politics from becoming even more polarized in the near term, as overwhelming a task as that might seem to be. The trouble is that zealots often work to explicitly undermine democratic processes. Powerful fanatical coalitions never compromise. Consider the National Rifle Association's tight grip on American firearm policy. When one's opponents are intransigent and incapable of making concessions, giving political ground in pursuit of compromise is a pointless exercise in appeasement.

And fanaticism seems to be on the upswing. Some readers might find it naive to preach the value of compromise and concession at a time when white supremacists have openly marched in one North Carolina college town and far-right populist parties are gaining seats in European parliaments. Some of my friends and colleagues point to the growing fanaticism of right-wing opponents as evidence for the need of an "illiberal" response. They argue that now is the time for more violent and exclusionary tactics, citing the Nazi regime's millions of victims to prove the folly of conciliatory politics with fascists.

There are several problems with this line of reasoning. First, whether an opposing political group is as dangerous as the Nazis is clear only in hindsight. As regretful as acquiescence in the face of fascism in the 1930s was, accusations of authoritarianism and fascist tendencies are so prevalent today that it is difficult to get any sense of proportion. Second, I think this reasoning fails to take seriously the full ramifications of full-blown fanaticism. Recall the case of the American Civil War. Restoring some semblance of pluralistic politics came only by fundamentally compromising the war's great achievement of emancipating America's slaves. The lesson seems to be that if compromise is to be avoided, then citizens need to be prepared to pursue either a complete fracturing of the political body or the utter decimation of their political opponents. Following the fanatical project to completion might mean the breakdown of the United States into separate geopolitical entities—divided along ideological lines—or viciously repressive policies and violence against political enemies. Citizens who feel uneasy with such possibilities should reconsider their attraction to "illiberal" action.

I have done my best to write a book that is fair to multiple sides of contentious debates, but I am sure that I fell short of that goal. I tried to be pro-democracy writ large rather than advocate for an exclusively leftist vision of democratic society. However, my own political commitments have likely colored my presentation of the issues. Despite whatever asymmetry there is in my treatment of contemporary political conflicts, I do not believe that democratic pluralism excludes conservative values. In fact, intelligent policy depends on the existence of conservative political actors to temper the zeal of progressives, who might otherwise forge ahead too readily with radical political changes. Skeptics on the right warn us that we may be throwing the baby out with the bathwater when leftists propose dispensing with traditional ideas, policies, or behaviors.

However, right-leaning readers could also use the strategies and reforms that I have outlined to achieve some of what they value in life, whether it be broader social support for family life, stronger community ties, or less-onerous bureaucratic red tape for small businesses. Learning about left-ists' values and experiences would help conservatives recognize collabora-tive opportunities. I know that I share conservatives' healthy distrust of large federal educational reforms such as Common Core and No Child Left Behind, albeit for different reasons. The same policy changes that enable the democratic schools that I want for my offspring would also give con-servatives the local autonomy over curriculum that they so often demand.

Another promising area for cross-cutting political coalitions is commu-nity life. Far too many leftists treat *community* as if it were an inherently prob-lematic word. Traditional, place-based communities are purportedly destined to be no different than the town depicted in the movie *Pleasantville*: invariably racist, sexist, and stifling of individuality. It has become almost commonsen-sical to believe that progress depends on dispensing with locally rooted forms of togetherness and on embracing the individualism found in hip urban sub-cultures or via online social networks. In my previous book, I challenged that view. Place-based forms of community have features that have yet to be replicated in networked societies. Rather than accept the anticommunitarian common sense of previous generations, it is worth experimenting with new ways of living together that will satisfy both the values of neighborliness and mutual aid as well as a respect for diversity.

But most people's options for social life are highly constrained, which is reflective of deep democratic deficits. The failure of epistocratic decision making is clear in the pitiful state of neighborhoods in the United States—and increasingly elsewhere in the world. Most residential areas have neither cafes nor pubs to provide a center for communal interactions because rigid zoning codes implemented by bureaucratic experts have left little room for public debate over "good" urban design. Liberal, expert-driven societies seem to offer citizens any kind of good life they desire, but only so long as it is a form of networked individualism.[9] Only a deepened commitment to the practice of democracy will permit citizens genuine choices regarding the shape of collective ways of life.

While in exile in New Zealand during World War II, the Austrian philosopher Karl Popper penned a powerful defense of democratic civilization. He championed "open societies," or political cultures rooted in citizens collectively deliberating the merits and consequences of public decisions.[10] But he believed that open societies were threatened and undermined by "historicisms," seemingly scientific theories that claimed to uncover the ideal and unstoppable direction of human history. The damage wrought by fascism and communism, in Popper's view, stemmed from the sense of inevitability they imparted regarding the possible instantiations of society, which in turn justified violent policy meant to ensure that humanity achieved its proper destiny. Fascists prophesied a chosen people or race taking their rightful place (of power) in the world, while communism foretold revolution by the lower classes. Popper argued that such ideologies were in fact responses to the discomfort brought on by the movement toward an open society. No longer could hierarchies and taken-for-granted practices be sanctioned by cosmologically derived taboos and other unquestioned dogma. Living in an open society demanded that citizens think more as individuals, which often left them feeling adrift in an ever-changing world of uncertainties. Popper hoped that citizens would eventually be capable of resisting the historicist slide back to quasi-tribalistic, closed societies.

Although my own argument owes a great debt to Popper's incisive analysis, I think he cast his net far too narrowly and misjudged the necessary degree of citizens' *individualism* within an open society. He did not anticipate the development of ideologies and political rhetoric that could be as fundamentalist as fascism or communism while still echoing the language of individual freedom that motivated his work. Although not exactly matching the grandeur of the narratives of fascism and communism, new fanatical historicisms have nevertheless filled the void. Commentators such as Francis Fukuyama depicted the late twentieth-century form of globalized, liberal-capitalist democracy as if it were the only viable alternative for organizing societies.[11] This historicism has run aground in the beginning of the twenty-first century as liberalism, capitalism, and democracy have become increasingly recognized as often at odds with each other and more citizens now question whether globalization and liberal democracy have really ever been or can continue to be guarantors of prosperity. Other historicisms have developed out of cultish conceptions of science and common sense, which usually treat this or that value-laden conception of progress as if it were objectively ordained. The threat to open societies comes more broadly from people's desire to believe in unerring truths, verities that obviate the need to do democratic politics, whatever their form.

The current era threatens to be like the time in which Popper wrote. An increasing number of democracies are beset with ever higher levels of economic inequality and instability, especially in the wake of the COVID-19 pandemic. Increasingly popular demagogues call for a return to some ostensible golden era when there were fewer immigrants or other racial minorities. Members of reactionary right-wing groups and antifascists clash violently in street protests. It is anyone's guess whether political instability will rise to levels witnessed in the decades leading up to World War II or if a period of renewed economic growth might arrive to damper populist agitation and relegitimate rule by elite epistocrats. Impending dilemmas seem to provoke sentiments nearly as inflammatory and fanatical as the battle among fascist, communist, and anarchist grand narratives in the early twentieth century. Proposals to address problems such as widespread gun violence, climate change, economic and racial inequality, dramatic losses in biodiversity, and numerous other issues evoke extreme levels of ire and distrust. Our opponents, so we are told, will lead us into fascist authoritarianism, communist tyranny, or global destruction unless they can be made to recognize the real facts and forced to see the (our) Truth.

The problems humanity now faces are far too important to leave to a fickle and often perverse globalized market system and far too complex and consequential to entrust to small groups of experts or populist firebrands. An alternative path lies in enabling a dynamic, intelligent, and minimally civil form of democratic tribalism. It may be possible that nations will resolve their most enduring and contentious conflicts without fostering the more open and pluralistic societies that I have urged here, but I doubt it.

NOTES

CHAPTER 1

1. Reid Nakamura, "Rose McGowan Says Trump Voters Are Victims of 'Cult Brainwashing,'" *SF Gate*, February 22, 2018, https://www.sfgate.com/entertainment/the-wrap/article/Rose-McGowan-Says-Trump-Voters-Are-Victims-of-12657034.php.

2. Jennifer Kavanagh and Michael D. Rich, *Truth Decay* (Santa Monica, CA: RAND, 2018).

3. Tom Nichols, *The Death of Expertise* (New York: Oxford University Press, 2017).

4. Chris Mooney, *The Republican Brain* (Hoboken, NJ: Wiley, 2012); Alex Berezow and Hank Campbell, *Science Left Behind* (New York: PublicAffairs, 2012); Ben Shapiro, *Brainwashed* (Nashville, TN: WND Books, 2010); Vox Day, *Social Justice Warriors Always Lie* (Kouvola, Finland: Castalia House, 2015).

5. John Vidal, "Schwarzenegger: Climate Change Is Not Science Fiction," *The Guardian*, July 21, 2015, https://www.theguardian.com/environment/2015/jul/21/arnold-schwarzenegger-climate-change-is-not-science-fiction; *Northern Journal*, "The Debate on Climate Change Is Over, Time for Action," June 15, 2015, https://norj.ca/2015/06/the-debate-on-climate-change-is-over-time-for-action/; Marc Sandalow, "Bush Claims Mandate, Sets 2nd-Term Goals," *SF Gate*, November 5, 2004, https://www.sfgate.com/politics/article/Bush-claims-mandate-sets-2nd-term-goals-I-2637116.php.

6. John R. Hibbing and Elizabeth Theiss-Morse, *Stealth Democracy* (New York: Cambridge University Press, 2001), 135.

7. Charles Lindblom criticizes viewing political preferences as if they were the same as "the taste for bananas." Tallying political preferences is not the same as counting subatomic particles in an accelerator or mapping out the tree species in a forest. Such a view fails to recognize that a person's understanding of issues develops over time and as he or she learns. See Charles Lindblom, "Who Needs What Social Research for Policymaking," *Science Communication* 7, no. 4 (1986): 360–361; Charles Lindblom, *Inquiry and Change* (New Haven, CT: Yale University Press, 1990).

8. Nina Eliasoph, *Avoiding Politics* (New York: Cambridge University Press, 1998), 136.

9. Tulsi Gabbard, "The Gun Control Debate," Sanders Institute, accessed January 10, 2019, https://www.sandersinstitute.com/blog/the-gun-control-debate-what -debate.

10. Sophia Rosenfeld, *Democracy and Truth* (Philadelphia: University of Pennsylvania Press), 137.

11. Graham Saul, "Environmentalists, What Are We Fighting For?," Metcalfe Foundation, October 2018, https://metcalffoundation.com/wp-content/uploads/2018 /09/2018-10-10-Environmentalists-what-are-we-fighting-for-web.pdf.

12. Amy Chua, *Political Tribes* (New York: Penguin Press, 2018), 11.

13. Charles Duhhig, "The Real Roots of American Rage," *The Atlantic*, January– February 2019, https://www.theatlantic.com/magazine/archive/2019/01/charles -duhigg-american-anger/576424/.

14. Katherine Cramer, *The Politics of Resentment* (Chicago: University of Chicago Press, 2016).

15. Ben Sasse, *Them* (New York: St. Martin's Press, 2018).

16. Taylor Dotson, *Technically Together* (Cambridge, MA: MIT Press, 2017).

17. Quoted in Rosenfeld, *Democracy and Truth*, 13.

18. Tom Regan, "When Contemplating War, Beware of Babies in Incubators," *CS Monitor*, September 6, 2002, https://www.csmonitor.com/2002/0906/p25s02-cogn .html; Joseph J. Ellis, "American Wars Often Start with a Lie," *Chicago Tribune*, July 7, 2014, https://www.chicagotribune.com/opinion/ct-xpm-2014-07-07-ct-war -obama-history-0707-20140707-story.html.

19. Teresa M. Bejan, *Mere Civility* (Cambridge, MA: Harvard University Press, 2017), 45; William Lee Miller, *Arguing about Slavery* (New York: Vintage Books, 1998), 370–371; Stephan Grossmann quoted in "Indiskretion," *Illustrierter Sonntag*, March 31, 1929, 4, author's translation; Susan Sonntag, "Fascinating Fascism," *New York Review of Books*, February 6, 1975, https://www.nybooks.com/articles /1975/02/06/fascinating-fascism/.

20. See Sergio Sismondo, "Post-truth?," *Social Studies of Science* 47, no. 1 (2017): 3–6; Harry Collins, Martin Evans, and Martin Weinel, "STS as Science or Politics?," *Social Studies of Science* 47, no. 4 (2017): 580–586.

21. Steve Fuller, *Post-truth* (New York: Anthem Press, 2018).

22. Bruno Latour, "Telling Friends from Foes in the Time of the Anthropocene," in *The Anthropocene and the Global Environmental Crisis*, ed. Clive Hamilton, Christophe Bonneuil, and François Gemenne (New York: Routledge, 2013), 145–155.

23. Rosenfeld, *Democracy and Truth*, 137–176.

24. See Evgeny Morozov, *The Net Delusion* (New York: PublicAffairs, 2011).

25. Yascha Mounk, *The People versus Democracy* (Cambridge, MA: Harvard University Press, 2018), 27.

26. Mounk, *The People versus Democracy*, 27.

27. Jason Brennan, *Against Democracy* (Princeton, NJ: Princeton University Press, 2016), 12.

28. There is a real debate to be had about children voting and what age participation is reasonable. Perhaps full voting rights go too far, but a more democratic society would permit them to influence policy through political interest groups, specially appointed representatives, or citizen assemblies.

29. Elizabeth Anderson, *Private Government* (Princeton, NJ: Princeton University Press, 2017); Langdon Winner, "Do Artifacts Have Politics?," *Daedalus* 109, no. 1 (1980): 121–136; Richard Sclove, *Democracy and Technology* (New York: Guilford Press, 1995).

CHAPTER 2

1. Andy Kroll, "Ted Cruz's Secret Weapon to Win the Right," *The Atlantic*, June 26, 2015, https://www.theatlantic.com/politics/archive/2015/06/ted-cruzs-secret-weapon-to-win-the-right/440019/.

2. "Sen. Cruz Confronts the Dogma of Climate Change Alarmism," U.S. Senator for Texas Ted Cruz, last modified December 8, 2015, https://www.cruz.senate.gov/?p=press_release&id=2548.

3. Leo Goldstein, "Renounce Climate Alarmism," *Watts Up with That?*, last modified May 24, 2017, https://wattsupwiththat.com/2017/05/24/renounce-climate-alarmism/; James Delingpole, "Climate Alarmists Finally Admit 'We Were Wrong about Global Warming,'" Breitbart, last modified September 19, 2017, http://www.breitbart.com/big-government/2017/09/19/delingpole-climate-alarmists-finally-admit-we-were-wrong-about-global-warming/; John Stossel, "The Climate Alarmists Are Wrong," *Reason*, September 13, 2017, http://reason.com/2017/09/13/thr-climate-alarmists-are-wrong/.

4. John E. Losey, Linda S. Raynor, and Maureen E. Carter, "Transgenic Pollen Harms Monarch Larvae," *Nature* 399 (1999): 214.

5. Anthony M. Shelton and Richard T. Roush, "False Reports and the Ears of Men," *Nature Biotechnology* 17 (1999): 832.

6. Mark K. Sears et al., "Impact of *Bt* Corn Pollen on Monarch Butterfly Populations: A Risk Assessment," *PNAS* 98, no. 21 (2001): 11937–11942; John M. Pleasants and Karen S. Oberhauser, "Milkweed Loss in Agricultural Fields Because of Herbicide Use: Effect on the Monarch Butterfly Population," *Insect Conservation and Diversity* 6, no. 2 (2013): 135–144.

7. See Sarah Fecht, "Monsanto v. Monarch Butterflies," Genetic Literacy Project, last modified March 25, 2013, https://geneticliteracyproject.org/2013/03/25/monsanto -v-monarch-butterflies; Lincoln Brower, "The Monarch and the *Bt* Corn Controversy," *Orion Magazine* 20 (2001): 32–41, https://orionmagazine.org/article/canary -in-the-cornfield/.

8. See Dan Charles, *Lords of the Harvest* (New York: Basic Books, 2001).

9. Rachel Aviv, "A Valuable Reputation," *The New Yorker*, February 20, 2014, https://www.newyorker.com/magazine/2014/02/10/a-valuable-reputation.

10. Rex Dalton, "Berkeley Accused of Biotech Bias as Ecologist Is Denied Tenure," *Nature* 426 (2003): 591; Charles Burress, "Embattled UC Teacher Is Granted Tenure," *SFGate*, May 21, 2005, http://www.sfgate.com/education/article/BERKELEY -Embattled-UC-teacher-is-granted-tenure-2669634.php.

11. Nicole Papsco, "North Carolina Denies and Defies Science in House Bill 819," *Columbia Undergraduate Law Review*, March 21, 2016, http://blogs.cuit.columbia.edu /culr/2016/03/21/north-carolina-denies-and-defies-science-in-house-bill-819/; Dave Dewitt, "The State That 'Outlawed Climate Change' Accepts Latest Sea-Level Rise Report," WUNC 91.5 (North Carolina Public Radio), May 4, 2015, http:// wunc.org/post/state-outlawed-climate-change-accepts-latest-sea-level-rise-report #stream/0.

12. Oliver Milman, "US Federal Department Is Censoring Use of Term 'Climate Change,' Emails Reveal," *The Guardian*, August 7, 2017, https://www.theguardian .com/environment/2017/aug/07/usda-climate-change-language-censorship -emails; also see Ted Steinberg, *Acts of God* (New York: Oxford University Press, 2006).

13. Reiner Grundmann, "The Legacy of Climategate," *WIREs Climate Change* 3 (2012): 281–288.

14. David Ian Wilson, "The Scientific and Political Method," cartoon, flickr, March 10, 2006, https://www.flickr.com/photos/wilsnod/110551839.

15. Brian Kennedy, "Most Americans Trust the Military and Scientists to Act in the Public Interest," Pew Research Center, October 18, 2016, http://www .pewresearch.org/fact-tank/2016/10/18/most-americans-trust-the-military-and -scientists-to-act-in-the-publics-interest/.

16. Naomi Oreskes and Erik M. Conway, *Merchants of Doubt* (New York: Bloomsbury, 2010).

17. Thomas O. McGarity and Wendy Wagner, *Bending Science* (Cambridge, MA: Harvard University Press, 2012), "contaminated" on p. 5. For more on "private-interest" science, see Kristin Schrader-Frechette, *Taking Action, Saving Lives* (New York: Oxford University Press, 2007).

18. Daniel Sarewitz, *Frontiers of Illusion* (Philadelphia: Temple University Press, 1996).

19. Sarewitz, *Frontiers of Illusion*; Daniel Greenberg, *Science, Money, and Politics* (Chicago: University of Chicago Press, 2001).

20. Gerald Shatten and Helen Schatten, "The Energetic Egg," *Medical World News* 23 (1984): 51, quoted in Emily Martin, "The Egg and the Sperm," *Signs* 16, no. 3 (1991): 485–501, 490.

21. John J. Strouse et al., "NIH and National Foundation Expenditures for Sickle Cell Disease and Cystic Fibrosis Are Associated with Pubmed Publications and FDA Approvals," *Blood* 122, no. 21 (2013): 1739; Julian Reiss and Philip Kitcher, "Biomedical Research, Neglected Diseases, and Well-Ordered Science," *Theoria* 24, no. 3 (2009): 263–282.

22. The examples in this and the next several paragraphs are drawn from Kevin C. Elliot, *A Tapestry of Values* (New York: Oxford University Press, 2017).

23. Ian Mitroff, *The Subjective Side of Science* (New York: Elsevier, 1974); also see Phillip Kitcher, "The Cognitive Division of Labor," *Journal of Philosophy* 87, no. 1 (1990): 5–22.

24. Harry Collins and Trevor Pinch, *The Golem*, 2nd ed. (New York: Cambridge University Press, 1998).

25. Neil deGrasse Tyson, *Science in America*, YouTube video, 4:42, April 17, 2017, https://www.youtube.com/watch?v=8MqTOEospfo.

26. Abby J. Kinchy, Daniel Lee Kleinman, and Robyn Autry, "Against Free Markets, against Science?," *Rural Sociology* 73, no. 2 (2008): 156.

27. See John P. A. Ioannidis, "Why Most Published Research Findings Are False," *PLOS Medicine*, August 30, 2005, https://doi.org/10.1371/journal.pmed.0020124; Monya Baker, "1,500 Scientists Lift the Lid on Reproducibility," *Nature* 533 (2016): 452–454.

28. See Harry Collins and Robert Evans, *Why Democracies Need Science* (Malden, MA: Polity, 2017).

29. Ragnar Fjelland, "When Laypeople Are Right and Experts Are Wrong," *HYLE—International Journal for Philosophy of Chemistry* 22, no. 1 (2016): 105–125.

30. Brian Wynne, "Sheepfarming after Chernobyl," *Environment* 31, no. 2 (1989): 10–15, 33–39; Brian Wynne, "Misunderstood Misunderstandings," in *Misunderstanding Science?*, ed. Alan Irwin and Brian Wynne (New York: Cambridge University Press, 1996), 19–46; Benjamin J. Paul, *Flint Fights Back* (Cambridge, MA: MIT Press, 2019).

31. Daniel Sarewitz, "How Science Makes Environmental Controversies Worse," *Environmental Science & Policy* 7, no. 5 (2004): 385–403.

32. Sylvia Tesh, *Uncertain Hazards* (Ithaca, NY: Cornell University Press, 2000).

33. Will Stor, "We Believe You Harmed Your Child," *The Guardian*, December 8, 2017, https://www.theguardian.com/news/2017/dec/08/shaken-baby-syndrome-war-over-convictions.

34. See Debbie Cenziper, "A Disputed Diagnosis Imprisons Parents," *Washington Post*, March 20, 2015; Niels Lynøe, Nilas Juth, and Anders Eriksson, "From Child Protection to Paradigm Protection," *Journal of Medicine and Philosophy* 44, no. 3 (2019): 378–390; Joelle Moreno and Brian Holmgren, "The Supreme Court Screws Up the Science," *Utah Law Review*, no. 5 (2013): 1357–1435; Daniel Lindberg et al., "The 'New Science' of Abusive Head Trauma," *International Journal on Child Maltreatment* 2 (2019): 1–16.

35. Sarewtiz, "How Science Makes Environmental Controversies Worse." Regarding the corrosion of copper canisters for nuclear waste, see Andrei Ozharovsky, "When Haste Makes Risky Waste," trans. Maria Kaminskaya, *Bellona*, August 9, 2016, http://bellona.org/news/nuclear-issues/radioactive-waste-and-spent-nuclear -fuel/2016-08-21710.

36. Abby Kinchy, *Seeds, Science, and Struggle* (Cambridge, MA: MIT Press, 2012).

37. Kinchy, Kleinman, and Autry, "Against Free Markets, against Science?," 158.

38. See Kelly A. Clancy, *The Politics of Genetically Modified Organisms in the United States and Europe* (New York: Palgrave Macmillan, 2017), 67–98.

39. See Sarah A. Vogel, *Is It Safe?* (Berkeley: University of California Press, 2013); Warren Cornwall, "In BPA Safety War, a Battle over Evidence," *Science*, February 9, 2017, http://www.sciencemag.org/news/2017/02/bpa-safety-war-battle-over -evidence.

40. James Madison, *Federalist Papers, No. 10,* in *The Federalist*, ed. Terence Hall (New York: Cambridge University Press, 2003), 44.

41. Tom Cutterham, "The Dark Side of Alexander Hamilton," *HistoryExtra*, July 15, 2020, https://www.historyextra.com/period/georgian/dark-side-alexander-hamilton -lin-manuel-miranda-musical-realistic-portrayal-founding-father/.

42. See Benjamin Schwarz, "What Jefferson Helps to Explain," *The Atlantic*, March 1997, https://www.theatlantic.com/magazine/archive/1997/03/what-jefferson-helps -to-explain/376800/; Paul B. Thompson, *The Agrarian Vision* (Lexington: University Press of Kentucky, 2010); Sean Wilentz, *The Politicians and the Egalitarians: The Hidden History of American Politics* (New York: Norton, 2017).

43. See Frank Fischer, *Democracy and Expertise* (New York: Oxford University Press, 2009).

44. Jason Brennan, *Against Democracy* (Princeton, NJ: Princeton University Press, 2016), 162. The libertarian Brennan's skepticism about democracy probably grows out of a belief that market liberties rather than democracy is a surer path to prosperity. Like the earlier Federalists, libertarians fear that an unpropertied democratic majority would prefer redistributive policies that harm the property rights of the affluent minority.

45. Neil deGrasse Tyson, Twitter post, June 29, 2016, 7:12 a.m., https://twitter.com /neiltyson/status/748157273789300736?lang=en; Richard Wike et al., "Globally,

Broad Support for Representative and Direct Democracy," Pew Research Center, October 16, 2017, http://www.pewglobal.org/2017/10/16/globally-broad -support-for-representative-and-direct-democracy/. Also see John Hibbing and Elizabeth Theiss-Morse, *Stealth Democracy* (New York: Cambridge University Press, 2002).

46. See Robert Pool, *Beyond Engineering* (New York: Oxford University Press, 1997), 63–84; Richard G. Hewlett and Jack M. Holl, *Atoms for Peace and War, 1953– 1961* (Berkeley: University of California Press, 1989).

47. As quoted in Pool, *Beyond Engineering*, 77.

48. Benjamin Sovacool, *Contesting the Future of Nuclear Power* (Hackensack, NJ: World Scientific, 2011), 47–48; Kristin Schrader-Frechette, *Nuclear Power and Public Policy* (Boston: Reidel, 1980), 82–87.

49. Caitlin Drummond and Baruch Fischoff, "Individuals with Greater Science Literacy and Education Have More Polarized Beliefs on Controversial Science Topics," *Proceedings of the National Academy of Sciences of the United States of America* 114, no. 36 (2017): 9587–9592; regarding expert disagreement, see Éric Montpetit, *In Defense of Pluralism* (Cambridge, UK: Cambridge University Press, 2016), 142–146.

50. See Bjørn Lomberg, ed., *Global Crises, Global Solutions* (New York: Cambridge University Press, 2004); Mike Hulme, *Why We Disagree about Climate Change* (New York: Cambridge University Press, 2009).

51. Adam Curtis, dir., "Goodbye Mrs. Ant," episode 4 of *Pandora's Box*, BBC Two, 1992; also see Sarewitz, "How Science Makes Environmental Controversies Worse."

52. Brennan, *Against Democracy*, 12–16.

53. See Steve Rayner and Robin Cantor, "How Fair Is Safe Enough?," *Risk Analysis* 7, no. 1 (1987): 3–9; Wynne, "Misunderstood Misunderstandings"; Pool, *Beyond Engineering*, 230–241; Joseph G. Morone and Edward J. Woodhouse, *The Demise of Nuclear Energy?* (New Haven, CT: Yale University Press, 1989), 133– 134; Charles Perrow, *Normal Accidents* (Princeton, NJ: Princeton University Press, 1999), 306–328.

54. Morone and Woodhouse, *The Demise of Nuclear Energy?*, 135.

55. *New York Times*, "Conflicts of Interest at the F.D.A.," April 13, 2015, https:// www.nytimes.com/2015/04/13/opinion/conflicts-of-interest-at-the-fda.html; Charles Seife, "Is the FDA Withholding Data about a Controversial Drug to Protect the Manufacturer?," *Scientific American*, November 29, 2017, https://www .scientificamerican.com/article/is-the-fda-withholding-data-about-a-controversial -drug-to-protect-its-manufacturer.

56. Michael Fumento, "A Confederacy of Boobs," *Reason*, October 1, 1995, http:// reason.com/archives/1995/10/01/a-confederacy-of-boobs/print; Gina Kolata, "A

Case of Justice, or a Total Travesty?," *New York Times*, June 13, 1995, http://www
.nytimes.com/1995/06/13/business/case-justice-total-travesty-battle-over-breast
-implants-took-dow-corning-chapter.html; William M. Evan and Mark Manion,
Minding the Machines (Upper Saddle River, NJ: Prentice Hall, 2002), 134–137; also
see Lawrence Susskind and Patrick Field, *Dealing with an Angry Public* (New York:
Free Press, 1996).

57. Alice Benessia and Bruna De Marchi, "When the Earth Shakes . . . and Science
with It," *Futures* 91 (2017): 35–45.

58. Collins and Evans, *Why Democracies Need Science*.

59. National Science Foundation, *FY 2016 Budget Request to Congress*, tables, accessed
December 13, 2017, https://www.nsf.gov/about/budget/fy2016/table.jsp.

60. Charles E. Lindblom, "The Science of 'Muddling Through,'" *Public Administration Review* 19, no. 2 (1959): 79–88; Charles E. Lindblom and Edward J. Woodhouse, *The Policy-Making Process*, 3rd ed. (Englewood Cliffs, NJ: Prentice-Hall,
1993), 23–32; Charles E. Lindblom, *The Intelligence of Democracy* (New York: Free
Press, 1965).

61. Charles E. Lindblom, *Inquiry and Change* (New Haven, CT: Yale University
Press, 1992).

62. Lindblom, *The Intelligence of Democracy*, 3.

63. Tom McNichol, "Roads Gone Wild," *Wired*, December 1, 2004, https://
www.wired.com/2004/12/traffic/; Todd R. LaPorte and Paula M. Consolini,
"Working in Practice but Not in Theory," *Journal of Public Administration Research
and Theory* 1, no. 1 (1991): 19–48.

64. Morone and Woodhouse, *The Demise of Nuclear Energy?*, 118–141.

65. Edward J. Woodhouse, "When Expertise Goes Awry, and When It Proves
Helpful," in *International Symposium on Technology and Society: Technical Expertise and Public Decisions* (Princeton, NJ: IEEE, 1996), 200–206; Matthias Hey-
mann, "Signs of Hubris: The Shaping of Wind Technology Styles in Germany,
Denmark, and the United States, 1940–1990," *Technology and Culture* 39, no. 4
(1998): 641–670.

66. Gene I. Rochlin, Todd R. La Porte, and Karlene H. Roberts, "The Self-
Designing High-Reliability Organization," *Naval War College Review* 51, no. 3
(1998): 97–113; see also Karl E. Weick and Kathleen M. Sutcliffe, *Managing the
Unexpected* (San Francisco: Jossey-Bass, 2001).

67. Paul R. Schulman, "The Negotiated Order of Organizational Reliability,"
Administration & Society 25, no. 3 (1993): 353–372; Pool, *Beyond Engineering*, 262–264.

68. See Karl E. Weick, "The Vulnerable System: An Analysis of the Tenerife Air
Disaster," *Journal of Management* 16, no. 3 (1990): 571–593; Muhammad Aftab

Alam, "Cockpit Learning in Power Distant Cockpits," *Journal of Air Transport Management* 42 (2015): 192–202.

69. Aaron Wildavsky argues that "what is wanted is not scientific neuters but scientists with differing points of view . . . who are numerous, dispersed, and independent" (*But Is it True?* [Cambridge, MA: Harvard University Press, 1997], 9). Also see Karl Popper, *The Logic of Scientific Discovery* (1959; reprint, New York: Routledge, 2005); Helen Longino, *Science as Social Knowledge* (Princeton, NJ: Princeton University Press, 1990); Jeroen Van Bouwel, "Towards Democratic Models of Science," *Perspectives on Science* 23, no. 2 (2015): 149–172; Ian I. Mitroff, *The Subjective Side of Science* (New York: Elsevier, 1974).

70. See Collins and Pinch, *The Golem.*

71. Collins and Evans, *Why Democracies Need Science.*

72. John Fleck, *Water Is for Fighting Over* (Washington, DC: Island Press, 2016).

73. For more on the relationship between consensus, exclusion, and democracy, see Chantal Mouffe, *The Democratic Paradox* (New York: Verso, 2000), and Michael Ignatieff, "Enemies vs. Adversaries," *New York Times*, October 16, 2013.

74. Lindblom and Woodhouse, *The Policy-Making Process*, 90–103.

75. See Leah Stokes, *Short Circuiting Policy* (New York: Oxford University Press, 2020).

76. Charles E. Lindblom, "The Market as Prison," *Journal of Politics* 44, no. 2 (1982): 324–336.

77. Stephen Bell and Andrew Hindmoor, "The Structural Power of Business and the Power of Ideas," *New Political Economy* 3 (2014): 470–486.

78. Martin Gilens and Benjamin I. Page, "Testing Theories of American Politics: Elites, Interest Groups, and Average Citizens," *Perspectives on Politics* 12, no. 3 (2014): 564–581.

79. Anne Skorkjær Binderkrantz, Peter Munk Christiansen, and Helene Helboe Pedersen, "A Privileged Position?," *Journal of Public Administration Research and Theory* 24, no. 4: 879–896.

80. Mouffe, *The Democratic Paradox.*

81. Lindblom, *Inquiry and Change*; Lindblom and Woodhouse, *The Policy-Making Process*, 114–124.

82. Edward Woodhouse and Jeff Howard, "Stealthy Killers and Governing Mentalities," in *Killer Commodities*, ed. Merrill Singer and Hans Baer (Lanham, MD: AltaMira, 2009), 35–66.

83. Keith Kloor, "GMO Worry Warts: This Is Your Brain on Ignorance and Ideology," *Discover*, April 7, 2013, http://blogs.discovermagazine.com/collideascape

/2013/04/07/gmo-worry-warts-this-is-your-brain-on-ignorance-and-ideology/;
Ethan A. Huff, "Bill Nye Aligns Himself with Greatest Science Fraud of the Century: GMO 'Safety,'" *Natural News*, March 5, 2015, https://www.naturalnews.com
/049163_Bill_Nye_GMOs_Monsanto.html.

84. Paul Krugman, "The Liberal Bias of Facts," *New York Times*, April 18, 2014,
https://krugman.blogs.nytimes.com/2014/04/18/on-the-liberal-bias-of-facts/;
Paul Krugman, "Facts Have a Well-Known Liberal Bias," *New York Times*, December
8, 2017, https://www.nytimes.com/2017/12/08/opinion/facts-have-a-well-known
-liberal-bias.html. For the "duped" thesis, see Thomas Frank, *What's a Matter with
Kansas?* (New York: Metropolitan Books, 2004); Courtney Kirchoff, "Liberals Are
Feeling the Issues, Not Thinking about Them," *Louder with Crowder* (podcast), August
30, 2015, https://www.louderwithcrowder.com/opinion-liberals-are-feeling-the
-issues-not-thinking-about-them/.

85. Reuben, "Being Anti-vaccine Might Be Some Sort of Mental Disorder," *The
Poxes Blog*, June 28, 2014, https://thepoxesblog.wordpress.com/2014/06/28/being
-anti-vaccine-might-be-some-sort-of-mental-disorder/; Ashutosh Jogalekar, "Top
5 Reasons Why Intelligent Liberals Don't Like Nuclear Energy," *Scientific American*,
February 6, 2013, https://blogs.scientificamerican.com/the-curious-wavefunction
/top-5-reasons-why-intelligent-liberals-dont-like-nuclear-energy/; Eric Armstrong,
"Are Democrats the Party of Science? Not Really," *New Republic*, January 10, 2017,
https://newrepublic.com/article/139700/democrats-party-science-not-really; Nick
Murray, dir., *Bill Nye Saves the World*, streaming video series, Netflix, 2017.

86. Steinberg, *Acts of God*, 138.

87. Mike Adams, "Carbon Dioxide Revealed as the 'Miracle Molecule of Life' for
Re-greening the Planet," *Natural News*, May 9, 2017, https://www.naturalnews
.com/2017-05-09-carbon-dioxide-revealed-as-the-miracle-molecule-of-life-for
-re-greening-the-planet.html.

88. See Lindblom, *Inquiry and Change*.

89. Nicole Russell, "I'm Sick of Your Moral Relativism," *The Federalist*, August 20,
2015, http://thefederalist.com/2015/08/20/im-sick-of-your-moral-relativism/,
cited in Brandon A. Weber, "One of the Most Thoughtful Videos about the Right
to Choose That I've Seen Yet," *Big Think*, March 29, 2016, http://bigthink.com
/brandon-weber/one-of-the-most-thoughtful-videos-about-the-right-to-choose
-that-ive-seen-yet.

90. Michael Bouchey and Jason Delborne, "Redefining Safety in Commercial
Space," *Space Policy* 30, no. 2 (2014): 53–61.

91. Neil Postman, *Technopoly* (New York: Vintage Books, 1993), 56–58.

92. The more highly educated are not immune to confirmation bias; they often
are simply more skilled at it. See Jonathan Haidt, *The Righteous Mind* (New York:
Vintage, 2012), 94–95.

93. Jacques Ellul, *Propaganda* (New York: Vintage, 1973), 52.

94. Adam Baidawi, "'No Jab, No Play,'" *New York Times*, July 24, 2017, https:// www.nytimes.com/2017/07/24/world/australia/vaccination-no-jab-play-pay .html; Mark A. Largent, *Vaccine: The Debate in Modern America* (Baltimore: Johns Hopkins University Press, 2012), 169.

95. See Largent, *Vaccine*; Emma Green, "Anti-vaxxers Aren't Stupid," *The Atlantic*, February 16, 2016, https://www.theatlantic.com/health/archive/2016/02/anti -vaxers-arent-stupid/462864/; Alva Noë, "Can We Trust Science?," NPR, February 10, 2017, https://www.npr.org/sections/13.7/2017/02/10/514466107/can -we-trust-science.

96. Cornelia Betsch and Robert Böhm, "Detrimental Effects of Introducing Partial Compulsory Vaccination," *European Journal of Public Health* 26, no. 3 (2016): 378–381; Catherine Helps, Julie Leask, and Lesley Barclay, "'It Just Forces Hardship,'" *Journal of Public Health Policy* 39 (2018): 156–169.

97. Marcia Angell, *The Truth about the Drug Companies* (New York: Random House, 2005).

98. Dianne E. Hoffman and Anita J. Tarzian, "The Girl Who Cried Pain," *Journal of Law, Medicine, & Ethics* 29, no. 1 (2001): 13–27; Maya Dusenbery, "Is Medicine's Gender Bias Killing Young Women?," *Pacific Standard*, March 23, 2015, https://psmag.com /social-justice/is-medicines-gender-bias-killing-young-women; Abby Ellin, "Endometriosis Is Often Ignored in Teenage Girls," *New York Times*, March 30, 2015, https://well .blogs.nytimes.com/2015/03/30/endometriosis-is-often-ignored-in-teenage-girls/.

99. Annaliese Griffin, "Women Are Flocking to Wellness Because Modern Medicine Still Doesn't Take Them Seriously," *Quartz*, June 15, 2017, https://qz.com /1006387/women-are-flocking-to-wellness-because-traditional-medicine-still -doesnt-take-them-seriously/.

100. Jordan Weissmann, "Whom Does the NRA Really Speak For?," *The Atlantic*, December 18, 2012, https://www.theatlantic.com/business/archive/2012/12 /whom-does-the-nra-really-speak-for/266373/.

101. Dominique Belpomme et al., "Thermal and Non-thermal Health Effects of Low Intensity Non-ionizing Radiation," *Environmental Pollution* 242 (2018): 643– 658; Christopher Ketcham, "Is 5G Going to Kill Us All?," *New Republic*, May 8, 2020, https://newrepublic.com/article/157603/5g-going-kill-us-all/; David Gorski, "The Nation Indulges in Fear Mongering about Cell Phones and Cancer," *Science Based Medicine*, April 2, 2018, https://sciencebasedmedicine.org/the-nation-indulges -in-some-particularly-egregious-fear-mongering-about-cell-phones-and-cancer/.

102. Daniel Sarewitz, "The Trouble with Climate Science," *Slate*, March 10, 2010, http://www.slate.com/articles/health_and_science/green_room/2010/03/the _trouble_with_climate_science.html.

103. Susskind and Field, *Dealing with an Angry Public*.

CHAPTER 3

1. Quoted in Philip Bump, "A Reporter Pressed the White House for Data. That's When Things Got Tense," *Washington Post*, August 2, 2017, https://www.washingtonpost.com/news/politics/wp/2017/08/02/a-reporter-pressed-the-white-house-for-data-thats-when-things-got-tense/?utm_term=.46c65ae6c7a0.

2. Sophia Rosenfeld, *Common Sense* (Cambridge, MA: Harvard University Press, 2014).

3. Rosenfeld, *Common Sense*, 7, emphasis in original.

4. Robert L. Ivie, "Speaking 'Common Sense' about the Soviet Threat," *Western Journal of Speech Communication* 48, no. 1 (1984): 39–50.

5. Jerry Haar, "On Trade, Trump Team Shows Ivy League Schooling No Match for Common Sense," *The Hill*, March 9, 2018, http://thehill.com/opinion/finance/377566-trump-team-shows-ivy-league-schooling-no-match-for-common-sense-on-trade; Scott Lincicome, "'Reciprocal' Trade Demands Defy Basic Economics and Common Sense," Cato Institute, March 7, 2018, https://www.cato.org/blog/reciprocal-trade-demands-defy-basic-economics-common-sense.

6. Kyle Kashuv, "Larry Elder, 'Common Sense Gun Control' Lacks Common Sense," *Daily Wire*, May 28, 2018, https://www.dailywire.com/news/31154/kashuv-common-sense-gun-control-lacks-common-sense-kyle-kashuv; Larry Elder, "Where's the Common Sense in 'Common Sense' Gun Laws?," *Townhall*, March 29, 2018, https://townhall.com/columnists/larryelder/2018/03/29/wheres-the-common-sense-in-common-sense-gun-laws-n2465644.

7. Michael Ramirez, "It's Called 'Weather,'" cartoon, *Trinity Press*, May 8, 2014, http://trinitypress.net/its-called-weather/.

8. Julie Stewart and Thomas Clark, "Lessons from *South Park*: A Comic Corrective to Environmental Puritanism," *Environmental Communication* 5, no. 3 (2011): 333.

9. Owen in GA, December 29, 2016, 4:09 a.m., comment on Eric Worrall, "Latest Liberal Climate Plan: Buy Off the 'Conservative Elites,' to Sway the Sheep," *Watts Up with That?*, December 28, 2016, https://wattsupwiththat.com/2016/12/latest-liberal-climate-plan-buy-off-the-conservative-elites-to-sway-the-sheep/; William Warren, "Global Warming Kool-Aid," cartoon, *PA Pundits—International*, November 22, 2009, https://papundits.wordpress.com/2009/11/22/global-warming-kool-aid/.

10. Ethan Siegel, "Newt Gingrich Exemplifies Just How Unscientific America Is," *Forbes Magazine*, August 5, 2016, https://www.forbes.com/sites/startswithabang/2016/08/05/newt-gingrich-exemplifies-just-how-unscientific-america-is/#1600650f5e47.

11. Jan-Werner Müller, *What Is Populism?* (Philadelphia: University of Pennsylvania Press, 2016), 102.

12. Bruce G. Charlton, "Clever Sillies: Why High IQ People Tend to Be Deficient in Common Sense," *Medical Hypotheses* 73, no. 6: 867–870; see also Satoshi Kanazawa, "If Liberals Are More Intelligent Than Conservatives, Why Are Liberals so Stupid?," *Psychology Today*, March 28, 2010, https://www.psychologytoday.com/us/blog/the-scientific-fundamentalist/201003/if-liberals-are-more-intelligent-conservatives-why-are.

13. See Stephen Jay Gould, "Sociobiology: The Art of Storytelling," *The New Scientist*, November 16, 1978, 530–533.

14. Rankfreudlite, May 19, 2015, 3:27 p.m., comment on Byanyothername, "An Aberration That Came with the Advent of Agriculture," *MetaFilter*, May 17, 2015, https://www.metafilter.com/149719/An-aberration-that-came-with-the-advent-of-agriculture.

15. Consider Natalie Angier, "Thirst for Fairness May Have Helped Us Survive," *New York Times*, July 4, 2011, https://www.nytimes.com/2011/07/05/science/05angier.html; Dylan Evans, "The Mask Falls," *Aeon*, January 17, 2013, https://aeon.co/essays/is-the-struggle-for-equality-a-fight-against-nature. For the roots of hierarchy and egalitarianism in human societies, see Christopher Boehm, *Hierarchy in the Forest* (Cambridge, MA: Harvard University Press, 2001).

16. Clifford Geertz, "Common Sense as a Cultural System," *Antioch Review* 33, no. 1 (1975): 5–26.

17. Don Norman, *The Design of Everyday Things* (New York: Basic Books, 2013).

18. Rosenfeld, *Common Sense*.

19. See Cas Muddle and Cristóbal Rovira Kaltwasser, *Populism in Europe and the Americas* (New York: Cambridge University Press, 2012); for a deeper look at right-wing populism, see Roger Eatwell and Matthew Goodwin, *National Populism* (London: Pelican, 2018).

20. Rick Perlstein, *Nixonland* (New York: Scribner's, 2008), 748.

21. Jean-Jacques Rousseau, *The Social Contract*, in *Political Philosophy*, ed. Louis Pojman (New York: McGraw-Hill, 2002), 51–63.

22. Nate Silver, "'Real' America Looks Different to Palin, Obama," *FiveThirtyEight*, October 18, 2008, https://fivethirtyeight.com/features/real-america-looks-different-to-palin/; Nate Silver, "Only 20 Percent of Voters Are 'Real Americans,'" *FiveThirtyEight*, July 21, 2016, https://fivethirtyeight.com/features/only-20-percent-of-voters-are-real-americans/.

23. Bonnie Kristian, "In 2008 Sarah Palin Introduced Us to 'Real America.' Now, the Clinton Camp Has Found 'New America,'" *The Week*, April 19, 2016, http://theweek.com/speedreads/619356/2008-sarah-palin-introduced-real-america-now-clinton-camp-found-new-america; Angie Drobnic Holan, "In Context: Hillary Clinton and the 'Basket of Deplorables,'" *Politifact*, September 11, 2016, http://www

.politifact.com/truth-o-meter/article/2016/sep/11/context-hillary-clinton-basket
-deplorables/.

24. See Müller, *What Is Populism?*; Patrick Kingsley, "Erdogan Claims Vast Powers
in Turkey after Narrow Victory in Referendum," *New York Times*, April 16, 2017,
https://www.nytimes.com/2017/04/16/world/europe/turkey-referendum-polls
-erdogan.html.

25. Chantal Mouffe, *For a Left Populism* (Brooklyn, NY: Verso, 2018).

26. Tomi Lahren, Twitter post, May 12, 2018, 2:23 p.m., https://twitter.com
/TomiLahren/status/995414096999661568; Ben Shapiro, Twitter post, March 13,
2017, 11:18 a.m., https://twitter.com/benshapiro/status/841352707826835456;
Ben Shapiro, Twitter post, August 8, 2017, 7:20 a.m., https://twitter.com/benshapiro
/status/894926259599298560.

27. Jordan B. Peterson, Twitter post, February 3, 2018, 10:16 p.m., https://twitter
.com/jordanbpeterson/status/960034290154184704.

28. The Common Sense Conservative, *About*, YouTube video, accessed December 15,
2020, https://www.youtube.com/channel/UCAJqGdQ-KO8jEcsEx4PA-Lg/about;
Steven Crowder, *Louder with Crowder* (podcast), https://www.louderwithcrowder
.com/top-5-liberal-fails-throughout-history.

29. The term *infowars* alludes to "globalists" attempting to censor Christian,
nationalist, and pro-gun news venues. Breitbart touts itself as a source for "stories leftists don't want you to read." Pundits on TheBlaze include Pat Gray and
Rabbi Daniel Lapin, who describe themselves as "restoring common sense" and
informing visitors about "how the world REALLY works" (emphasis in original).
Rebel Media's website claims that it provides people with the stories the "consensus media ignores [*sic*]."

30. Istanbul Bilgi, University Center for Migration Research, "Dimensions of
Polarization in Turkey," February 5, 2018, https://goc.bilgi.edu.tr/media/uploads
/2018/02/06/dimensions-of-polarizationshortfindings_DNzdZml.pdf.

31. Pew Research Center, "Partisanship and Political Animosity in 2016," June 22,
2016, https://www.pewresearch.org/politics/2016/06/22/partisanship-and-political
-animosity-in-2016/; *PBS Newshour*, "How Political Opponents Became Enemies
in the U.S.," April 1, 2018, https://www.pbs.org/newshour/show/how-political
-opponents-became-enemies-in-the-u-s; Lee Drutman, Larry Diamond, and Joe
Goldman, "Follow the Leader," Democracy Fund: Voter Study Group, March 2018,
https://www.voterstudygroup.org/publications/2017-voter-survey/follow-the
-leader.

32. Dinesh D'Souza, *The Big Lie* (Washington, DC: Regnery, 2017), 229–247.

33. As quoted in Joshua Phillip, "Jorden Peterson Exposes the Postmodern-
ist Agenda," *The Epoch Time*, June 21, 2017, https://www.theepochtimes.com

/jordan-peterson-explains-how-communism-came-under-the-guise-of-identity
-politics_2259668.html; Samantha Beattie, "U of T Prof's Proposed Website
Would Target Professors Teaching Women's and Ethnic Studies," *Toronto Star*,
November 10, 2017, https://www.thestar.com/news/gta/2017/11/10/u-of-t-profs
-proposed-website-would-target-professors-teaching-womens-and-ethnic-studies
.html.

34. Jesse Kelly, "America Is Over, but I Won't See It Go without an Epic Fight,"
The Federalist, June 21, 2018, https://thefederalist.com/2018/06/21/america-wont
-see-go-without-epic-fight/; Tribune Media Wire, "Alabama Newspaper Editor
Calls for Return of the Ku Klux Klan, Lynching," WGN-TV, February 19, 2019,
https://wgntv.com/2019/02/19/alabama-newspaper-editor-calls-for-return-of
-the-ku-klux-klan-lynching.

35. Kurt Weyland, "The Threat from the Populist Left," *Journal of Democracy* 24,
no. 3 (2013): 18–32.

36. Carlos de la Torre, "Trump's Populism: Lessons from Latin America," *Postco-
lonial Studies* 20, no. 2 (2017): 187–198; Greg Sargent, "In New Interview, Trump
Openly Rages at Checks on His Authoritarianism," *Washington Post*, November
3, 2017, https://www.washingtonpost.com/blogs/plum-line/wp/2017/11/03/in
-new-interview-trump-openly-rages-at-checks-on-his-authoritarianism/?utm
_term=.461ae679a320.

37. Steven Levitsky and Daniel Ziblatt, *How Democracies Die* (New York: Crown,
2018), 72–117.

38. Levitsky and Ziblatt, *How Democracies Die*, 97–117.

39. Müller, *What Is Populism?*, 32; *NBC News*, "Trump: Clinton Can't Win Pennsylvania Unless There's Cheating," August 12, 2016, https://www.nbcnews.com/video
/trump-clinton-can-t-win-pennsylvania-unless-there-s-cheating-743559747525
?v=a; Peter Baker and Maggie Haberman, "In Torrent of Falsehoods, Trump Claims
Election Is Being Stolen," *New York Times*, November 5, 2020, https://www
.nytimes.com./2020/11/05/us/politics/trump-presidency.html.

40. Quoted in Müller, *What Is Populism?*, 26.

41. See Peter Dorey, "The Oratory of Margaret Thatcher," in *Conservative Orators
from Baldwin to Cameron*, ed. Richard Hayton and Andrew S. Crines (Manchester,
UK: Manchester University Press, 2015), 103–120.

42. D'Souza, *The Big Lie*, 242–243.

43. Rudiger Dornbusch and Sebastian Edwards, *The Macroeconomics of Populism in
Latin America* (Chicago: University of Chicago Press, 1991).

44. See William R. Kelly, *Criminal Justice at the Crossroads* (New York: Columbia University Press, 2015); Marc Santora, "City's Annual Cost per Inmate Is
$168,000, Study Finds," *New York Times*, August 23, 2013, https://www.nytimes

.com/2013/08/24/nyregion/citys-annual-cost-per-inmate-is-nearly-168000-study
-says.html; Nancy Gertner and Chiraag Bains, "Mandatory Minimum Sentences Are
Cruel and Ineffective. Sessions Wants Them Back," *Washington Post*, May 15, 2017,
https://www.washingtonpost.com/posteverything/wp/2017/05/15/mandatory
-minimum-sentences-are-cruel-and-ineffective-sessions-wants-them-back/?utm
_term=.43deb4cc7eff; Seena Fazel and Achim Wolf, "A Systematic Review of Crimi-
nal Recidivism Rates Worldwide," *PLOS One*, June 18, 2018, http://journals.plos
.org/plosone/article?id=10.1371/journal.pone.0130390.

45. Downtrend, *This Is How Libtard Michael Moore Thinks America Should Coddle Killers*, video, February 16, 2016, https://downtrend.com/dtvideos/this-is-how-libtard
-michael-moore-thinks-america-should-coddle-killers-video/; Team Crowder, "Liberal Utopia Sweden," *Louder with Crowder* (podcast), August 17, 2015, https://www
.louderwithcrowder.com/liberal-utopia-sweden-where-murder-and-rape-are-easy
-to-do/; John Hanna, "Kansas to Air-Condition Next Prison as Heat Becomes Concern," *Atlantic Broadband*, August 12, 2017, http://www.atlanticbb.net/news/read
/category/National/article/the_associated_press-kansas_to_aircondition_next_pri
son_as_heat_becomes-ap.

46. A Google search of the keywords *Trump* and *meme* and *authoritarian* uncovers
dozens of such memes. Also see John G. Messerly, "Yes, America Is Descending in
Totalitarianism," Institute for Ethics and Emerging Technologies, January 8, 2017;
Adam Roy, "Yes, You Should Be Comparing Trump to Hitler," *Forward*, June
19, 2018, https://forward.com/opinion/403515/yes-you-should-be-comparing
-trump-to-hitler/; Stephen M. Walt, "Top 10 Signs of Creeping Authoritarianism, Revisited," *Foreign Policy*, July 27, 2017, https://foreignpolicy.com/2017/07
/27/top-10-signs-of-creeping-authoritarianism-revisited/.

47. Levitsky and Ziblatt, *How Democracies Die*, 145–175.

48. Consider Magnus Linden, "Trump's America and the Rise of the Authoritarian Personality," *The Conversation*, February 16, 2017, https://theconversation.com
/trumps-america-and-the-rise-of-the-authoritarian-personality-72770.

49. See Müller, *What Is Populism?*, 16, 87, 103.

50. Noah Rothman, "An Unpopular Approach to the Populism Problem," *Commentary Magazine*, March 8, 2018, https://www.commentarymagazine.com/politics
-ideas/an-unpopular-approach-trade-populism-problem. Others even argue that
Trump-supporting communities are negative economic and moral assets that "deserve
to die": see Kevin Williamson, "Chaos in the Family, Chaos in the State," *National
Review*, March 17, 2016, https://www.nationalreview.com/2016/03/donald-trump
-white-working-class-dysfunction-real-opportunity-needed-not-trump/.

51. Tom Jacobs, "Research Finds That Racism, Sexism, and Status Fears Drove
Trump Voters," *Pacific Standard*, April 24, 2018, https://psmag.com/news/research
-finds-that-racism-sexism-and-status-fears-drove-trump-voters; Charles M. Blow,

"The White Rebellion," *New York Times*, April 26, 2018, https://www.nytimes.com/2018/04/26/opinion/the-white-rebellion.html.

52. Margaret Wente, "The Original Sin of White Privilege," *Globe and Mail*, May 27, 2017, https://www.theglobeandmail.com/opinion/the-original-sin-of-white-privilege/article35124053/; Roland Merullo, "In Defense of the White Male," *Boston Globe*, July 3, 2017, https://www.bostonglobe.com/opinion/2017/07/02/defense-white-male/Me9UoUrcPbcljxRkPFlXAP/story.html#comments.

53. Robert A. Dahl, "Is Civic Virtue a Relevant Ideal in a Pluralist Democracy?," in *Diversity and Citizenship*, ed. Gary Jeffrey Jacobsohn and Susan Dunn (Lanham, MD: Rowman and Littlefield, 1996), 3.

54. Levitsky and Ziblatt, *How Democracies Die*.

CHAPTER 4

1. Rob Lindeman, "Attachment and Sleep: Dr. Sears Is Wrong," *Essentially Healthy Child*, March 28, 2016, http://www.essentiallyhealthychild.com/2016/03/28/attachment-sears-wrong/; Dan Broadbent, "It's Not OK to Sleep Next to Your Infant Child," *A Science Enthusiast*, September 17, 2016, https://ascienceenthusiast.com/infant-co-sleep-deadly/.

2. One NPR article raised ire among safe-sleep advocates: Michaeleen Doucleff, "Is Sleeping with Your Baby as Dangerous as Doctors Say?," NPR, May 21, 2018, https://www.npr.org/sections/goatsandsoda/2018/05/21/601289695/is-sleeping-with-your-baby-as-dangerous-as-doctors-say. James McKenna and Thomas Dade point out the limitations and cultural assumptions of existing studies in "Babies Should Never Sleep Alone," *Pediatric Respirator Reviews* 6 (2005): 134–152. For reports on the congenital defects in sudden infant death syndrome (SIDS), see Linda Geddes, "SIDS Deaths Linked to Brain Defect," *New Scientist*, November 1, 2006, https://www.newscientist.com/article/mg19225763-700-sids-deaths-linked-to-brain-defect/, and Ariana Eunjung Cha, "Genetics May Make Some Babies Vulnerable to SIDS or 'Crib Death,' Study Says," *Washington Post*, March 28, 2018, https://www.washingtonpost.com/news/to-your-health/wp/2018/03/28/genetics-may-make-some-babies-vulnerable-to-sids-or-crib-death/?utm_term=.ddc5859c44c9. For an early study on observed benefits of co-sleeping, see James McKenna et al., "Experimental Studies of Infant–Parent Co-sleeping," *Early Human Development* 38, no. 3 (1994): 187–201.

3. Susan D. Stewart, *Co-sleeping* (Lanham, MD: Rowman and Littlefield, 2017).

4. Ileana Llorens, "Milwaukee Co-sleeping Ad of Baby with Knife Aims to Warn Parents of Dangers, Causes Controversy," *Huffington Post*, December 6, 2017, https://www.huffingtonpost.com/2011/11/16/co-sleeping-ad-baby-knife-dangers_n_1097170.html; Cindy Powers, "Newborn's Suffocation Prompts a Warning," *Bend Bulletin*, June

22, 2008, https://www.bendbulletin.com/news/1462914-151/newborns-suffocation
-prompts-a-warning.

5. Bryan Polcyn and Leeann Watson, "'I Just Don't Want Any Baby to Die': Law-makers Struggle for Consensus on Co-sleeping Legislation," *Fox6Now*, January 25, 2015, https://fox6now.com/2015/01/25/i-just-dont-want-any-baby-to-die-the -challenge-in-finding-a-solution-to-co-sleeping-deaths/.

6. Victoria Lambert, "The Case for Co-sleeping," *The Guardian*, September 12, 2008, https://www.theguardian.com/lifeandstyle/2008/sep/13/family2; Tracy Gil-lett, "Why Babies (and Parents) Love Co Sleeping," *Raised Good*, November 20, 2015, https://raisedgood.com/why-co-sleeping-is-best-for-babies-and-parents/.

7. James McKenna, "Breastfeeding & Bedsharing: Still Useful (and Important) after All These Years," *International Chiropractic Pediatric Association* 9 (2006), http:// icpa4kids.org/Wellness-Articles/breastfeeding-a-bedsharing-still-useful-and -important-after-all-these-years/All-Pages.html.

8. Mike Hulme, *Why We Disagree about Climate Change* (New York: Cambridge University Press, 2009).

9. Marcia Frellick, "Safe Sleep Recommendations: Parents Are Not Buying Them," *Medscape*, September 22, 2017, https://www.medscape.com/viewarticle/886109.

10. See Alan Levinovitz, *Natural* (Boston: Beacon Press, 2020).

11. Janet Hook, "Americans Still Like Tech Industry—but Not Telecom," *Wall Street Journal*, May 6, 2014, https://blogs.wsj.com/washwire/2014/05/06 /snowden-effect-americans-still-like-tech-industry-but-not-telecom/; Edelman, *Edelman Trust Barometer* (2018), http://cms.edelman.com/sites/default/files/2018 -02/2018_Edelman_TrustBarometer_Executive_Summary_Jan.pdf.

12. Examples of overhyped, deterministic, and disagreement-stifling rhetoric include Max Opray, "The End of Cars Is Coming, so What Will Happen to the Petrol-heads?," *The Guardian*, March 21, 2016, https://www.theguardian.com/sustainable -business/2016/mar/22/the-end-of-cars-is-coming-so-what-will-happen-to-the -petrolheads; and Ian Andrew, "The Environmental Benefits of Driverless Cars," *Greener Ideal*, August 31, 2017, https://greenerideal.com/news/vehicles/driverless -cars-environmental-benefits/.

13. According to Virginia Postrel in *The Future and Its Enemies* (New York: Free Press, 1998), the future's "enemies" are critics of laissez-faire, market-led techno-logical drift. But the market isn't the only decentralized mechanism for coordinat-ing collective action; the addition of decentralized democratic control enhances the intelligence of innovation. See Charles E. Lindblom, *The Market System* (New Haven, CT: Yale University Press, 2002).

14. See Kristin Shrader-Frechette, *Taking Action, Saving Lives* (New York: Oxford University Press, 2007), 95–96; Robert Pool, *Beyond Engineering* (New York: Oxford University Press, 1997).

15. Nidhi Kalra and Susan M. Paddock, *Driving to Safety* (Santa Monica, CA: RAND, 2016), https://www.rand.org/pubs/research_reports/RR1478.html.

16. David Noland, "How Safe Is Tesla Autopilot?," *Christian Science Monitor*, October 14, 2016, https://www.csmonitor.com/Business/In-Gear/2016/1014/How-safe-is-Tesla-Autopilot-A-look-at-the-statistics.

17. R. Anthony Steele, "Driver-less Cars Need Not Equate to Starving Drivers," *RAnt(hony)-ings@WP*, February 27, 2015, http://ranthonysteele.com/?cat=315; Sam Altman quoted in Suzi Feay, "Secrets of Silicon Valley, BBC2," *Financial Times*, August 4, 2017, https://www.ft.com/content/bab5c208-78a9-11e7-90c0-90a9d1bc9691.

18. Hiroko Tabuchi, "How the Koch Brothers Are Killing Public Transit Projects around the Country," *New York Times*, June 19, 2018, https://www.nytimes.com/2018/06/19/climate/koch-brothers-public-transit.html; Yves Engler, "Are Tolls a 'Flat Tax' or One Step in Building a Sane (Carless) Society?," December 18, 2016, https://yvesengler.com/2016/12/18/are-tolls-a-flat-tax-or-one-step-in-building-a-sane-carless-society/.

19. Pool, *Beyond Engineering*, 63–84.

20. Charles Perrow, *Normal Accidents* (Princeton, NJ: Princeton University Press, 1999).

21. See Donald A. Norman, "The 'Problem' with Automation," *Philosophical Transactions of the Royal Society B* 327, no. 1241: 585–593; Nicholas Carr, *The Glass Cage* (New York: Norton, 2015); Shoshana Zuboff, *In the Age of the Smart Machine* (New York: Basic Books, 1988); also see Don Norman, *Things That Make Us Smart* (Reading, MA: Addison-Wesley, 1993).

22. See Adam Thierer, *Permissionless Innovation* (Arlington, VA: Mercatus Center, 2014), 7, for an example of the "illusion of harmony" at work; also see Taylor Dotson, "Technological Determinism and Permissionless Innovation as Technocratic Governing Mentalities," *Engaging Science, Technology, and Society* 1 (2015): 98–120.

23. Neil Postman, *Technopoly* (New York: Knopf, 1992), 170.

24. See Joseph Morone and Edward Woodhouse, *Averting Catastrophe* (Berkeley: University of California Press, 1986); David Collingridge, *The Management of Scale* (New York: Routledge, 1992); Taylor Dotson, *Technically Together* (Cambridge, MA: MIT Press, 2017); Audley Genus, *Decisions, Technology, and Organization* (New York: Routledge, 2018).

25. Quoted in Chantal Mouffe, *For a Left Populism* (Brooklyn, NY: Verso, 2018), 4.

26. Christopher Lasch, *The True and Only Heaven* (New York: Norton, 1991), 24.

27. Jeffrey Dorfman, "10 Essential Economics Truths Liberals Need to Learn," *Forbes*, June 5, 2014, https://www.forbes.com/sites/jeffreydorfman/2014/06/05/10-essential-economic-truths-liberals-need-to-learn/#163606404e73; Daniel B. Klein,

"Are You Smarter Than a Fifth Grader?," *Wall Street Journal*, June 8, 2010, https://www.wsj.com/articles/SB10001424052748703561604575282190930932412?mod=WSJ_WSJ_US_PoliticsNCampaign_6; Jonathan Chait, "Study Proves Libertarian Economists Ignorant," *The New Republic*, June 7, 2010, https://newrepublic.com/article/75399/study-proves-libertarian-economists-ignorant; Wayne Allyn Root, "Economic Ignorance Gap between Liberals and Conservatives," TheBlaze, June 6, 2012, emphasis in original, https://www.theblaze.com/contributions/the-economic-ignorance-gap-between-liberals-and-conservatives.

28. Ha-Joon Chang, "Economics Is for Everyone!," *The RSA*, July 15, 2016, https://www.thersa.org/discover/videos/rsa-animate/2016/economics-is-for-everyone; Ha-Joon Chang, *Economics: The User's Guide* (New York: Bloomsbury Press, 2014).

29. Zubin Jelveh, Bruce Kogut, and Suresh Naidu, "Political Language in Economics," Columbia Business School Research Paper no. 14-57, 2018.

30. Annemarie Duran, "Seattle's Mayor Caught 'Fixing' the Berkeley Study on Minimum Wage," *Swipeclock*, August 8, 2017, https://www3.swipeclock.com/blog/seattles-mayor-caught-fixing-the-berkeley-study-on-minimum-wage/; John Burbank, "UW Minimum Wage Study: Disconcerting, Distorted, and Biased," Economic Opportunity Institute, July 10, 2017, https://www.eoionline.org/blog/uw-minimum-wage-study-disconcerting-distorted-and-biased/.

31. See Lindblom, *The Market System*; *Rolling Alpha*, "Singapore: A Success Story, Not a Free Market One," March 23, 2015, http://www.rollingalpha.com/2015/03/23/singapore-a-success-story-not-a-free-market-one/; Alana Semuels, "Why Does Sweden Have so Many Start-ups?," *The Atlantic*, September 28, 2017, https://www.theatlantic.com/business/archive/2017/09/sweden-startups/541413/.

32. For a primer on and defense of economic democracy, see Tom Malleson, *After Occupy* (New York: Oxford University Press, 2014); for more on "private governments," see Elizabeth Anderson, *Private Government* (Princeton, NJ: Princeton University Press, 2017).

33. See Michael Meeropol, *Surrender: How the Clinton Administration Completed the Reagan Revolution* (Ann Arbor: University of Michigan Press, 1998); Bruce Japsen, "Despite Clinton's Claims, Obamacare Is More Romneycare Than Hillarycare," *Forbes*, January 23, 2016, https://www.forbes.com/sites/brucejapsen/2016/01/23/obamacare-is-more-romneycare-than-hillarycare-2/#594e6805523b; Abigail Tracy, "D.N.C. Chair Purges Dissenters in Surprise Shake-up," *Vanity Fair*, October 19, 2017, https://www.vanityfair.com/news/2017/10/tom-perez-dnc-shake-up; Lawrence Douglas, "The Democratic Party Is Now Publicly Attacking Progressive Candidates," *The Guardian*, February 26, 2018, https://www.theguardian.com/commentisfree/2018/feb/26/democratic-party-laura-moser-texas.

34. Richard Denniss, "Spreadsheets of Power," *The Monthly*, April 2015, https://www.themonthly.com.au/issue/2015/april/1427806800/richard-denniss/spreadsheets-power.

35. Denniss, "Spreadsheets of Power"; CBC Ideas, *It's the Economists, Stupid*, podcast, CBC Radio, September 9, 2015, https://www.cbc.ca/radio/ideas/it-s-the -economists-stupid-1.3219471.

36. Julie Nelson, *Economics for Humans* (Chicago: University of Chicago Press, 2010), 115, emphasis in original.

37. For brief introductions to Modern Monetary Theory, see Atossa Araxia Abrahamian, "The Rock-Star Appeal of Modern Monetary Theory," *The Nation*, May 8, 2017, https://www.thenation.com/article/the-rock-star-appeal-of-modern-mone tary-theory/; Zach Carter, "Stephanie Kelton Has the Biggest Idea in Washington," *Huffington Post*, May 5, 2018, https://www.huffingtonpost.com/entry/stephanie -kelton-economy-washington_us_5afee5eae4b0463cdba15121.

38. For positive studies of right-to-work laws, see Stan Greer, "Research Bolsters Economic Case for State Right to Work Laws," National Institute for Labor Relations, January 17, 2017, http://www.nilrr.org/2017/01/17/research-bolsters -economic-case-state-right-work-laws/; negative views include Lonnie K. Stevans, "The Effect of Endogenous Right-to-Work Laws on Business and Economic Conditions in the United States," *Review of Law and Economics* 5, no. 1 (2009): 595– 614; Elsie Gould and Will Kimball, "'Right-to-Work' States Still Have Lower Wages," Economic Policy Institute Briefing Paper no. 395, April 22, 2015, https:// www.epi.org/publication/right-to-work-states-have-lower-wages/.

39. Library of Parliament, "Legislative Summer of Bill C-51," Parliament of Canada, June 19, 2015, https://lop.parl.ca/About/Parliament/LegislativeSummaries /bills_ls.asp?ls=c51&Parl=41&Ses=2&Language=E#a10; Shawn McCarthy, "'Anti-petroleum' Movement a Growing Security Threat to Canada, RCMP Say[s]," *Globe and Mail*, February 17, 2015, https://www.theglobeandmail.com/news/politics/anti -petroleum-movement-a-growing-security-threat-to-canada-rcmp-say/article 23019252/.

40. Patrik Jonsson, "New Protest Bills: Stamping Out 'Economic Terrorism' or Chilling Free Expression?," *Christian Science Monitor*, March 16, 2017, https:// www.csmonitor.com/USA/Justice/2017/0316/New-protest-bills-Stamping-out -economic-terrorism-or-chilling-free-expression; Mitch Smith and Michael Wines, "Across the Country, a Republican Push to Rein in Protestors," *New York Times*, March 2, 2017, https://www.nytimes.com/2017/03/02/us/when-does-protest-cross -a-line-some-states-aim-to-toughen-laws.html.

41. See Leah Carlson, "Pink Slime by Any Other Name Is Still Finely Textured Beef," *Drake Journal of Agricultural Law* 19, no. 2 (2004): 191–216; Jacob Gershman, "'Pink Slime' Lawsuit: Food-Libel Laws Explained," *Wall Street Journal*, March 14, 2017, https://www.wsj.com/articles/pink-slime-lawsuit-food-libel-law-explained -1489542437; Aman Batheja, "The Time Oprah Winfrey Beefed with the Texas Cattle Industry," *Texas Tribune*, January 10, 2018, https://www.texastribune.org /2018/01/10/time-oprah-winfrey-beefed-texas-cattle-industry/.

42. Steve Dunning, "How to Fix Stagnant Wages," *Forbes*, July 26, 2018, https://
www.forbes.com/sites/stevedenning/2018/07/26/how-to-fix-stagnant-wages
-dump-the-worlds-dumbest-idea/#302528af1abc; Matthew Yglesias, "Elizabeth
Warren Has a Plan to Save Capitalism," *Vox*, August 15, 2018, https://www.vox.com
/2018/8/15/17683022/elizabeth-warren-accountable-capitalism-corporations; Elizabeth Warren, "Companies Shouldn't Be Accountable Only to Shareholders," *Wall
Street Journal*, August 14, 2018, https://www.wsj.com/articles/companies-shouldnt
-be-accountable-only-to-shareholders-1534287687.

43. Stephen Barr, "Clinton Orders Government to Use Only Recycled Paper," *Los
Angeles Times*, September 20, 1998, https://www.latimes.com/archives/la-xpm
-1998-sep-20-me-24592-story.html; Cristina Maza, "Is Economic Opportunity a
Catalyst for Peace at Israeli Company SodaStream—or PR for Israel—or Both?,"
Newsweek, June 25, 2019, https://www.newsweek.com/2019/07/05/economic
-opportunity-catalyst-peace-israeli-company-sodastream-pr-israel-both-1445859
.html.

44. Mary Ann Glendon, *Rights Talk* (New York: Free Press, 1991).

45. Steven Shapin and Simon Schaffer, *Leviathan and the Air-Pump* (Princeton, NJ:
Princeton University Press, 1985).

46. Shapin and Schaffer, *Leviathan and the Air-Pump*, 100–102.

47. Shapin and Schaffer, *Leviathan and the Air-Pump*, 104.

48. Richard J. Evans, *The Coming of the Third Reich* (New York: Penguin Press,
2004), 350–354.

49. See Robert A. Dahl, *A Preface to Economic Democracy* (Berkeley: University of
California Press, 1985), 13–31.

50. Robert A. Dahl, "Decision-Making in a Democracy: The Supreme Court
as a National Policy-Maker," *Journal of Public Law* 6 (1957): 179–295; for mid-
twentieth-century public opinion on integration, see Mildred A. Schwartz, *Trends
in White Attitudes toward Negroes* (Chicago: National Opinion Research Center,
University of Chicago, 1967).

51. See Jeremey Waldron, "Judicial Review and the Conditions of Democracy,"
Journal of Political Philosophy 6, no. 4 (1998): 335–355.

52. Steven Levitsky and Daniel Ziblatt, *How Democracies Die* (New York: Crown,
2018).

53. See David R. Roediger, *The Wages of Whiteness* (New York: Verso, 1991) for
a detailed history of race and labor organizing; also see Joshua Zeitz, "Does the
White Working Class Really Vote against Its Own Interests?," *Politico*, December
31, 2017, https://www.politico.com/magazine/story/2017/12/31/trump-white
-working-class-history-216200.

CHAPTER 5

1. Quoted in Sophia Rosenfeld, *Common Sense* (Cambridge, MA: Harvard University Press, 2014), 250.

2. Benjamin Barber, *Strong Democracy* (Berkeley: University of California Press, 2003), 178.

3. Robert A. Dahl, "Is Civic Virtue a Relevant Ideal in a Pluralist Democracy?," in *Diversity and Citizenship*, ed. Gary Jeffrey Jacobsohn and Susan Dunn (Lanham, MD: Rowman and Littlefield, 1996), 1–16.

4. Charles Lindblom, *Inquiry and Change* (New Haven, CT: Yale University Press, 1990).

5. See Maria Konnikova, "Why We Need Answers," *The New Yorker*, April 30, 2013, https://www.newyorker.com/tech/elements/why-we-need-answers; Ming Hsu et al., "Neural Systems Responding to Degrees of Uncertainty in Human Decision-Making," *Science* 310, no. 5754 (2005): 1680–1683; Judith E. Glaser, "Your Brain Is Hooked on Being Right," *Harvard Business Review*, February 28, 2013, https://hbr.org/2013/02/break-your-addiction-to-being.

6. Diego Gambetta and Steffan Hertog, *Engineers of Jihad* (Princeton, NJ: Princeton University Press, 2016), 149.

7. Phillip M. Fernbach et al., "Political Extremism Is Supported by an Illusion of Understanding," *Psychological Science* 24, no. 6: 939–946.

8. Éric Montpetit, *In Defense of Pluralism* (New York: Cambridge University Press, 2016), 111.

9. For a number of examples of the precautionary principle's application, see Peter L. deFur and Michelle Kaszuba, "Implementing the Precautionary Principle," *Sciences of the Total Environment* 288 (2002): 155–165.

10. Aaron Wildavsky, *Searching for Safety* (Piscataway, NJ: Transaction, 1988), 19.

11. See Joseph Morone and Edward Woodhouse, *Averting Catastrophe* (Berkeley: University of California Press, 1986); David Collingridge, *The Management of Scale* (New York: Routledge, 1992); Audley Genus, *Decisions, Technology, and Organizations* (Burlington, VT: Gower, 2000).

12. Joseph Morone and Edward Woodhouse, *The Demise of Nuclear Energy?* (New Haven, CT: Yale University Press, 1989); Adam Curtis, dir., "A Is for Atom," episode 6 of *Pandora's Box*, BBC Two, 1992. The United Kingdom's roll-out of nuclear was similar. See Collingridge, *The Management of Scale*; Matthew Cotton, *Nuclear Waste Politics* (New York: Routledge, 2017).

13. See Robert O. Keohane and David G. Victor, "Cooperation and Discord in Global Climate Policy," *Nature Climate Change* 6 (2016): 570–575; David Roberts, "The Argument for Incrementalism in Global Climate Negotiations," *Vox*, May 26,

2016, https://www.vox.com/2016/5/26/11766252/international-climate-incremen talism; Elinor Ostrom, *A Polycentric Approach to Coping with Climate Change* (Washington, DC: World Bank, 2009).

14. See Jill Grant, *Planning the Good Community* (New York: Routledge, 2006); Sharon Crowther, "Airport Redevelopment Project Taking Off," *Globe and Mail*, November 12, 2017, https://www.theglobeandmail.com/real-estate/calgary-and -edmonton/edmontons-blatchford-airport-redevelopment-project-takingoff /article35882291/.

15. See Taylor Dotson, "Trial and Error Urbanism," *Journal of Urbanism* 9, no. 2 (2016): 148–165; Taylor Dotson, *Technically Together* (Cambridge, MA: MIT Press, 2017).

16. Matthias Heyman, "Signs of Hubris," *Technology and Culture* 29, no. 4 (1998): 641–670.

17. For a few examples of the idealization of politics in earlier eras, see Bruce Thornton, "Three Cheers for Political Incivility," Hoover Institution, September 22, 2015, https://www.hoover.org/research/three-cheers-political-incivility.

18. Michael Sandel makes calls for a renewed practice of reasoned public deliberation in *Justice* (New York: Farrar, Straus, and Giroux, 2009). Also see Christina Pazzanesse, "Making a Case for Democracy," *Harvard Gazette*, January 16, 2015, https://news.harvard.edu/gazette/story/2015/01/making-a-case-for-democracy/; *CBC News*, "Why Democracy Depends on How We Talk to Each Other," November 28, 2017, https://www.cbc.ca/radio/ideas/why-democracy-depends-on-how-we -talk-to-each-other-1.4422725.

19. Brian Resnick, "Watch: This Scientifically Proven Method to Reduce Anti-transgender Prejudice," *Vox*, April 8, 2016, https://www.vox.com/2016/4/8 /11392298/reduce-prejudice-transgender.

20. See David Broockman and Joshua Kalla, "Durably Reducing Transphobia," *Science* 352, no. 6282 (2016): 220–224; Geoff Kaufman and Lisa K. Libby, "Changing Beliefs and Behavior through Experience-Taking," *Journal of Personality and Social Psychology* 103, no. 1 (2012): 1–19; Fernanda Herrera, "Building Long-Term Empathy," *PLOS One*, October 17, 2018, https://journals.plos.org/plosone /article?id=10.1371/journal.pone.0204494. Regarding motivated skepticism of experts' credentials, see Dan Kahan et al., "Cultural Cognition of Scientific Consensus," *Journal of Risk Research* 14, no. 2 (2011): 147–174.

21. Frances Marlin-Tackie and Jessica M. Smith, "Key Characteristics Influencing Risk Perceptions of Unconventional Energy Developing," *Journal of Cleaner Production* 251, no. 1 (2020): 119644.

22. Sónia Gonçalves, "The Effects of Participatory Budgeting on Municipal Expenditures and Infant Mortality in Brazil," *World Development* 53 (2014): 94–110; Michael Touchton and Brian Wampler, "Improving Social Well-Being through New

Democratic Institutions," *Comparative Political Studies*, December 27, 2013, http:// journals.sagepub.com/doi/abs/10.1177/0010414013512601.

23. Tim Alberta, "Kent Sorenson Was a Tea Party Hero. Then He Lost Everything," *Politico*, September 21, 2018, https://www.politico.com/magazine/story /2018/09/21/kent-sorenson-was-a-tea-party-hero-then-he-lost-everything -220522.

24. Sonia Kruks, *Retrieving Experience* (Ithaca, NY: Cornell University Press, 2001), 80–88.

25. See Adam Rubenstein, "Steven Pinker: Identity Politics Is 'an Enemy of Reason and Enlightenment Values,'" *Weekly Standard*, February 15, 2018, https://www .weeklystandard.com/adam-rubenstein/steven-pinker-identity-politics-is-an-enemy -of-reason-and-enlightenment-values; J Oliver Conroy, "Mark Lilla: The Liberal Who Counts More Enemies on the Left Than the Right," *The Guardian*, December 21, 2017, https://www.theguardian.com/media/2017/dec/21/mark-lilla-identity -politics-liberals; Michael Shermer, "How Classical Liberalism Can Heal the Bonds of American Affection," *Quillette*, April 30, 2018, http://quillette.com/2018/04/30 /classical-liberalism-can-heal-bonds-american-affection/; Amy Chua, *Political Tribes* (New York: Penguin Random House, 2018).

26. Chua, *Political Tribes*, 190.

27. *Sputnik News*, "#WhatAboutMe?: Male Sexual Assault Victims Feel Left Out by #MeToo Movement," April 19, 2018, https://sputniknews.com/society/20180419 1063726889-male-sexual-victims-me-too-movement/; Chandra Bozelko, "Why We Let Prison Rape Go On," *New York Times*, April 17, 2015, https://www.nytimes .com/2015/04/18/opinion/why-we-let-prison-rape-go-on.html; Jenna Birch, "The Number of Men Who Suffer Domestic Abuse Is Shockingly High," *Yahoo Lifestyle*, October 26, 2015, https://www.yahoo.com/lifestyle/the-number-of-male-domestic -1284479771263030.html; Noah Berlatsky, "When Men Experience Sexism," *The Atlantic*, May 29, 2013, https://www.theatlantic.com/sexes/archive/2013/05/when -men-experience-sexism/276355/; C. J. Pascoe, *Dude, You're a Fag* (Berkeley: University of California Press, 2011); Matt Wray, *Not Quite White* (Durham, NC: Duke University Press, 2006); Cooper Thompson, "A White Man's Experience of Oppression in a Life of Privilege," *The Diversity Factor*, Spring 2008, http://www.cooper -thompson.com/essays/PDF/AWhiteMan'sExperienceOfOppressionInALifeOfPriv ilege.pdf.

28. Asking white men to listen silently is a common call in anti-oppression activism. See Katherine Kirkinis, "The Scientific Way to Train White People to Stop Being Racist," *Quartz*, April 11, 2016, https://qz.com/656159/the-scientific-way-to-train -white-people-to-stop-being-racist/; Greta Christina, "The Part about Black Lives Mattering Where White People Shut Up and Listen," *Humanist.com*, June 23, 2015, https://thehumanist.com/magazine/july-august-2015/fierce-humanism/the-part -about-black-lives-mattering-where-white-people-shut-up-and-listen. However,

such a call functions too similarly to political scientistic calls to pipe down and listen to the facts.

29. Sonia Kruks makes the same argument: "groups that espouse particularistic identity politics must also actively seek areas of common ground with others" if they are to move beyond the potential divisiveness of it, "even as they rightly continue to insist on the specificity of their own experiences" (*Retrieving Experience*, 106).

30. Montpetit, *In Defense of Pluralism*, 36.

31. Jonathon Haidt, *The Righteous Mind* (New York: Vintage Books, 2012).

32. Avnika B. Amin et al., "Association of Moral Values with Vaccine Hesitancy," *Nature Human Behavior* 1 (2017): 873–880.

33. Human physiology is far more complex than the mechanistic model of medicine implies. The placebo effect can be seen as a biochemical process with some healing potential rather than as a bug. Learning from alternative medicine might make standard medicine more effective. See Gary Greenberg, "What If the Placebo Effect Isn't a Trick?," *New York Times Magazine*, November 7, 2018, https://www.nytimes.com/2018/11/07/magazine/placebo-effect-medicine.html.

34. See Paul Menzel and Donald Light, "A Conservative Case for Universal Access to Health Care," *Hastings Center Report* 36, no. 4 (2006): 36–45.

35. John Metta, "Racism and the Black Hole of Gun Control in the US," Al Jazeera, November 23, 2019, https://www.aljazeera.com/indepth/features/racism -black-hole-gun-control-191121115131565.html; David D'Amato, "Actually, Gun Restrictions Will Target the Black Community," *The Hill*, August 5, 2019, https:// thehill.com/opinion/criminal-justice/456243-actually-gun-restrictions-will-target -the-black-community.

36. Andrew Hoffman, "Talking Past Each Other? Cultural Framings of Skeptical and Convinced Logics in the Climate Change Debate," *Organization & Environment* 24, no. 1 (2011): 3–33.

37. Also see Naomi Oreskes and Erik M. Conway, *Merchants of Doubt* (New York: Bloomsbury Press, 2010), 240–265.

38. Sean Mowbray, "Trump and the Military Are at Odds on Climate Change," *Pacific Standard*, January 18, 2018, https://psmag.com/environment/our-government -is-in-two-minds-over-climate-change; Craig Morris and Arne Jungjohann, *Energy Democracy* (London: Palgrave, 2016).

39. Dashka Slater, "North Dakota's Norway Experiment," *Mother Jones*, July–August 2017, https://www.motherjones.com/crime-justice/2017/07/north-dakota-norway -prisons-experiment/.

40. Matthew Feinberg and Robb Willer, "From Gulf to Bridge," *Personality and Social Psychology Bulletin* 41, no. 12 (2015): 1665–1681; Peter Beinart, "*Republican* Is

Not a Synonym for *Racist*," *The Atlantic*, December 2017, https://www.theatlantic
.com/magazine/archive/2017/12/conservatism-without-bigotry/544128/.

41. Timothy D. Wilson, *Redirect* (New York: Back Bay Books, 2015).

42. Wilson, *Redirect*, 14–17.

43. David Webber et al., "Deradicalizing Detained Terrorists," *Political Psychology* 39,
no. 3 (2018): 539–556; Arie Kruglanski, "Drivers of Deradicalization," *Huffington
Post*, January 11, 2015, https://www.huffingtonpost.com/arie-kruglanski/drivers
-of-deradicalizati_b_6117334.html; Wes Enzinna, "Inside the Radical, Uncomfortable Movement to Reform White Supremacists," *Mother Jones*, July–August
2018, https://www.motherjones.com/politics/2018/07/reform-white-supremacists
-shane-johnson-life-after-hate/.

44. Robert Putnam, *Bowling Alone* (New York: Simon and Schuster, 2000), 355.

45. Juliet Eilperin, *Fight Club Politics* (Lanham, MD: Rowman and Littlefield,
2006), 32–35.

46. See John Fleck, *Water Is for Fighting Over* (Washington, DC: Island Press, 2016),
53–64; Elinor Ostrom, "Beyond Markets and States," *Annual Economic Review* 100
(2010): 641–672.

47. David Braybrooke and Charles E. Lindblom, *A Strategy of Decision* (New York:
Free Press, 1963), 134–138.

48. Guian McKee, "Why Are Republicans Trapped on Health Care?," *Washington Post*, June 26, 2017, https://www.washingtonpost.com/news/made-by-history
/wp/2017/06/26/why-are-republicans-trapped-on-health-care-because-democrats
-stole-their-best-idea/?utm_term=.af257d786d91; Norm Ornstein, "The Real Story
of Obamacare's Birth," *The Atlantic*, July 6, 2015, https://www.theatlantic.com
/politics/archive/2015/07/the-real-story-of-obamacares-birth/397742/.

49. Raina Delisle, "Should All Babies Receive the Hepatitis B Vaccine at Birth?,"
Today's Parents, August 28, 2017, https://www.todaysparent.com/baby/baby-health
/should-all-babies-be-getting-the-hepatitis-b-vaccine-at-birth/.

50. Nadja Durbach, *Bodily Matters* (Durham, NC: Duke University Press, 2005),
199–200.

51. Alan Irwin, "The Politics of Talk," *Social Studies of Science* 36, no. 2 (2006):
299–320; Javier Lezaun and Linda Soneryd, "Consulting Citizens," *Public Understanding of Science* 16 (2007): 279–297; Nina Eliasoph, *Avoiding Politics* (New York:
Cambridge University Press, 1998).

52. See Nancy Fraser, *Justice Interruptus* (New York: Routledge, 1997), 78; Rebecca
Comay, "Interrupting the Conversation," *Telos* 69 (1986): 125.

53. David Adler, "Centrists Are the Most Hostile to Democracy, Not Extremists,"
New York Times, May 23, 2018, https://www.nytimes.com/interactive/2018/05

/23/opinion/international-world/centrists-democracy.html?mtrref=undefined &assetType=opinion.

54. Ad Fontes Media, *Media Bias Chart, Version 4.0*, August 2018, https://www .adfontesmedia.com/.

55. Michael Starr Hopkins, "Bernie Is Not Even a Democrat, so Why Is He Ripping Our Party Apart?," *The Hill*, September 27, 2017, https://thehill.com/opinion /campaign/352632-bernie-sanders-is-not-a-democrat-so-he-should-stop-tearing -us-apart; James Rodgers Bush, "Bernie Sanders, Donald Trump, Hillary Clinton, and the Impossible American Dream (Revisited)," Facebook Note, February 5, 2016, https://www.facebook.com/notes/james-rogers-bush/bernie-sanders-donald-trump -hillary-clinton-and-the-impossible-american-dream-re/1541233445932986/.

56. See Charles Lindblom, *The Intelligence of Democracy* (New York: Free Press, 1965), 44–53.

57. Edward J. Woodhouse and Jeff Howard, "Stealthy Killers and Governing Mentalities," in *Killer Commodities*, ed. Merrill Singer and Hans Baer (Lanham, MD: Rowman and Littlefield, 2008), 46.

58. Woodhouse and Howard, "Stealthy Killers and Governing Mentalities."

59. See Ian Mitroff, *The Subjective Side of Science* (New York: Elsevier, 1974).

60. See Hélène Landemore, "Democratic Reason and Distributed Intelligence," presentation at the annual meeting of the American Political Science Association, Chicago, August 31, 2007). I borrow the coffee example from Charles E. Lindblom, *The Market System* (New Haven, CT: Yale University Press, 2001), 35–51; Christopher Lasch, *Revolt of the Elites* (New York: W.W. Norton, 1995), 171.

61. A similar argument about pluralism and relativism is made in Andrew Sayer, *Why Things Matter to People* (New York: Cambridge University Press, 2011), 135.

62. Teresa M. Bejan, *Mere Civility* (Cambridge, MA: Harvard University Press, 2017), 166.

63. Barber, *Strong Democracy*, 185.

64. Lindblom, *Inquiry and Change*, 291.

65. Quoted in Kate Bowler, *Blessed* (New York: Oxford University Press, 2013), 152.

66. Bowler, *Blessed*; also see Chua, *Political Tribes*, 153–156.

67. Joel Olson, "The Freshness of Fanaticism," *Perspectives on Politics* 5, no. 4 (2007): 685–701; Joel Olson, "Friends and Enemies, Slaves and Masters," *Journal of Politics* 71, no. 1 (2009): 82–95.

68. Olson, "The Freshness of Fanaticism" and "Friends and Enemies, Slaves and Masters"; Lena Zuckerwise incisively critiques the "cruelty" of "racial compromises" throughout US history, which served to prop up oppressive practices, in her essay "There Can Be No Loser," *American Political Thought* 5, no. 3 (2016): 467–493.

69. Quoted in DeNeen L. Brown, "Martin Luther King Jr.'s Scorn for 'White Moderates' in His Birmingham Jail Letter," *Washington Post*, January 15, 2018, https://www.washingtonpost.com/news/retropolis/wp/2018/01/15/martin-luther-king-jr-s-scathing-critique-of-white-moderates-from-the-birmingham-jail/.

70. Olson, "The Freshness of Fanaticism," 697.

71. Jim Powell, "Was the Civil War a Terrible Mistake?," History News Network, February 4, 2008, https://historynewsnetwork.org/article/46037.

72. Steven Levitsky and Daniel Ziblatt, *How Democracies Die* (New York: Crown, 2018), 143.

73. Susan Matthews, "How *Scientific American* Ended Up at the Center of a Massive Twitter War," *Scientific American*, December 3, 2019, https://slate.com/technology/2019/12/jen-gunter-jennifer-block-scientific-american.html.

CHAPTER 6

1. Jared Diamond, *Collapse* (New York: Penguin, 2005), 236–238.

2. Regarding citizens' distrust of politics, see Quinnipiac University Poll, "Deep Dissatisfaction among U.S. Voters, Quinnipiac University Poll Finds," April 5, 2016, https://poll.qu.edu/national/release-detail?ReleaseID=2340; Pew Research Center, "Beyond Distrust: How Americans View Their Government," November 23, 2015, http://www.people-press.org/2015/11/23/beyond-distrust-how-americans-view-their-government/; David Smith, "Most Americans Do Not Feel Represented by Democrats or Republicans," *The Guardian*, October 25, 2016, https://www.theguardian.com/us-news/2016/oct/25/american-political-parties-democrats-republicans-representation-survey; Mark Evans, Gerry Stoker, and Max Haulpka, "Australians' Trust in Politicians and Democracy Hits an All-Time Low," *The Conversation*, December 4, 2018, https://theconversation.com/australians-trust-in-politicians-and-democracy-hits-an-all-time-low-new-research-108161.

3. Quoted in Amy Gutmann and Dennis Thompson, "The Mindsets of Political Compromise," *Perspectives on Politics* 8, no. 4 (2010): 1136.

4. Emily Singer, "What If We Didn't . . . Have Endless Political Campaigns?," *Mic*, April 10, 2018, https://mic.com/articles/188447/what-if-we-didnt-have-endless-political-campaigns#.6yt4U7SGh; *CBC News*, "Other Things That Happened during Marathon Election Campaign," October 19, 2015, https://www.cbc.ca/news/canada/windsor/other-things-that-happened-during-marathon-election-campaign-1.3274141.

5. Arend Lijphart, "Polarization and Democratization," in *Solutions to Political Polarization in America*, ed. Nathaniel Persily (New York: Cambridge University Press, 2015), 75.

6. Arend Lijphart, *Patterns of Democracy*, 2nd ed. (New Haven, CT: Yale University Press, 2012).

7. Josep M. Colomer, "Spain: From Civil War to Proportional Representation," in *Handbook of Electoral System Choice*, ed. Josep M. Colomer (New York: Palgrave Macmillan, 2004), 253–264.

8. Martin Gilens and Benjamin I. Page, "Testing Theories of American Politics," *Perspectives on Politics* 12, no. 3 (2014): 576, emphasis in original.

9. Glenn Greenwald, "Brazil's Bolsonaro-Led Far Right Wins a Victory Far More Sweeping and Dangerous Than Anyone Predicted. Its Lessons Are Global," *The Intercept*, October 8, 2018, https://theintercept.com/2018/10/08/brazils-bolsonaro -led-far-right-wins-a-victory-far-more-sweeping-and-dangerous-than-anyone -predicted-its-lessons-are-global/.

10. Christopher Achen and Larry Bartels, *Democracy for Realists* (Princeton, NJ: Princeton University Press, 2016), esp. 32–35, 175–176, 276–284, 312; Ben Casselman and Jim Tankersley, "Feeling Good about the Economy? You're Probably a Republican," *New York Times*, June 15, 2018, https://www.nytimes.com/2018/06 /15/business/economy/survey-trump-economy.html.

11. Mogens Herman Hansen, *The Athenian Democracy in the Age of Demosthenes*, trans. J. A. Crook (Norman: University of Oklahoma Press, 1999), 160; also see Tom Malleson, "Beyond Electoral Democracy," *Jacobin*, June 29, 2018, https:// jacobinmag.com/2018/05/legislature-lot-electoral-democracy-real-utopias.

12. Hélène Landemore, "Deliberation, Cognitive Diversity, and Democratic Inclusiveness," *Synthese* 190 (2013): 1209–1231.

13. Feng Shi et al., "The Wisdom of Polarized Crowds," *Nature Human Behaviour*, March 4, 2019, https://www.nature.com/articles/s41562-019-0541-6.

14. Patrick Fournier et al., *When Citizens Decide* (New York: Oxford University Press, 2011), 39.

15. For more on these democratic deficits, see Yascha Mounk, *The People versus Democracy* (Cambridge, MA: Harvard University Press, 2018).

16. Lawrence Susskind and Patrick Field, *Dealing with an Angry Public* (New York: Free Press, 1996), 60–75.

17. Claudia Chwalisz, *The People's Verdict* (Lanham, MD: Rowman and Littlefield, 2017), 3; Achen and Bartels, *Democracy for Realists*, 30–31, 73–75; Brian Martin, "Democracy without Elections," *Social Anarchism* 21 (1995–1996): 18–51; Alina Selyukh, "After Brexit Vote, Britain Asks Google: 'What Is the EU?,'" *All Tech Considered*, NPR, June 24, 2016, https://www.npr.org/sections/alltechconsidered/2016/06/24 /480949383/britains-google-searches-for-what-is-the-eu-spike-after-brexit-vote.

18. Chwalisz, *The People's Verdict*; James C. Petersen, ed., *Citizen Participation in Science Policy* (Amherst: University of Massachusetts Press, 1984); Gail Heyman and Nicholas Christenfeld, "Seeing the Other Side," *Journal of Experimental Social Psychology* 59 (2015): 18–23.

19. Christopher Hare and Keith Poole, "The Polarization of Contemporary American Politics," *Northeastern Political Science Association* 46, no. 3 (2014): 414.

20. Ian Haney López, *Dog Whistle Politics* (New York: Oxford University Press, 2014).

21. Haney López, *Dog Whistle Politics*, xiii–xiv, 151.

22. Jack H. Nagel, "Expanding the Spectrum of Democracies," in *Democracies and Institutions*, ed. Markus M. L. Crepaz, Thomas A. Koelble, and David Wilsford (Ann Arbor: University of Michigan Press, 2000), 113–128.

23. For overviews of utopian perspectives of what the internet can do for society, see Matthew Hindman, *The Myth of Digital Democracy* (Princeton, NJ: Princeton University Press, 2009), 1–8; Evgeny Morozov, *The Net Delusion* (New York: PublicAffairs, 2011); Robert McChesney, *Digital Disconnect* (New York: New Press, 2014), 5–8.

24. Siva Vaidhyanathan, *Anti-social Media* (New York: Oxford University Press, 2018), 106–108.

25. See Cass Sunstein and Reid Hastie, *Wiser* (Boston: Harvard Business Review Press, 2015).

26. Eli Pariser, *The Filter Bubble* (New York: Penguin, 2011).

27. Vaidhyanathan, *Anti-social Media*, 163–172; Craig Silverman, "Cambridge Analytica Says It Won the Election for Trump. Here's What It's Actually Talking About," *BuzzFeed News*, March 20, 2018, https://www.buzzfeednews.com/article/craigsilverman/cambridge-analytica-says-they-won-the-election-for-trump.

28. Casey Michel, "These Are the Facebook Posts Russia Used to Undermine Hillary Clinton's Campaign," *Think Progress*, October 6, 2017, https://thinkprogress.org/russia-facebook-clinton-campaign-d6d76b2a2e82/; Phillip Bump, "All the Ways Trump's Campaign Was Aided by Facebook, Ranked by Importance," *Washington Post*, March 22, 2018, https://www.washingtonpost.com/news/politics/wp/2018/03/22/all-the-ways-trumps-campaign-was-aided-by-facebook-ranked-by-importance/.

29. Boaz Hameiri et al., "Paradoxical Thinking as a New Avenue of Intervention to Promote Peace," *PNAS* 111, no. 30 (2014): 10996–11001.

30. Jack M. Balkin and Jonathan Zittrain, "A Grand Bargain to Make Tech Companies Trustworthy," *The Atlantic*, October 3, 2016, https://www.theatlantic.com/technology/archive/2016/10/information-fiduciary/502346/; Jack M. Balkin, "Information Fiduciaries and the First Amendment," *UC Davis Law Review* 49 (2016): 1183–1234.

31. McChesney, *Digital Disconnect*.

32. Hindman, *The Myth of Digital Democracy*, 90–101.

33. Daniel C. Hallin and Paolo Mancini, *Comparing Media Systems* (New York: Cambridge University Press, 2004).

34. Charles Lindblom, "Who Needs What Social Research for Policymaking?," *Science Communication* 7, no. 4 (1986): 345–366.

35. In *Inquiry and Change* (New Haven, CT: Yale University Press, 1990), Charles Lindblom argues that experts' role within a democracy is to aid citizens' and policy makers' ability to probe social problems critically. For journalists' negative portrayal of disagreement, see Nina Eliasoph, *Avoiding Politics* (New York: Cambridge University Press, 1998), 210–229; Éric Montpetit, *In Defense of Pluralism* (New York: Cambridge University Press, 2016).

36. McChesney, *Digital Disconnect*, 88.

37. Elizabeth Suhay et al., "Forging Bonds and Burning Bridges," *American Politics Research* 43, no. 4 (2015): 643–679.

38. David A. Walsh, "How the Right Wing Convinces Itself That Liberals Are Evil," *Washington Monthly*, July–August 2018, https://washingtonmonthly.com /magazine/july-august-2018/how-the-right-wing-convinces-itself-that-liberals -are-evil/; Zach Varda and Lily Masila, "Ben Shapiro Draws Conservative Crowd, Liberal Protest," *The Lantern*, November 13, 2018, https://www.thelantern.com /2018/11/ben-shapiro-draws-conservative-crowd-liberal-protests/; Lucas Nolan, "Milo in Orlando," Breitbart, June 15, 2016, https://www.breitbart.com/social -justice/2016/06/15/milo-gays-save-dont-import-muslims/.

39. Neil Postman, *Amusing Ourselves to Death* (New York: Viking Penguin, 1985), 79.

40. See Vaidhyanathan, *Anti-social Media*.

41. John R. Hibbing and Elizabeth Theiss-Morse, *Stealth Democracy* (New York: Cambridge University Press, 2002), 129.

42. For more on the folly of reducing complex sociopolitical problems into technological ones, see Morozov, *The Net Delusion;* Evgeny Morozov, *To Save Everything, Click Here* (New York: PublicAffairs, 2014); Michael Huesemann and Joyce Huesemann, *Techno-Fix* (Gabriola Island, Canada: New Society, 2011); Ozzie Zehner, *Green Illusions* (Lincoln: University of Nebraska Press, 2012).

43. Yascha Mounk, *The People vs. Democracy* (Cambridge, MA: Harvard University Press, 2018), 99–131.

44. Jonathan Haidt, *The Righteous Mind* (New York: Vintage Books, 2013), 296–313, 336–343.

45. Eric J. Oliver, *Democracy in Suburbia* (Princeton, NJ: Princeton University Press, 2001).

46. M. P. Baumgartner, *The Moral Order of a Suburb* (New York: Oxford University Press, 1988).

47. Setha Low, Gregory T. Donovan, and Jen Gieseking, "Shoestring Democracy," *Journal of Urban Affairs* 34, no. 3 (2012): 279–296.

48. For a provocative polemic against schooling, see John Taylor Gatto, "Against School," *Harper's Magazine*, September 2003.

49. Tim Walker, "The Testing Obsession and the Disappearing Curriculum," *NEA Today*, September 2, 2014, http://neatoday.org/2014/09/02/the-testing-obsession -and-the-disappearing-curriculum-2/; Quinn Mulholland, "The Case against Standardized Testing," *Harvard Political Review*, May 14, 2015, http://harvardpolitics .com/united-states/case-standardized-testing/; Nikhil Goyal, *Schools on Trial* (New York: Doubleday, 2016).

50. Survey data find that a surprising number of Americans are uncomfortable with political discussions of any kind; see Hibbing and Theiss-Morse, *Stealth Democracy*, 135.

51. Steve Klees, "Measurement Fetish," *Worlds of Education*, July 16, 2015, https:// worldsofeducation.org/en/woe_homepage/woe_detail/4812/measurement -fetishism.

52. Diego Gambetta and Steffan Hertog, *Engineers of Jihad* (Princeton, NJ: Princeton University Press, 2016).

53. Kelly Wang, "Study on the Careers of MIT Mechanical Engineering Undergraduate Alumni," BS thesis, Massachusetts Institute of Technology, 2015.

54. National Academy of Engineering, *Engineering as a Social Enterprise* (Washington, DC: National Academies Press, 1991).

55. For more on the politics of urban technologies, see Taylor Dotson, *Technically Together* (Cambridge, MA: MIT Press, 2017).

56. Jonathan Haidt and Greg Lukianoff, "How to Play Our Way to a Better Democracy," *New York Times*, September 1, 2018, https://www.nytimes.com/2018/09/01 /opinion/sunday/democracy-play-mccain.html. I make the same point in *Technically Together*; also see Steven Horwitz, "Cooperation over Coercion," *Cosmos+Taxis* 3, no. 1 (2015): 3–16.

57. Elizabeth Anderson, "How Bosses Are (Literally) Like Dictators," *Vox*, September 3, 2017, https://www.vox.com/the-big-idea/2017/7/17/15973478/bosses -dictators-workplace-rights-free-markets-unions; Joshua Rothman, "Are Bosses Dictators?," *The New Yorker*, September 12, 2017, https://www.newyorker.com/books /page-turner/are-bosses-dictators.

58. Peter Gray, *Free to Learn* (New York: Basic Books, 2013).

59. See Tom Malleson, *After Occupy* (New York: Oxford University Press, 2014); Pater Walsh, Michael Peck, and Ibon Zugasti, "Why the U.S. Needs More Worker-Owned Companies," *Harvard Business Review*, August 8, 2018, https://hbr.org/2018/08/why -the-u-s-needs-more-worker-owned-companies; Corey Rosen and Michael Quarrey, "How Well Is Employee Ownership Working?," *Harvard Business Review*, September 1987, https://hbr.org/1987/09/how-well-is-employee-ownership-working.

60. Daniel T. Beito, *From Mutual Aid to the Welfare State* (Chapel Hill: University of North Carolina Press, 2000).

61. Dotson, *Technically Together*.

62. For an overview of the barriers to civic participation, see Robert Putnam, *Bowling Alone* (New York: Simon and Schuster, 2000).

63. John Nichols and Robert W. McChesney, *Dollarocracy* (New York: Nation Books, 2013); *The Economist*, "As Inequality Grows, so Does the Political Influence of the Rich," July 21, 2018, https://www.economist.com/finance-and-economics/2018/07/21/as-inequality-grows-so-does-the-political-influence-of-the-rich.

64. Michel Crozier, Samuel P. Huntington, and Joji Watanuki, *The Crisis of Democracy* (New York: New York University Press, 1975).

65. Achen and Bartels, *Democracy for Realists*, 325.

66. Quoted in Putnam, *Bowling Alone*, 340.

67. Robert A. Dahl, *Democracy and Its Critics* (New Haven, CT: Yale University Press, 1989), 326.

68. Citizens United v. Federal Election Commission, 558 US 310 (2010).

69. Lee Drutman, "The Political One Percent of One Percent," Sunlight Foundation, December 13, 2011, https://sunlightfoundation.com/2011/12/13/the-political-one-percent-of-the-one-percent/; Ian Vandewalker and Lawrence Norden, "Small Donors Still Aren't as Important as Wealthy Ones," *The Atlantic*, October 18, 2016, https://www.theatlantic.com/politics/archive/2016/10/campaign-finance-fundraising-citizens-united/504425/.

70. Jerry Useem, "Power Causes Brain Damage," *The Atlantic*, July–August 2017, https://www.theatlantic.com/magazine/archive/2017/07/power-causes-brain-damage/528711/; David Owen and Jonathan Davidson, "Hubris Syndrome," *Brain* 132, no. 5 (2009): 1396–1406.

71. Nathan Brooks and Katarina Fritzon, "Psychopathic Personality Characteristics among High Functioning Populations," *Crime Psychology Review* 2, no. 1 (2016): 22–44. This article was retracted, not due to flawed methods or data but because it was a case of—possibly inadvertent—self-plagiarism.

72. Roger Eatwell and Matthew Goodwin, *National Populism* (London: Pelican, 2018).

73. Mehdi Hasan, "Time to Kill the Zombie Argument," *The Intercept*, September 18, 2018, https://theintercept.com/2018/09/18/2016-election-race-class-trump/; Daniel Cox, Rachel Lienesch, and Robert Jones, *Beyond Economics: Fears of Cultural Displacement Pushed Working Class to Trump* (Washington, DC: PRRI, 2017), https://www.prri.org/research/white-working-class-attitudes-economy-trade-immigration-election-donald-trump/; Arlie Hochschild, *Strangers in Their Own Land* (New York: New Press, 2018).

74. Steve Benen, "Alabama Congressman Perceives a Democratic 'War on Whites,'" MSNBC, August 5, 2014; Greg Sargent, "President Trump and the Fantasy of a Race War against White People," *Washington Post*, September 10, 2018, https://www.washingtonpost.com/blogs/plum-line/wp/2018/09/10/donald-trump-and-the-dream-of-a-race-war-against-white-people/?noredirect=on&utm_term=.1d4c111acf7c.

75. Noel Ignatiev, *How the Irish Became White* (New York: Routledge, 1995).

76. Personality and individual initiative also contribute to success, but they are nevertheless difficult to disentangle from environment. For instance, my own work ethic comes in part from the example that my father set for me. Such complexity makes the perpetuation of inequality a wicked problem. See Priyanka Boghani, "How Poverty Can Follow Children into Adulthood," *Frontline*, November 22, 2017, https://www.pbs.org/wgbh/frontline/article/how-poverty-can-follow-children-into-adulthood/; Mimi Kirk, "How Some Kids Escape Poverty," *City Lab*, May 19, 2017, https://www.citylab.com/solutions/2017/05/how-some-kids-escape-poverty/527409/.

77. Nate Cohn, "More Hispanics Declaring Themselves White," *New York Times*, May 21, 2014, https://www.nytimes.com/2014/05/22/upshot/more-hispanics-declaring-themselves-white.html.

78. Haney López, *Dog Whistle Politics;* James B. Steward, "Rich Farmers, Bigger Subsidies," *New York Times*, July 19, 2013, https://www.nytimes.com/2013/07/20/business/richer-farmers-bigger-subsidies.html; Andrew Woo and Chris Salviati, "Imbalance in Housing Aid," *Apartment List*, October 11, 2017, https://www.apartmentlist.com/rentonomics/imbalance-housing-aid-mortgage-interest-deduction-vs-section-8/.

79. Chris Ladd, "Unspeakable Realities Block Universal Health Coverage in America," *Forbes*, March 13, 2017, https://www.forbes.com/sites/chrisladd/2017/03/13/unspeakable-realities-block-universal-health-coverage-in-the-us/#33121868186a.

80. Jonathan Rieder, *Canarsie* (Cambridge, MA: Harvard University Press, 1987), 121.

81. Hansi Lo Wang, "2020 Census Will Ask People More about Their Ethnicities," NPR, February 1, 2018, https://www.npr.org/2018/02/01/582338628/-what-kind-of-white-2020-census-to-ask-white-people-about-origins.

82. Zachary B. Wolf, Curt Merrill, and Daniel Wolfe, "How Voters Shifted During Four Years of Trump," *CNN*, November 4, 2020, https://www.cnn.com/interactive/2020/11/politics/election-analysis-exit-polls-2016-2020/; Lizette Alvarez, "Latinos Can Be Racist, Too. My Community Shows How," *Washington Post*, July 28, 2020, https://www.washingtonpost.com/opinions/2020/07/28/latinos-can-be-racist-too-my-community-shows-how/.

83. In Adam Curtis, dir., *Century of the Self*, documentary series, BBC Two, 2002. For more on how people are socialized to be individualistic consumers rather than community-minded citizens, see Stephen A. Marglin, *The Dismal Science* (Cambridge,

MA: Harvard University Press, 2010); Juliet Schor, *Born to Buy* (New York: Scribner, 2004).

84. Dotson, *Technically Together*.

85. J. C. Mathes and Donald H. Gray made this observation in their incisive article "Engineer as Social Radical," *The Ecologist* 5, no. 4 (1975): 119–125.

86. Howard Gillette, *Civitas by Design* (Philadelphia: University of Pennsylvania Press, 2012).

87. The philosopher of science Karl Popper distinguished "piecemeal social engineering" from more "utopian" forms in that it proceeds incrementally and democratically and focuses on addressing great harms and evils. It is not an attempt to discern the ultimate good and realize it through sweeping social transformations. See Karl Popper, *The Open Society and Its Enemies* (Princeton, NJ: Princeton University Press, 2013); Karl Popper, "Piecemeal Social Engineering," in *Popper Selections*, ed. David Miller (Princeton, NJ: Princeton University Press, 1985), 304–318.

88. Friedrich A. Hayek, "The Use of Knowledge in Society," *American Economic Review* 35, no. 4 (1945): 519–530.

CHAPTER 7

1. Marshall D. Sahlins, "Poor Man, Rich Man, Big Man, Chief," *Comparative Studies in Society and History* 5, no. 3 (1963): 285–302; Paul Richardson, "New Religious Movements and the Search for Melanesian Spirituality," *Melanesian Journal of Theology* 2, no. 1 (1986): 66–75.

2. Peter M. Worsley, "50 Years Ago: Cargo Cults of Melanesia," *Scientific American*, May 1, 2009, https://www.scientificamerican.com/article/1959-cargo-cults-melanesia/. Cargo cults are far more complex than my metaphorical use of them shows. Anthropologists are divided about their underlying causes and whether colonialism or Melanesians' underlying desires for political autonomy or moral salvation was more significant than the cargo. See Lamont Lindstrom, "Cargo Cults," in *The Cambridge Encyclopedia of Anthropology* (Cambridge: Cambridge University Press, March 29, 2018), https://www.anthroencyclopedia.com/entry/cargo-cults.

3. Nathan Pippenger, "Is Trump Panic More Dangerous Than Trumpism?," *Democracy: A Journal of Ideas*, October 23, 2017, https://democracyjournal.org/arguments/is-trump-panic-more-dangerous-than-trumpism/.

4. The democratic pluralist system seems to be what Nassim Nicholas Taleb would call an "antifragile" system. Dissent is a stressor on policy making. Within a democratic pluralist system, dissent aids the achievement of intelligent policies and helps governments maintain stability and legitimacy. See Taleb's book *Antifragile* (New York: Random House, 2012).

5. Readers interested in a more thorough defense of pluralism should read Charles Lindblom, Robert Dahl, and contemporary neopluralists.

6. Regarding the roots of political apathy and nonpolitical framings of political problems, see Nina Eliasoph, *Avoiding Politics* (New York: Cambridge University Press, 1998).

7. Karl Popper, *The Open Society and Its Enemies* (Princeton, NJ: Princeton University Press, 2013).

8. Edward J. Woodhouse, "(Re)Constructing Technological Society by Taking Social Construction Even More Seriously," *Social Epistemology* 19, nos. 2–3 (2005): 199–223; Taylor Dotson, *Technically Together* (Cambridge, MA: MIT Press, 2017).

9. Dotson, *Technically Together*.

10. Popper, *The Open Society*.

11. Francis Fukuyama, *The End of History and the Last Man* (New York: Free Press, 1992); Timothy Stanley and Alexander Lee, "It's Still Not the End of History," *The Atlantic*, September 1, 2014, https://www.theatlantic.com/politics/archive/2014/09/its-still-not-the-end-of-history-francis-fukuyama/379394/.

INDEX